My Father's Shadow

Sam Mahon is an artist who lives in North Canterbury in a reconstructed flour mill. He is a painter, sculptor – mostly in bronze – and a printmaker: he's a superb draughtsman and builds everything from musical instruments to miniature rockets, as well as orchestrating mock-battles.

His first book *The Year of the Horse* won the Best First Book of Prose Award in 2003. This was followed by the much-acclaimed *The Water Thieves* in 2006; a lament for the rivers and 'a fine literary achievement'.

Sam's most recent exhibition of portraits 'Talking Heads' was shown in Christchurch in 2007, at the COCA Gallery.

My Father's Shadow

A PORTRAIT OF JUSTICE PETER MAHON

SAM MAHON

Longacre Press

Acknowledgments
I wish to thank Geoffrey Saunders and Dr George Barton QC.
I am grateful to Creative New Zealand, whose grant in 2006
enabled this book to be written.

My thanks also to Barbara, Annette and Nicky at Longacre for giving this
portrait a frame, an audience and the necessary paring of critique.

First published with the assistance of

ISBN 978 1 877460 17 3

A catalogue record for this book is available
from the National Library of New Zealand.

First published by Longacre Press, 2008
30 Moray Place, Dunedin, New Zealand.
Reprinted 2009

Book design: IslandBridge
Cover design: Nick Wright/Christine Buess
Cover image: portrait of Peter Mahon painted by Sam Mahon, 1987
Printed by Astra Print, Wellington

www. longacre.co.nz

Contents

Bassanio: '...And I beseech you,
            Wrest once the law to your authority:
            To do a great right, do a little wrong;
            And curb the cruel devil of his will.'

Portia: 'It must not be; there is no power in Venice
            Can alter a decree established;
            'Twill be recorded for a precedent;
            And many an error, by the same example,
            Will rush into the state: it cannot be.'

The Merchant of Venice, William Shakespeare

'Man is driven to the use of metaphor owing to the fact that he is too short-lived to carry out his tremendous self-imposed task. It is this disparity between the brevity of his life and the greatness of his task which forces him to gaze eagle-eyed at all things, and to make his meaning clear by instantaneous flashes. That is what poetry is. Metaphor is the shorthand of a great individuality, the handwriting of the soul.'

Boris Pasternak, in *Dante the Maker* by William Anderson

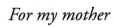

For my mother

Introduction

My initial intent in writing this book was to present a biography of Peter Mahon QC. What little of the man I knew beyond whatever part of him he presented to me as my father I meant to faithfully represent in the following chapters. I had hoped it would be enough. But it happens that it is not.

My father, if he had been alive now, would have turned eighty-four this year and many of his friends, most of the people I would have been pleased to interview about his life, are no longer around. Also, he was an emotionally private man and he kept his professional life almost entirely separate from his family. The only path, really, along which we can hope to track the tendency of his heart, is through his many letters in which he weaves language like a master of tapestry, every coloured stitch placed precisely to present a desired effect. And even then, it is a matter of reading between the lines, for apart from one or two letters written to colleagues at the time of Erebus, he never said anything plainly.

So in the face of so little evidence, in order to fill the broad territory between points of fact, I have had to cast opinion and make best guesses. At first this greatly annoyed me, for I hold in deep respect the biographer who manages in his work to sublimate his own voice. Accordingly, because there simply does not exist enough material, I have to accept that this book must be more of a memoir than a biography; a sketch if you like, with smudges and rubbings out, and my fingerprints all over it.

Sam Mahon

Part One

Lago Como, Italy

The wind comes off the lake like a feather, reminding me of home. I walked along the road last night, my shadow lengthening and diminishing beneath the street lamps, dark at my feet then stretching out to dissolve amid the cobbles like dust. Now and then I paused to glance back at the empty street, as if there were someone there, remembering how he had walked in the middle of the road, a pistol in his pocket, a cigarette in his teeth.

So I sit with a cappuccino and wait, staring across the water and trying to imagine how it must have been for him at twenty-one, unaccountably alive and in the presence of the ancient Roman beauty of Como.

The light is beginning to go out on the slopes of Brunate, it catches a window or two and gold bars burn for a minute in the black water. The funicular, where I found the winding track twitching with spring lizards, is lit now like a string of beads. Como's lapping the flagstones a few metres away, jetsam at its hem: a bloated fish, bits of wood, leaves, a little plastic; the cobbles at my feet are neatly grouted with cigarette butts. Nearby, tethered boats tink like cheap alloy dangling in a window breeze. They have nowhere to go but up and down this lake, nowhere to go until morning, gently heaving on the swell like breathing. Two fishermen stand close, their rods tapering out to nothing. It's evening, and as the heat at last begins to drain from the day, as the shadows deepen in the hollow of the elms, the promenaders appear like courteous thieves. Hand in hand they come to walk the lake front, arm in arm, young and old, singly with a walking stick, singly with quick eyes; and all the women look like my sister. And I understand, now, the allure, why he would dream of this place, how at twenty-one, on leave from Trieste, from the discomfort of inaction, he came here and it was printed against his memory for ever; a place to come back to one day.

He said he wanted to write; when it was all over, when the fuss had died down. He would come here, he said, find a room near the lake, a room with a view; and with a beautifully manicured, steady hand, sketch the madding crowd in undulating lines of aquamarine blue. He didn't make it, so I have come here instead: to Italy, to write the last chapter of his book.

I watched a hawk this afternoon turning slowly against a lightly toasted sky.

'There was an albatross,' he wrote from the troop ship. 'It followed us for half a day, effortless.'

If we shared anything at all it was this, an intimate observation of nature. That and a bloody-minded Irish obstinacy; and it is the latter, more than some vague filial duty, that has brought me here. After all, I had easier things to do.

(From an article written for the *Sunday Star Times*: 2004)

In *Voyage Around My Father*, John Mortimer examines a man he wished in some way to live up to, to impress or perhaps to exorcise. He studies the little he knows of him in much the same way an archaeologist studies shards of pottery or bone and on the scant evidence before him, makes a guess at its true form. The best we can do is to suppose. As far as our parents are concerned, always we are too near to see them clearly and it is possible that I might portray with more accuracy a stranger on a bus with whom I have shared a brief five minutes' journey, than the man who presided over nearly a third of my life.

We were partially orphaned by the war, those of us whose fathers had dwelt among the dead and dying for too long, their memories too bitter to share, afraid, perhaps, that intimacy might un-cage a flock of half-forgotten horrors. My father communicated best from a distance, in an exchange of letters, and even then we had to work to find him between the lines.

I remember the shape of him, the grey coat and hat, the briefcase and perpetual cigarette, and the long journeys in his small car that took him away from us to some far flung provincial courtroom where he plied his extraordinary acumen for a minimal fee. He never spoke about his work. He spoke instead about the Canada geese in the autumn, the swallows in the spring and the heron that strutted in the winter ponds below our house like a disillusioned cleric.

I remember my father arriving home late one evening and depositing, with a magician's flourish, a newly dead falcon in the middle of the dinner table; an act designed to draw opprobrium from his wife and delight from his sons. And, probably, this is where his life and mine intersected; in the no man's land of endless summer fields, skylarks' nests and speckled eggs. So it was not surprising that as soon as his report on the Erebus Inquiry was signed and delivered, he should make a rare visit to the hills, don a worsted great-coat and loiter amid the willows of a cold autumn evening, listening again for the sibilant whisper of wings. I remember the wind riffling the black pond and the restlessness of the trees. I remember him lighting a cigarette in the niche of his lapel, the shotgun broken in the crook of his arm, the brief smoke shredding in a wind pouring from an empty sky. 'Tomorrow,' he said, 'all hell's going to break loose.' And it did.

He was not a religious man but he maintained, according to my mother, one underlying certainty. 'Nothing matters,' he used to say. 'But surely something must,' she would reply. Had he read too much Shakespeare, too much Dante, seen at first hand too much of man's inhumanity to entertain any philosophy more complex than this simple mantra? There's a line of Greene's that goes vaguely like this, 'Truth is of no earthly use to the ordinary man. It is a tool for mathematicians and philosophers and the best we can offer each other is lies and kindness.'

Greene was one of his favourites along with Maugham and Thurber, their acerbic wit matching his own, a sense of the absurd wrought from the comedy of man taking himself far too seriously. It is said that melancholy is genius' constant, shadowy attendant, that clarity of thought leads inevitably to pessimism, perhaps to the private conviction that, after all, 'nothing matters'.

And yet, apparently, the law mattered to him very much and he dedicated his life to weaving those fine threads that bind us all, a social order without which we would take up knives in the dark and devour one another. His findings as Royal Commissioner into the air disaster on Mt Erebus brought him into direct conflict with Prime Minister Muldoon, who sought then to undermine the man he had so confidently appointed. At my father's funeral I thought it fitting, therefore, to read an extract from *A Man for all Seasons*. It is part of Thomas More's reply when asked to amend the law in favour of the king, and in so doing, save his own life.

...If you cut a great road through the law, Roper, to get after the Devil and find the Devil turned round on you – where will you hide, the laws all being flat? This country's planted thick with laws from coast to coast – and if you cut them down do you really think you could stand upright in the winds that would blow then?

My father was once counselled by Sir Arthur Donnelly that if he wished to be a good lawyer he should take the law as his mistress and avoid the distractions of family. I imagine he already recognised Peter's potential and as a bachelor himself was simply wishing the best for his protégé. Perhaps Sir Arthur hadn't read *To Kill a Mockingbird*, or perhaps he had and took the character of Atticus Finch for an invention of American sentimentalism, a little like the first amendment. But domesticity must have appealed to my father's sense of order for he acquired it nevertheless, and I doubt if it made him any less of a jurist.

Andrew Wyeth, the American painter, once said of his father, 'We were a drag on him, we held him back. He would have been a great artist, but he loved us too much...' In this role of family man, my father often portrayed himself, with calculated inaccuracy, as a kind of Walter Mitty, weighed down by familial responsibilities. He describes a nocturnal walk with my mother and the family Labrador: 'We made a curious trio. If an impartial observer had directed his attention to the tall, humble, grey-haired gentleman with the distinguished features he might have fancied he discerned in the dim light the shadowy outline of a third leash...'

Nothing could have been further from the truth. For the most part my father pleased himself and he was at no one's behest. He was an individual who moved easily amongst his fellow men while keeping his thoughts to himself and it seemed to me that he was most at one with the world when he was alone with a glass of old malt and his books, communing with the thoughts of men most of whom were long dead. There's a comment by Cicero, 'I am never less lonely than when I am by myself.' And, as a youth, I felt this instinctively as I tip-toed past his sanctuary, less inclined to disturb him with his ghosts than if he were in the company of solid men.

Some believe that the Erebus Inquiry and its aftermath unravelled his health and took him from us too soon. That may be so. But he was an artist in his way and Erebus was his masterwork. It is inconceivable that he would have turned down the challenge of untangling that extraordinary mystery.

To attempt a biography of Peter Mahon would be impossible. He moved through our lives like a character from a book, admirable and yet ultimately unreachable, like le Carré's Smiley strolling through the London mist. It was difficult enough for those of us closest to him to keep him in focus and, as I said, the best we can do is to suppose.

Helga Testorf was Andrew Wyeth's muse for fifteen years. 'Art is selfish,' she said.

'Do you think I'm selfish?' asked Andrew.

'Yes,' she said, 'but you call it love.'

The law was my father's brush and palette and it was his medium, and who among us can argue the right to interrupt genius? Nevertheless, it is spring now and fantails have built a nest in the barn woven from spiderwebs. I would have liked him to see it.

A year after writing this I am sitting across a coffee table from Geoff Saunders LLB, senior partner of his own firm, Christ's College to the bone, collector of art and pivoting on retirement at fifty-four. My latest manuscript is lying between us, the coffee cups smoking like pistols. 'You're being a little unkind,' he says glancing off to his right, a quirk he has when delivering truths. 'The bit about Max's girlfriend – the girl "Buttercup" – I think you should drop it.' He turns back to me, meets my eye. 'Unless you're very sure.' He grins and I can see the boy peeking out from three decades of over-painting. I see him again in the shadow of the cloisters, stiff buttoned collar, arms full of books and already an hereditary haughtiness that disdains friendship. But there is also that dimpled, mischievous smile.

'Otherwise,' he says, 'I think it's okay. I must say,' he adds, 'and it's no disrespect to your first book, but I think this one's better.'

We've finished coffee. We've talked art and of his imminent change in direction. I'm aware that time is precious here and I lean forward, palms on knees. 'Well. Thanks, Geoff…' But he stops me.

'Have you ever thought of writing your father's biography?' He is still seated, one long leg crossed over the other, one arm flung along the back of the couch. He has taken me by surprise. I slump back again into my seat.

'Well, I've thought about it, yes. But…' I remember the very neat piece of writing for the *Sunday Star Times* and my conclusion that it would be impossible for anyone to do it. For who among us knew him? Certainly not me.

'I'd say you've got about five years to do it,' he said. 'After that the people you need to talk to just won't be there.' He is gazing off to the right again. 'You should do it. You have the ability,' he says, gesturing towards the neat white pile of paper between us. 'I used to see him at Shirley sometimes, at the clubhouse after a round of golf, playing cards with the old boys. I'd like to have been a fly on the wall.' He grinned again. 'And the whisky. And all of them climbing into their cars and driving on home afterwards.' He shook his head. 'They were more liberal days.'

And I am aware of the *should*. It keeps echoing all the way home and I can't shake it. 'You have five years.' Should is my nemesis. When I was twenty and thrown out of Art School I heard a lot of shoulds and rejected them all because the easiest thing in the world would have been to go back. The hardest was to get down and get painting. And it was then, right when I was at my weakest, that my father offered me a trip to Nepal. It was another should, but this time I accepted because it was harder to go than to stay. It would be easier not to do this, this piece of writing. I have paintings to paint, sculptures that have been waiting in line for years to be transmuted from thought to bronze. And if I am to write at all it would be about something dearer to my heart. But there it is, Geoff's *should*, and if I have inherited anything from my father at all, it is an obstinate refusal to back down in the face of adversity.

I suppose I should follow the biographic rules; start at the beginning with his grandparents, my own Irish forebears, followed fairly soon by faded black and white photographs of himself in a christening shawl. But I don't think he would ever forgive me.

I'm not trained to write, and I have never had the patience for recipes. I'm an artist, after all, a portraitist in paint and bronze, and I would like to approach this subject in the same way I would carve a piece of stone; take the raw material and start whacking away at it from all angles, shaping it roughly and then working in from every direction in the slow fining up of the features until, *voilà*, I have gone far enough. And that is always the most difficult part, the far enough.

A few months ago I did exactly this, carved a bust of my father and cast it in bronze for the law library at Auckland University. Within quarter of an hour of setting the plaster on the mandrel I had him in the abstract, and it was startling to walk into the studio and catch that first impression and feel his presence. But I continued to work away with my files and saw blades and, although, once or twice I lost him completely, in the end I got very close and I am happy enough with it now in the bronze. Still, I can't forget that first rough outline of his head with the dust of the studio caught in the slanted rays of evening light. It was startling. For isn't that how we see our closest? We don't notice if they've grown a beard or sprouted a carbuncle on the chin because we know them too well. We are looking for gestures and mood, indicators of the currents stirring beneath the surface. 'Give me ten minutes to talk away my face, and I'll woo the queen of France,' said Voltaire. And he's right. It's the man within, the gesture that's everything.

And here with this 'sculpture' I will whack away at the air around him and try to rough out the shape he inhabited by attempting to make solid the stories and memories that surrounded him; and to hell with the intricate stitch-work of his christening shawl.

So, having first cleverly convinced myself that it is impossible to write about my father, I find myself asking where do I start? Where do I begin to look for a man I so vaguely know?

I suppose if it were a detective story, if I had been brought in to search for a missing person, it would begin with articles of clothing, objects left behind or picked up along the trail. Cigarette butts innumerable, half-drained glasses countless, crumpled copies of the *Racing Times* enough to light up Ellerslie. And those few characters left whose paths his briefly intersected. Briefly, yes. For after all, friendship at its best is incomplete; it is only betrayal that we can depend on.

All right, so what is there? What solid clues did he leave behind?

Let us just take it that he came into this world in the usual way, that his father was a cantankerous Catholic, green thumbed and highly virtuous, and his mother a laced Anglican saint. I'm not one for collecting: collecting is tinged with regret, and regret I find too often a sort of cancer that withers people from the inside. But there are tangible odds and ends among the memories, just a few. So, by way of a tentative beginning, let me deal with them one by one and see where they lead.

Exhibit A:
His Baikel under-and-over shotgun

It was always a little too stiff in the breach, the safety hard to push forward when your fingers were cold. And if the weather was perfect for duck shooting, then your fingers were, inevitably, next to numb. When I press the walnut to my cheek I can smell a number of things: the oil from the breach, the linseed oil from the stock and the scent of burned powder. And I can smell the Neatsfoot oil I used to rub into my boots, staining them dark, caring for the leather in the tender way a rider cares for his tack. I still have my guns but I don't care for them any longer. I don't care for the lands and grooves, I don't hold the things to the light in case there might be one stray grain of unburned powder to mar the burnished steel. I don't care for hunting now, but then ... then, it was everything.

Peter, visiting me once at the cottage deep in the hills of North Canterbury, woke me one early morning to point out a large hare on the drive. 'Where's the rifle,' he asked.

'Leave him, Dad,' I said. 'He's company.'

He looked surprised. He sighed, shook his head sadly and turned away to watch the beautiful animal for a while where it peacefully cropped the verge. Then Peter wandered off to brew himself a consoling cup of tea.

My father was an early riser. The only time I ever beat him was during duck season on those mornings my schoolmate, Tim, arrived noiselessly in his side-valve Humber to tap his knuckle against my bedroom window. Invariably I'd part the curtains, blink at him in the half-light, then roll over and go back to sleep for a few moments until he woke me again. Tim and I would stalk the ponds by foot, trying to pick out a blur of wings in the autumn mist.

But shooting with my father was a different business altogether. It was mechanised and it was furious and it was driven by the volatile substance of a young Englishman called Christopher Flemming.

Chris was a nephew of the famous writer and it seemed to me that everything in his life was to be absolutely shaken, never simply stirred. He had bought a huge tract of land that began at the edge of the city and ended at the summit road and overlooked just about everything. He had purchased his farm from the Cracroft-Wilson family and for Chris it had been easy money. He owned the land for five years, made twice what he paid, and then disappeared back to England and his own set. I didn't know anything about the business of farming or the intricacies of commercial law and subdivision, I know next to nothing of them today. What I do know is that during those few years, Chris provided me with some of the brightest moments of my life.

'Flemming's asked us over for a shoot tonight,' my father announced on our way into town one morning. That evening he arrived home with the brand new Baikel and two boxes of cartridges. 'Apparently it has stainless steel bores,' he said. 'You don't have to clean it.' I wonder if he chose the gun primarily for this feature given his experience during the war where he was issued with a rifle that had a flaw in the barrel. His sergeant always took it for powder residue and ordered him to clean it repeatedly until the day my father found an opportunity to let it slip over the balustrade of a bridge they happened to be crossing and he was issued with a new one.

Usually, for the duck hunts, my father borrowed one of Chris's side by sides, light and snappy with fine checkering in the pistol grip. This Russian gun was a little coarse and I never quite got used to the barrels lying one over the other. Mine was a single-barrelled British gun, fully choked, paid for out of a good number of back-breaking hours in the potato field.

We were a little late, and by the time we arrived at the estate, we found Chris leaning on the fence of the manager's cottage with his shotgun broken over one arm and a duck dangling by the feet from his free hand. He was wearing tweed and gumboots with a fore and aft cap on his head. He held the bird aloft for us to see, his round face breaking into a grin as he described how it had passed overhead a minute earlier and he'd taken a crack at it anyway. 'First kill,' he said. 'Off to an early start. Don't know where William's got to. Better get on with it, though. Light'll beat us. Come on chaps,' and he tore open the door of the Land Rover and squeezed his corpulent frame behind the wheel. My father climbed in beside him while I positioned myself on the deck. A car swung into the driveway, spitting gravel.

'William,' Chris yelled from the cab. 'Jump on the back with Sam.' The newcomer swung a gun from the back seat of his car and barely made it aboard before, with a yelp of glee, Chris had the rover careening up the farm track toward the farthest pond, his best pond, the first of his litigious creations. And that, apparently, is how my father and he met: over a pond.

How strange to observe that when my father was my age he was defending a man who repeatedly defied the then Catchment Authority by bulldozing his own reservoirs without the necessary consents. And here I am two years into fighting similar men who would turn our best rivers into reservoirs; albeit slightly bigger ponds along with a slightly higher disregard for the commons. What discussions we could have had, my father and I. What, I wonder, would he have made of the Resource Management Act, that controversial document of conservation, so brilliant on the one hand, so artless on the other. But in those careless days I knew nothing of the Catchment Board and my father rarely discussed his work. I was simply along for the ride and my mind quite properly was on ducks.

The pond as I say was Chris's earliest transgression and there was a nice thicket of cover already established around its border. I was positioned on one side of the mouth of the pond and William on the other, forty yards away. My father and Chris disappeared toward the valley end to hunker in the shadows beneath some young willows. Soon I heard the faint tink of cut glass tumblers and guessed they were discussing topics more broad than the incoming flock. I cast them from my mind. Immobile among the tussocks, one knee pressed into the damp soil, I focused every nerve on the waning sky. The rise of the hill was black against the pale glow of the distant city and this was the portion to watch, for here the dark shapes would be seen first, before the faint whistle of wings could reach us. But the weather was dry. The cloud was slight, the sky clear, and the ducks were not moving around as they would if it were misty or if we were suffering under a light drizzle. As the night settled around us the frogs began to chirrup and from far away a lonely bull trumpeted in rising harmonics. Once I heard the faint whisper of feathers and turned my face down. But there was no rush of air, no long slash of white water on the black pond, nor the chuckle of a satisfied bird. A shape came in diagonally but not in a descending arc. I swung the barrel up and covered it, led it, but there was something wrong. And sure enough, as it passed overhead I recognised the stubby wings of an owl. I still had the gun to my shoulder when I saw the second bird. It was a duck coming in at his full seventy miles an hour with no intention of stopping. I gave him a four foot lead and fired. He crumpled, tumbling along an almost horizontal trajectory for a moment until I lost him against the black hill. Damn, I thought. I won't find him.

Fifty yards away my father, scarved to the chin, pouring whisky into Chris's raised glass, had the balaclava knocked from his head by a duck crashing through the fragile branches of the willow they had been sheltering under. 'By god,' said Chris, reaching to pick up the lifeless form. 'That boy's getting damned good.'

When night had fallen fully and the ducks were all down, we swept the paddocks with the headlights of the battered rover making slow zigzags over the low hills, picking out the hares, lean as whippets, hunched like Fagin, and the rabbits, wide eyed and slow. But when they ran the Land Rover ran with them, revving and swerving, thistle-heads exploding against the flaking paint-work as we clung desperately to the roll bar, trying not to ruin our guns on the roof of the cab. Once a goose lifted into the air and came down to William's gun and Chris, as usual, when any game tumbled to a good shot, let out a boyish yelp of glee. And this is what was so marvellous in him: his intense enjoyment of life even while we dispatched it on either side.

There was a pond at the top of the farm that Chris had been feeding illegally. The grim minions of the Catchment Board had spotted it and staked a sign in the water warning it was strictly off limits for the season. Chris, ever the poacher, drove his Rover up a winding track by the light of the stars and waited till we were ten yards from the water before snapping on the headlights. There before us sat two fine drakes. 'Quick!' he yelled. William and I let drive simultaneously and both decoys blew into myriad pieces, scattering across the surface of the empty pond like champagne corks. Chris laughed all the way down to the flats, sobering only as we turned into the bottom lane where our headlights picked out the cold metallic livery of a police car parked at the gate. As we drew alongside two constables climbed out and wandered over to us.

'Christ,' muttered William.

Chris leaned from the cab. 'Good evening officers,' he said. 'Are you lost?'

'No sir,' replied the first constable. 'We're not lost, sir. It's just that we've had a complaint of shots being fired in the vicinity.'

'Oh,' said Chris, and frowned, pretending to scan recent events. I remembered that he had shot the first duck while standing by the gate of the manager's cottage only a short distance from the urban fringe, and none of us had any doubts about the cause of the complaint.

'Well,' said Chris, 'I suppose it must have been us.' He appeared to consider the possibility. 'Yes, it must have been us,' he said, and then added a little stridently, 'trying to do the Rabbit Board's job for them. Don't know why we bother paying rates, do you? Look here,' he said, with hardly a pause, 'you boys care for a goose?' And without waiting for an answer, Chris stepped down from the cab and reached over into the shadows of the deck where William and I were sitting motionless trying to blend into the woodwork. We felt the feathers slide between us and next moment Chris was beaming like Saint Nick himself as he held the bird aloft. There was a moment, a hesitation, very slight, and then one of the policemen grinned, pushed his cap back with his thumb and forefinger and grasped the gift by its orange ankles.

'Why not,' he said. 'Very kind, indeed, sir.' We watched dumbly as they popped the animal into the boot of the patrol car, gave us a cheerful wave, and then drove away into the felonious night.

'Cheeky bastard,' said William. 'That was my bloody dinner!'

We would always retire to the cottage after these evening shoots so the men could revive their chilled limbs with a few glasses of whisky. For me there was a glass of cocoa although the cold never really bothered me. And while the conversation floated above my head, I would relive our recent adventure, rehearsing the telling of it at school the next day. Clearly, my father enjoyed Chris's company, and his stories that always crossed borders.

Often William was in attendance. William, Chris's nephew, the remittance man who was spending a little time in the colonies while a beautiful Jewess from Haifa searched vainly the home counties for the father of her child. He was witty, well travelled, and too wealthy for his own good. 'I'm what you might call a bit of a Hooray Henry,' he once admitted, and even here, on the opposite side of the world from Sloane Square, he seemed to treat authority like a school yard game. He was arrested once for urinating on the median strip of Bealey Ave and he caused a certain amount of panic around the quiet country lanes bordering the Cracroft estate by sneaking up on the cars of young lovers and discharging a shotgun close to their ears.

'Never seen tits and knickers move with such alacrity,' he chortled, and everyone laughed with him. Until he took my sister out on a date and then I noticed a little tension around the dinner table. I noticed my father's lids a little lower over his blue-grey eyes, and the ready smile contract into pursed lips at the mention of William's name. I should have been warned if I were William. I should have slipped my stories of the Six Day War in my back pocket and headed for the nearest pine tree.

And I remember one of those stories overheard in the manager's cottage. One that I pluck now from what I can best describe as the floating conversation, that mostly indecipherable murmur that hangs like mist over our heads when we're children. I remember it as I remember all things that involve paradox.

Chris, on a brief business trip to Timaru, had pushed his Jaguar faster than the law allowed. Accordingly, my father was called on to defend him in the Magistrates Court. My father asked that Chris do one thing in preparation for the case. He advised him to don his old school tie.

'I happened to know that the judge was an old Harrovian,' explained my father. 'As Chris and I mounted the steps of the court house we met his honour who had also just arrived. I took the opportunity to introduce "my client". I saw the judge glance down at Chris's tie, and in that moment I knew we'd won.'

Exhibit B:
Thoreau's *Walden*

Nature and all its works evoke delicate threads of thought. The lake at the golf course is his Walden pond and he the Sage of Middlemore, self-mocking...[however] he may not align himself wholeheartedly with [Thoreau's] essay on the Duty of Civil Disobedience...

George Barton in a review of *Dear Sam*

I find on the frontispiece the inscription, 'To Sam from Peter Mahon, 1978'. It was an indulgence. He had given me many books before, but never with a personal inscription. I was living in France at the time, surviving on very little, trying to be a painter. And although he may not have completely understood what I was doing or why I had chosen such a difficult route, I think, quietly, he was pleased. I think the direction I had taken was beginning to appeal to his sense of romance and he wanted to acknowledge it. And, after all, living in Fontainebleau meant that I was surrounded by forty-five thousand acres of forest, a forest that was teeming with wildlife. It provided an unending source of material with which to embellish the letters back home.

'Why should we be in such desperate haste to succeed and in such desperate enterprises?' wrote Thoreau, rather famously. 'If a man does not keep pace with his companions, perhaps it is because he marches to the beat of a different drummer, no matter how measured or far away.' They were adequate words to excuse my life. They were noble enough for him to accept.

Dante the Maker, by William Anderson

I don't know how it ended up here. I do remember the *New Zealand Listener* wanted it reviewed and he never had the time, or perhaps the endurance in the end. It was when he was very ill.

(Letter to Janet, my sister: 1977)

I hope you will keep up with your Italian studies despite the change of tutors, and in this letter I am setting out a few excerpts from Dante together with two or three examples of the way in which English poets have sometimes adopted the imagery or phraseology of *The Divine Comedy*. This is an allegorical work on the grand scale, drawn together in all its parts by the author's conception of Christian and moral philosophy but the effect is achieved by all the meetings with many individuals, some legendary, some real, during Dante's progress through the three regions. These encounters are described in lines that are clear and compressed and uncomplicated, and the language can be translated without much difficulty, making allowance for various archaisms.

In my youth I was a close student of the master, and on consulting a couple of my old books I see various pencil notes in the margins referring to some of what follows. One note, picked up from some commentator, indicates how Milton, evidently, copied one of Dante's descriptions, and there are one or two others which I will set out which I think I picked up myself. Though doubtless many erudite scholars have noted these in the past, and many more.

In canto 34 of the *Inferno*, there is a description of Satan:

> *O quanto parve a me gran maraviglia*
> *quando vidi te facce alla sua testa!*

> Oh how great a marvel seemed to me
> when I saw three faces on his head!

The canto goes on to describe how each face bore a different colour, representing the different aspects of anger, envy and despair which held Satan transfixed in the last confines of hell, reserved for traitors such as Judas and Cassius, and faithless Albert.*

When Dante descends into the second circle of hell he finds there the spirits of those who are being punished for sins of lust and incontinence, such as the licentious Queen of Babylon, Cleopatra, Helen of Troy, Achilles, and many others. Among them he sees the celebrated pair of adulterers Paolo and Francesca. Francesca was a beautiful girl living in Rimini, an Adriatic town captured by your father and his companions in September1944, and she was married by way of political alliance to the deformed son of the lord of Rimini. But she became enamoured of Paolo, her husband's handsome brother, and one day when she was reading him Galeotto's account of the romance of Lancelot and Guinevere, they were so carried away by the intensity of the tale that they laid aside the book, and shortly afterwards were surprised in adultery by the deformed husband who stabbed them both to death. The punishment inflicted on these carnal sinners consisted in their being whirled incessantly through the air by violent gales of wind, symbolic of the gusts of passion to which they yielded in mortal life:

> I came into a place void of all light,
> Which roars, like the seas in a tempest,
> When it is fought by warring winds.
> The hellest storm which never rests,
> leads the spirits with its sweep;
> Whirling and buffeting, it torments them.

I see by my pencilled note of long ago a reference to *Measure for Measure* in which a similar punishment is referred to. A young man named Claudio has been convicted of getting a young lady with child, and has been condemned to death. The following dialogue describes his offence:

---

* The Albert Peter was referring to was the family cat, which had abandoned him and taken up residence next door.

Clown: 'Yonder man is carried to prison.'

Bawd: 'Well: What has he done?'

Clown: 'A woman.'

Bawd: 'But what's his offence?'

Clown: 'Groping for trouts in a peculiar river.'

Claudio in prison is apprehensive of his fate. He endeavours, at first, to be philosophical:

> If I must die,
> I will encounter darkness as a bride,
> And hug it in mine arms.

But later he reflects upon his fate in the next world:

> Ay, but to die, and go we know not where;
> To lie in cold obstruction and to rot;
> This sensible warm motion to become
> A kneaded clod; and the delighted spirit
> To bathe in fiery floods, or to reside
> In thrilling regions of thick-ribbed ice;
> To be imprisoned in the viewless winds,
> And blown with restless violence round about
> the pendent world.

The parallel with Dante's description is so close that it seems almost certain to have been inspired by Dante's lines. This is reinforced by the previous reference to 'fiery floods' and 'thick-ribbed ice', which seems to be derived from canto 3 where Charon, the eternal ferryman, greets the spirits of the dead as they reach the river Acheron, on the other side of which lies eternal punishment:

> Woe to you depraved souls!
> Hope not ever to see heaven:
> I come to lead you to the other shore,
> into eternal darkness, into fire and ice.

Measure for Measure was written in about 1604. *The Divine Comedy* was written in about 1300 and was first printed in 1472.

The other adaptation by an English writer of a phrase written by Dante, one which I found myself, so far as I remember, occurs in the sonnet of Keats, which starts:

> When I have fears that I may cease to be
> before my pen has gleaned my teaming brain…

Further on the sonnet proceeds:

> And when I feel fair creature of an hour!
> That I shall never look upon thee more…

Now compare canto 29 of the *Purgatorio*, where the following description of Eve appears:

> …the only woman,
> Creature of an hour,
> endured not restraint of any veil;

The phrase *pur testa formata* (only just formed) has always conventionally been translated 'creature of an hour'. Dante is referring to Eve as being newly created, and being responsible for original sin by her lack of any raiment when she offered Adam the forbidden fruit, whereas Keats uses the phrase for its sound alone, the words being meaningless in their context because although it refers plainly enough to a woman, the allusion is unconnected.

Here is an extract from *The Waste Land* by T.S. Eliot:

> Under the brown fog of a winter dawn,
> A crowd flowed under London bridge, so many,
> I had not thought death had undone so many.

This is meant to convey, as you will see, that these workers trudging into the city are doomed souls with nothing to live for. The lines are taken from canto 3 of the *Inferno*. In the following passage, Dante is describing the spirits of the dead as they file in a long column towards the river Acheron:

> ...so long a train
> of people, that I would not have believed
> That death had undone so many.

...and finally, Janet, if you are not asleep by this time, here is the finest passage in the whole of *The Divine Comedy*, the inscription which Dante sees written on the gate of the Inferno. The middle three lines carry a subtle meaning. They refer to the concept that the entrance of Hell, and the inferno itself, were made by the Great One through his love and sense of justice to all mankind, which necessarily required that mortal sinners must forfeit their claim to paradise. Then comes the last line, once quoted to you as we drove one morning past the Supreme Court building in Waterloo Quadrant. You have to imagine that the gate itself is speaking:

> Through me is the way to the city of sorrow;
> Through me the way into eternal suffering;
> Through me the way among the lost people.
>
> Justice moved my High Maker;
> Divine Power made me, and
> Wisdom Supreme, and primeval love.
>
> Before me were no things created,
> That were not eternal; and eternal I endure;
> Abandon every hope, ye who enter here.

Ciao, Janet, *e buona fortuna, dalla tutta famiglia.*

It was spring when Channel Nine came to town looking for Peter. Erebus was big news even in Australia. They had come to make a documentary on the judge at odds with his government's prime minister and they had sent the most beautiful woman in the southern hemisphere to conduct the interview, Jana Wendt. I was in Auckland at the time visiting for a few days.

It was autumn because I remember cicadas in the tiny orchard at the back of their Parnell weather-board house. Peter was showing me the apricots with his customary air of astonishment whenever confronted by the miracle of vegetation doing as it was told. His father had been famous for his ability to conjure fruit of any kind effortlessly from the black soil of Marshlands and Moncks Bay, but it was a talent in which my father was entirely devoid and it left him marvelling, just as he had marvelled at the first fax machine he ever encountered. 'Look at that thing, my boy. The words on this bit of paper will very soon be printed out on a similar machine on the other side of the world,' and he shook his head as if he had just seen water turned to wine. And yet we had had television for thirty years, telephones for a lot longer. Magnetic impulses had been driving our world for a long time, only in different forms. He was a strangely unpractical man. If the hose connection broke he would call on the neighbour to fix it, if the windscreen wiper came adrift he would take it to the garage. I never doubted that my father could have solved many mysteries of the electronic and mechanical world if he had wanted to, I tend to think he simply chose not to. He had other things on his mind.

Jana was due in an hour. Everything was a little tense. But it was autumn, as I said, and the cicadas were singing. As my father turned to adore another fruit, I pinched one of the plump insects by the wings and popped it into my mouth. When he turned back to offer me an apricot I was buzzing. He frowned at me. I opened my mouth and the cicada flew free. My father squeezed his eyes shut and shook his head. 'Don't do that,' he said, and ambled away toward the house.

The crew had brought only one camera with them and it was necessary to film Jana asking the occasional question or nodding from time to time so that it could be spliced in later to give the interview a broader dimension.

'Just talk to me and I will nod,' she said.

'What do you want me to say?' asked my father.

'You can say anything,' she replied.

The camera rolled. Jana fixed my father with an enquiring, yet conspiratorial stare, and my father began to speak to her in Italian. The beautiful Czechoslovakian held out for only a few seconds and then her face cracked into a broad smile.

'What did he say,' asked the director.

'He's reciting from Dante,' she replied.

EXHIBIT D:
A stack of seventy-eights, predominantly Bing Crosby and Satchmo

On one long summer's day my father and I drove to Port Underwood where we were to share a seaside house for a couple of weeks during the Christmas holidays. I don't remember how my mother and sister travelled up; I don't think my brother had been born, or if he had he was still of limited significance in my life – significance depending on his ability to walk upright and present a steady target for the pinecone grenadiers that infested the broom-blushed hills of home. So my father and I were travelling alone, singing all the songs in his repertoire to wile away the miles: Dean Martin, Frank Sinatra, Satchmo and Crosby, everything set to the key of the cruising engine.

To my ear, my father had a marvellous voice. It was as rich as Crosby's and he used his unique phrasing; that effortless, almost conversational way he had of rendering a line. 'I'm as restless as a willow in a windstorm, I'm as jumpy as a puppet on a string…' You could imagine the old crooner taking a draw from his pipe after every line. I loved my father's voice and, although as we grew older there was less of it, I do remember my mother at the piano when particular old friends came by, standing close, glasses in hand, their voices blending. And when we travelled anywhere as a family we sang every mile of the journey, chopping the songs into four parts, each of us seeking the unoccupied harmony line.

Dean Martin's *Little Old Wine Drinker Me* was on our lips when we stopped at a small town ostensibly for Peter to find some floating board that I would be able to use in the sea during the holiday. My father wanted me to swim well. He could, I couldn't. Maybe the board would encourage me. We pulled up beside a sports store with boating equipment in the window. I stayed in the car while my father went to investigate. He glanced in at the window of the sports store, shook his head, and then detoured to the liquor store from which he returned with a bottle of whisky. 'They don't have anything,' he said.

I was a little disappointed. 'What did you ask for,' I replied, 'a boat on the rocks?'

I thought this was really funny. I still do, although I don't remember that he acknowledged it. And yet I must have been about ten at the time. It was almost as witty as the line delivered by eleven-year-old Evan Marks two days later as he leaned over the side of the dinghy from which we were all fishing. He was frowning at his line which seemed to have become stuck in the unfathomable depths.

'Kelp?' asked his father.

'No Dad,' he replied, studying the water. 'I think I've hooked the continental shelf.'

This was a cleverness that our parents enjoyed, the distorted keystones in the architecture of their casual conversation. Unconsciously we imitated them, trying to turn language around on itself, to make it absurd and yet more meaningful at the same time.

When he first heard *White Christmas* it was Italy. His platoon was hunkering down in the snow somewhere so I guess it must have been 1944. 'That song will be a hit, boys,' he announced. 'It will be eternal.' He was proud to have been the first to recognise it. And I can't hear *True Love* without thinking of Peter crooning Bing's part and Mum putting Grace Kelly in the shade. It is hard to say, of course, but that might well have been his favourite song. 'She can't sing a note,' my father informed us. 'Bing had to coach her through every line.' That scene from the film, Bing, with his sleepy eyes and his captain's cap askew and Kelly resting in his arms, was one that rated for my father as highly as the moment the cat nuzzles against the shins of Harry Lime in *The Third Man*.

In 1978 I went to live in Fontainebleau, to paint; to try and find an authentic voice in a foreign land. A few years ago I wrote a memoir of that time:

> ...I was painting when Joe called. The scent of distilled oils filled the room and it was comforting. It reminded me of the first days of Art School. The smell of duck canvas and turpentine that drew imagination to the surface like a poultice drawing poison from a wound.

'Sam, you wanna come?' I looked at my work, at the veneer of ochre that covered my drawing, enough warmth to take the chill out of the muddy blue sky to come. 'I can't, Joe. If it dries now I'll have to start again.'

'Oh,' said Joe. He shrank a little in his black jacket. 'Okay. I'm sorry though. She'd like to meet you, I know.' I gestured helplessness and regret. Joe brightened. 'Hey, did you hear Crosby died?'

I stared at him, expressionless. This strange young man with his grasshopper mind. What did he mean, 'Crosby died?'

'You know, the crooner.' Joe seemed happy. Happy? Or just pleased to have something of value to pass on. That Bing Crosby could become such tawdry tender revolted me.

'Dead?'

'Yesterday, I guess. Annette told me. She's...' he shrugged, 'You know, musical. You two'd get along well.'

'I'm sorry,' I said.

'Ah that's okay,' said Joe.

'I mean, about Bing Crosby. He was the best.'

'Yeah, I guess so,' said Joe, reflectively. 'He was one of the better crooners.' He glanced at his watch. 'Okay, I better scoot. Listen, I'm heading out of here tomorrow. All the best, huh?' He put out his hand.

'Same to you, Joe.'

Joe pulled his hood over his head. It made him look even taller.

'This's a great jacket. Looks mean, don't you think? No one's going to mess with this dude.' He grinned, waved his hand and turned away. I closed the door. All I could think of was my father, twelve thousand miles away, where the only music had come to an end.

Peter travelled to New Orleans once simply to hear some old time jazz. But he had left it too late. They were playing new tunes by then, smart licks, a little too experimental for his taste. No one was playing *The Basin Street Blues* anywhere.

EXHIBIT E:
The table on which he wrote
Verdict on Erebus

Was there, after the verdict, a criminal investigation? If not, why not?
It seems to me there was criminal negligence, at the least.

Letter from Dr Karl Popper

It is made of oak, sturdy, with rolled legs and ivory casters. The varnish is worn now and instead of volumes of paper, it bears an assortment of kinetic sculptures, wax maquettes and a constant film of dust.

I remember him sitting at this table hour after hour, tracking his pen across the white sheets, a cigarette poised in his left hand, reading-glasses half way down his nose, composing a novel that would grasp the public's imagination like a fist.

While a huge amount has been written about the tragedy itself, not a lot has been written about the impact on the families concerned. I know at this time of writing that the author, Owen Scott, is constructing a novel based on the effect the crash had on the lives of the pilot's families, and in some small way our lines of research have intersected; particularly concerning Sir Owen Woodhouse, the senior appeal judge. Of the five judges who reviewed Peter's findings concerning the Erebus Commission, Owen and Judge McMullin had gone, my father believed, beyond their brief by saying there was no evidence that my father had been lied to by witnesses for the airline. My father cited this minority decision as the sole reason for his resignation from the bench, arguing that the judgment effectively undermined public confidence in his ability to perform his job. In truth, there would have been at this time no judge in the country the public trusted more.

Woodhouse is a curious figure, and it is not enough just to say that he and my father held opposing opinions with regard to this matter. Concepts don't tend to exist in isolation; all of our points of view are connected, some to the extent that they constitute keystones and their removal or adjustment threatens to bring down whole architraves of perception.

Was there a gradual accumulation of dislike between the two men, or were their world viewpoints grounded so far apart to begin with that it was inevitable that they should disagree? How can the structure of law, so clear in its intent* be interpreted with such variance by two men of high intelligence and profound legal experience?

Peter by his own admission was a conservative. This is true only to a certain extent, of course. His sense of social responsibility is illustrated in these pages, and it was evident also in the courtroom. I remember a letter, which unfortunately we no longer possess, sent to him at the height of the Erebus controversy. It was from a man whom Peter had once sentenced to prison. It was a letter of support and it alluded to his moment in court before my father, thanking him for his fairness.

Peter was not at all the hard-bitten reactionary he liked to portray himself as being. Woodhouse and my father's sense of social justice would not have been that dissimilar I would have thought, and yet there it is, this constant undermining of each other leading to the crisis which, apparently, left my father with no choice but to walk away from the thing he loved most, the law.

But before attempting to review the relationship between Peter and Sir Owen Woodhouse, it is necessary, once more, to review Erebus. Using my father's book, *Verdict on Erebus*, as source material, I will relate the story as briefly as possible for those who may have missed it.

On 28 November 1979, a DC10 aircraft, operated by Air New Zealand, flew into the side of Mt Erebus in the Antarctic. It was the fourth worst air disaster in aviation history, killing 257 passengers and crew.

---

* 'The right of arrest is not controlled by uncertain standards, or disfigured by fluctuating jurisprudence. It is closely limited and clearly defined, so much so that in all cases, the ultimate answer is the legal response to a question of fact.' (From a judgment of Peter Mahon's, see p. 210.)

In due time my father was appointed as a one-man commissioner into the tragedy, with David Baragwanath QC assisting. Peter notes at the beginning of *Verdict on Erebus*:

> I could not foresee the obdurate and implacable series of obstructions and evasions which were to be created by the airline itself in a bold attempt to thwart the discovery of the truth.

And the truth was this: the aeroplane had been flying at a permitted low level in clear air on a course wrongly programmed into its navigational computer. Because of a trick of Antarctic light, the mountain was invisible to everyone on board the plane. Without any apprehension on the part of the pilots, they flew straight into it.

If everyone giving evidence at the commission had combined to discern the truth, the hearings would have been over in a very short time. However, the airline knew that if it were found to have been negligent or reckless, it would have been liable to limitless insurance claims. Consequently, it moved very cautiously, presenting only evidence designed to lead the commission in a direction that served the best interests of the company. Eight months passed between the opening of the hearing and the delivery of my father's report to parliament.

The Chief Inspector of Air Accidents, Ron Chippindale, had arrived at an early conclusion in his own investigations into the cause of the accident. He was of the fixed opinion that the aircraft had been flying far below the minimum altitude designated by the company and more importantly, that it had been flying in thick cloud when it hit the mountain.

However, among the first items of evidence produced before the Royal Commission were photographs collected from the crash site. These were printed from the dozens of cameras strewn across the ice, many of which were still intact. The photographs, some of which had been taken just split seconds before impact, showed the air on either side of the plane to be clear with almost limitless visibility to the east and west. (There were no photographs to the south, to where the slopes of the mountain rose to meet the overlying cloud layer. This is something that was never explained fully. One correspondent, however, wrote to my father saying that when the plane was flying toward Erebus no one could see forward except the pilots. And when it turned in its descending loop, the plane would have rolled, tilting the wing that faced south upward so that the only substance visible would have been the unbroken cloud layer five hundred feet above.) However, the photographs completely dispelled the notion that the pilots were lost in cloud, a notion that Ron Chippindale never completely relinquished.

To my father's great annoyance, the Chippindale Report was published a few days before the commission opened. Peter had written to the Prime Minister suggesting that it would be a very unwise move, but he was ignored and the Government Press was put into top gear to get the report into the public arena as soon as possible. My father, some time later, reviewing the way the airline had presented its evidence, reflected on the possible reasons for printing the Chippindale Report in such haste. It became clear that much of what the inspector believed about the accident would not have stood up under cross-examination during the commission hearing, and therefore would never have seen the light of day. It was advantageous to the government, however, the major shareholder in the airline company, to have the blame for the accident placed squarely on the heads of the dead pilots. Subsequent insurance claims against the company would be minimal. If my father found the company culpable, then his findings could always be discounted in favour of Chippindale's view. But if the Chippindale Report was never printed then there would never be any such 'other view'.

One of the most unfortunate effects of publishing the Chippindale Report before the commission had a chance to look at the evidence, was that the public was led to believe the pilots were to blame, and the pilots' families had to bear the brunt of the public's anger. Marie Collins, the senior pilot's widow, had two teenage daughters at the time who were still in school. It was very hard on them indeed.

Giving evidence, the company held that there had always been a minimum flying altitude of 6000 feet over the viewing area, and they produced witness after witness to give evidence to that effect. But Captain Collins, one of the most fastidious pilots in the airline, had taken his plane down to 1500 feet, apparently flouting all the rules.

There was also an early controversy over the 'black box' tapes that had been sent to Washington for translation. Chippindale had gone with them and then, oddly, had taken them to Farnborough, England, to a different facility where the audio transcriptions were amended.

Counsel for ALPA (Airline Pilots Association) gave notice that they did not accept this version of the black box tapes. They asserted that Chippindale's interpretation of an indistinct voice saying, 'A bit thick here, eh Bert?...', a phrase meant to suggest the plane was flying in cloud, never appeared on the Washington transcription.

My father was struck by the fact that where a commission is set up to weigh evidence alone, counsel for the airline seemed to be setting up the inquiry to play like an adversarial contest. This was evidenced first when he was told that the airline would not make any opening address.

I must admit that when I heard the news that the airline did not propose to make any opening submissions 'at this stage' I began to entertain a slight doubt as to their motives. They seemed to me to be regarding themselves in the same light as defendants in a court case. And there is very often a good reason why counsel for the defendant in a court case will elect not to make an opening submission in the sense of describing what the evidence is going to be. When this occurs in the courtroom, the usual explanation is that counsel for the defendant is not quite certain what his witnesses will say under cross-examination.

Against the company's repeated assertions, evidence started to accumulate supporting the fact that planes had often been flying as low as 2000 feet for some time, and this had been reported in at least four newspapers which had sent journalists along for a ride over the ice. None of the witnesses for the company admitted to any knowledge of the articles, the most prominent of which appeared in *The Travelling Times*, one of the airline's own magazines, distributed to all pilots and members of the airline. The air accident officer himself had received a complaint from McMurdo base that some planes were flying as low as 1000 feet over the base. He had done very little about it at the time, which was odd, given that low flying was one of the base reasons given by him for the accident.

> Again, the thought crossed my mind that Air New Zealand might be running the inquiry as if it were a court case in which they were defendants. Admit nothing unless compelled to do so. Do not volunteer evidence. If a witness is in doubt how to answer a dangerous question, then spar for time until the evening adjournment. These are all commonplace courtroom situations. Sometimes they are 'councils of perfection', especially the 'sparring for time' tactics for although such measures are usually identifiable, they often succeed...
>
> It became a standard feature of the inquiry for someone in management to monitor the daily record of evidence and to correct or patch up any defect in the company's case which cross-examination appeared to reveal. The stage was reached where, during the normal conference at the end of the day, Messrs Baragwanath and Harrison and I would identify some evidential setback which the airline seemed to have suffered, and we would then wait for that evidential fact to be modified or explained and, in some cases, contradicted by the same witness the next day. We were able to predict with considerable accuracy these future shifts and changes in the evidence...

Chapter seven, in *Verdict on Erebus*, deals with the evidence of Chief Pilot Captain Gemmel. Possibly in my father's mind he might have wished to call this chapter something like, 'The Third Man'. It is quite clear to the reader that he wants us to take note of this character with special reference to his previous observation that someone was modifying the company's evidence. Later in the book, when my father describes the chief executive Morrie Davis's demeanour under cross-examination, he goes to some lengths to dissuade us from suspecting that Morrie is as malignant as he looks. For all his posturing and threatening from the heights of his office, on the witness stand he looks weary and beaten. It is Gemmel's portrait that receives the closest attention, and it is for a very clear reason. But it has to be remembered that nowhere in Peter's narrative could he afford to step over the line into defamation. Many times he leads us to the edge of discovery and then steps back a pace, leaving us to come to our own conclusions.

Captain Gemmel was 'one of the dominant figures in the airline' and was said to be a close friend of Morrie Davis. He was one of the architects of the original plan for the Antarctic flights.

...the answers he gave [under cross-examination] were unhesitating and positive. When possible, his answers were monosyllabic and he seemed to treat the various counsel with thinly veiled contempt. His lean figure, standing upright with an almost military stance, reminded me of someone; but I could not for the moment remember who it was. I looked at his bronzed, immobile, aquiline features and his close-cut grey hair, and I surveyed his uncompromising demeanour. Then I remembered who it was that the captain reminded me of. In his general appearance he was very similar to photographs I had seen of the celebrated Field Marshal von Manstein, probably the most brilliant army commander of the present century. And as the hearing went on, I came to see that his similarity to the Field Marshal was not exclusively visual.

As I have indicated, his answers were given with almost military precision. Everything he said was clear and brief. If he considered a question repetitive, he did not hesitate to say so. After he was asked a question, he would immediately lean forward toward the microphone, pronounce his answer, then lean backward and regain his former posture. Under cross-examination the Chief Pilot maintained his iron composure. He was completely unperturbed and his answers continued to be concise and clear. No matter how valid some criticism seemed to be, his attitude never varied. He plainly maintained the view that the planning of the flights by the airline had been impeccable in all respects.

...the evidence of Captain Gemmel had come to an end. He stepped down from the witness stand and departed as he had arrived – intelligent, taciturn and impregnable. He walked to the back of the courtroom and sat down with the management contingent. Right through the long hearing, throughout all the weeks which lay ahead, Captain Gemmel sat day by day behind the airline counsel.

It was also admitted about this time that someone had typed incorrect data into the flight navigation system of the plane. This was a pretty serious point given that jets of that nature were not piloted in the way smaller and non-commercial planes were. The computer aboard the airliner took a fix on the centre of the earth and measured its position accordingly; I guess in a similar way to GPS systems today, except their reference points are geo-stationery satellites.

When describing this phenomenon of 'flight' to Sharon Crosbie on National Radio, one of the most instructive of all the interviews, Peter likened the pilots to train drivers. 'Imagine a railcar heading from Christchurch to Picton,' he said. 'Wherever the track is laid down, that is where you will expect the train to go. Now, the driver has been told the track goes to Picton via the coast. But if someone, without telling the driver, picks up the track and sets it down in a direct line with one of the nearby mountains, who would be to blame for the subsequent crash?'

It seemed to my father that the computer error might be of more significance than the company was admitting. The position they held was that it would not matter if the error had been made so long as the plane stuck to the rule of a 6000 foot minimum. At one point they held that the computer track was correct where it showed a heading that took the craft directly over Erebus, an active volcano. My father, counsel for ALPA and their pilots were astounded to think this could be seriously proposed as a safe practice.

The way the 'defence' were playing their witnesses was likened by Peter to a hand of cards:

I had already marked [Grundy] down as an ideal public relations man so far as the airline was concerned. If one desired to make a favourable early impression on a tribunal, then Captain Grundy was just the type of witness to be used for that purpose. Here I should explain that the decision as to the order of witnesses is always of importance in a jury case... It would not do, for example to call as a first witness a man who might be rude or self-assertive or otherwise liable to set the tribunal against him and therefore against the party calling him. So there is a standard procedure in jury cases whereby you select ... a person who is not only a reliable witness, but also with a demeanour which will favourably impress itself upon the tribunal. I strongly suspected that this manoeuvre had been attempted here. If so, I could only regret its occurrence. This inquiry was in no sense a court case. In addition it was being heard by a man who had spent all his working life in courtrooms. It was idle to expect that I could be taken in by this type of device.

There were also moments of sheer madness. The moment when Captain Kippenberger, in the face of evidence that there was no whiteout, suggested that the pilot, Captain Collins, had been struck by some malady at the crucial moment. Unfortunately for this hypothesis to have substance, the mystery illness would have had to strike both pilots simultaneously and probably the flight commentator, Peter Mulgrew, as well. But the tapes certainly didn't bear any of this out. I remember my brother, who had been visiting the hearing regularly, reported that from time to time the whole court would be trembling with mirth at some of the evidence given, it was so palpably unbelievable. It seemed there was a kind of desperation on the part of the company to adhere to their story no matter how absurd it became with the passing of the days. And the reason, probably, was that they were trying to avoid unlimited liability. The fact that neither of the two pilots on that fateful trip had ever flown to Antarctica before, was a fatal departure from international standards. If they had complied with the rule, then one of them would have noticed that the clear landmarks of Beauford Island and Cape Bird were in the wrong place. Peter Mulgrew, the commentator on that flight, had been to the ice with Hillary. Unfortunately he had never taken part in any previous flights so that when he mistook Cape Tennyson for Cape Bird there was no one with experience to correct him.

One reason why the company had not adhered to the usual rule was that these flights were a kind of perk, a departure from the usual routine for their pilots. However, there were many pilots working for Air New Zealand at the time, and they all wanted to have the chance to go down to the ice. One at a time would have taken too long.

It took twenty-four witnesses and ten weeks of commission hearings before someone from the defence admitted at last, that flights below 6000 feet over McMurdo were permissible. This evidence came from Captain

Wilson. My father remarks as an aside that this officer had flown in the Pacific Campaign and had been awarded the Air Force Cross. He was implying that it took a man of considerable courage to depart from the company line. He notes also that it is clear that the final paragraphs of this officer's prepared statement were typed on a different machine. Peter must have suspected that Captain Wilson had typed the appendment himself.

But apart from the unreliability of the evidence given by witnesses for the company, there was still one outstanding puzzle in the case. It was clear that the pilots had been flying lower than the summit of Mt Erebus, and that it was permitted. It was clear also that they were diligently following an incorrect course prescribed by the inboard computer. It had been proved that they were flying in clear air. The tapes, right up to impact showed that the plane was operating perfectly and that there was no hint of apprehension in the voices of the pilots or any member of the crew. The words translated by Chippindale as meaning 'a bit thick here, eh Bert?' were re-transcribed by the Washington experts as 'That's Cape Bird'. So something absolutely unexpected must have happened.

It took an exceptional pilot, Captain Gordon Vette, to discover what it was. Vette had begun his own investigations when the plane went down and it was now his firm view, supported by a professor of navigation whom he brought to the Commission from Australia, that the pilots had been victims of whiteout. They had been flying 500 feet beneath a layer of cloud that met the mountainside halfway up. What the pilots saw was the unblemished flank of the mountain rising up to meet the cloud, forming a line, which in the absence of texture gave the illusion of a long flat expanse which is exactly what they expected to see if they had been flying toward McMurdo Sound. The line where the cloud met the mountain was a false horizon and was never distinguished as being otherwise. Even when the ground proximity alarm sounded the pilots registered no apprehension. They must have thought the alarm faulty. Nevertheless, Captain Collins ordered, 'Go round power', the term used when a landing must be aborted, and had barely begun to push the throttle forward when the plane struck.

The disaster had involved a number of components: apart from the white-out phenomenon and the altered computer track, the forward radar on the plane was ineffective in Antarctic conditions given that the surface ice is dry, the radar only responds to moisture. It was also unfortunate that the radar operators at the US base at McMurdo had failed to switch to high frequency when TE109 slipped behind the mountain. When they lost contact with it they should have known why and if they had changed frequencies they could have warned the pilots that they were heading for disaster.

Peter travelled to Washington and to London, interviewing expert witnesses in relation to the black box recordings and trying to speak with the radar operators who had been whisked home by the Americans after the crash. The radar recordings were played but it was found that the four minutes of relevant sound, the time the aeroplane was out of contact, had been erased from the tapes.

One of the most significant events of Peter's journey took place when he was in London. He was phoned by a Mr Martin from Lloyds Insurance Agency, asking for a meeting, 'without prejudice'.

Mr Martin wanted to tell the judge that Lloyds was upset that the airline's witnesses clearly were not being taken seriously. He was afraid that their lack of credibility might reflect on Lloyds.

> By this stage Mr Martin had made his point. He plainly regarded the altitude and navigation evidence which I had listened to as being false, but he wanted it clearly understood that neither he nor Lloyds were in any way implicated and that when findings of credibility were made against the airline, it would be unfair for me to make any statement suggesting that the airline's insurers must necessarily have been involved.

Many months later a document was leaked to the press. It was a letter sent by Mr Martin to their brokers throughout the world, including those in Auckland. It stated that while the commission judge had been in London he had met with Mr Martin and they had had a brief discussion which revealed 'some anxiety' on the part of the court about how evidence had been presented. The following is an extract from that letter:

> ...as a result there has been further discussion of the whole matter between
> [legal representatives of Lloyds and legal representatives of airline] and there
> has been some considerable modification of certain proposals for evidence
> which have resulted in a far better impression of Air New Zealand having been
> given during recent days than previously. The evidence of Mr Davis, the chief
> executive, is still to be given and it is very much to be hoped that he will come
> up to proof and not be damaged by hostile cross-examination.

Well, I don't suppose Mr Davis did really come up to proof. He did what he
felt was required of him; he defended the company and attempted to defend
his reputation. Not with any real evidence as such, but by his belligerent
stance toward cross-examination and later by attacking the Commissioner.

> One of my final questions [to Morrie Davis] was how the airline could have
> published one million copies of *The Travelling Times* without his knowledge.
> To this he gave no verbal answer. He simply turned towards me and spread
> his arms outwards in a despairing gesture. He was indicating his total lack of
> comprehension that such a thing could have happened. I knew the feeling.

My father delivered his 160 page report on Erebus to the government printers
and then came down to spend a few days with me in the backwoods. I had
very little idea of what was going on. When my father was appointed to the
bench I was in my last year of school. I chose to remain in Christchurch
while the rest of the family moved to Auckland, and it was then that, to a
large degree, I lost track of the unfolding events of their lives. Maybe that's
why he chose to come down when he'd written the report; to get away from
the beginnings of what he knew was to be a firestorm.

And that was the first I knew of it, those few words spoken at the edge
of the pond that evening. Peter standing with his gun broken over his arm,
with the characteristic cigarette, staring out across the grey broken water,
surrounded by the leafless willows and waiting for gunfire. 'Tomorrow
all hell's going to break loose.' Tomorrow was when the report would be

delivered to parliament and the waiting press. And I wonder now if he used that army expression on purpose. He had waited at the Senio River for six months for the gun-fire to begin, and when it did, the common expression among the troops was 'Suddenly, all hell broke loose.'

I was twenty-five. I didn't understand. I glanced at him and I remember his face turned to the hills with his eyes set on that bright line where the sun had just gone down.

It was as if a stone had been thrown into the pond, the wake of it crashing against the shore in all directions. Unexpectedly, he had exonerated the pilots and placed the blame for the disaster on a string of administrative blunders. It was what the government and the company had most feared. If unchallenged, his findings would open the door to a flood of compensation claims, to a further decline of faith in the airline, and to an inevitable restructuring of the company from the top down. The pilots had been blamed for the disaster by Chippindale and that had suited most people very well. But now my father, finding in the pilots' favour, was to bear the disapproval of powerful men, men scrambling desperately to save their jobs and their reputations.

> I get pissed off when people lord the gentleman, who, in terms of that determination, was incompetent.
>
> Mr M.R. Davis in *North and South* magazine

And nearly everyone had something to say. Even the diminutive leader of the opposition, Bill Rowling, called from overseas suggesting there should be a new commission. He hadn't read the report of course, how could he have. Most people hadn't. But it didn't seem to matter.

And the stone was pretty: 'An orchestrated litany of lies'. It sticks. It was designed to. It is written in perfect iambic pentameter, the rhythm of Shakespeare, of true speech, and he knew exactly what he was doing. Here is a shard from a letter to a friend in which Peter is offering a critique on some poems written by his friend's son:

What I think produces the desired impact, in a short poem, is a final couplet clearly closing off the theme.

Here is one of unearthly beauty, with which Keats rounded off his reverie on sleep, and you will remember how many of his sonnets ended in that manner:

Turn the key deftly in the oiled words
And seal the hushed casket of my soul.

Exhibit F:
Great Battlefields of the World,
by John Macdonald

The second page bears the inscription: *'For Peter Mahon, to assist in planning those battles on the eastern front. Bill Hodge.'*

'There's a cafe called Gouchos,' he had said. 'Down the bottom of Federal Street, just past the Catholic church. There's a small garden outside and a rock fountain.'

And so there was. I arrived early, quarter past seven, not wanting to keep the associate professor waiting. I knew him slightly from television appearances where opinions or explanations concerning elements of constitutional law were required. He is an academic, the type of lawyer my father most disliked. But Bill is no type, and my father clearly enjoyed his company very much. He is American, near sixty but looks ten years younger. He bikes and runs very far and the first impression is one of compressed energy, detachment and evaluation.

'Why battlefields?' I asked.

'Because we had that in common. I served four years in the army.'

'Vietnam?'

He nodded. 'Artillery. I wasn't on the front line like your father, but it was something we shared and he liked to talk about it.'

'So why law?'

'Well, it's strange really how these things happen. I'd completed a history degree at Harvard before joining up with no real idea of where that would lead me. And then one day I was required to attend a court martial. I remember sitting in that courtroom and thinking 'this is me, this is exactly what I want to do'. So as soon as I got out I went to Stanford.'

'Did you know that Dad applied for a job at Canterbury University, but that they re-advertised the position without even replying to his application?'

'I'd heard something…'

'So who made the job for him up here?'

'Oh, I think it would have been Jack Northey.'

'Did he like it here?'

'Peter? I had the impression that when one of the students asked him about some judgment of his, he found it a bit boring. But if I said to him something like, well, that I'd noticed more thrushes about in the mornings than blackbirds, he would sit up a little and get really interested.'

'I wondered,' I said, 'many times, actually, if Dad had become bored with the bench. That if it hadn't been for Erebus he might have left anyway. That his resignation wasn't only precipitated by Woodhouse's report, that it might have been a convenient way out.'

Bill looked away, tilted his grey head a little. 'I couldn't say,' he said.

'Did he ever complain about Woodhouse?'

'Not that I remember.'

'Would you describe Woodhouse as a social engineer?'

'Oh yes, certainly. He would describe himself as a social engineer. And this was the thing that probably annoyed your father. Woodhouse could draw the broad picture but people like your father had to deal with the detail, had to apply it to the real world. It seemed as if Woodhouse's mission on earth was to remake the law.'

'Peter wrote once of Woody that he employed the broad view, and that taking a broad view was a convenient substitute for thought.'

He laughed. 'Yes, that's good.'

'Palmer. How did you find him?'

'I never warmed to him,' he said, frowning, and then smiled. 'Some people say that when he became a politician he became arrogant.' He paused, his eyes sparked with mischief. 'But that's not true,' he added.

I grinned and nodded.

Palmer had been Lange's Attorney General when, following the Erebus affair, two petitions to honour Peter were rejected by the Labour government. Palmer would have been stongly positioned to influence this decision. But Palmer, the pipe smoking academic from what my father used to describe as 'the left bank', was Woodhouse's man, and it is possible that in honouring Peter he might have felt he would have been dishonouring Woodhouse.

'One of your father's great talents was torts, of course,' said Bill, and his face lit up a little. 'Law evolves as society evolves,' he said. 'For example, nuisance to do with barking dogs might well be covered by precedent, but what about the nuisance of, say, radioactivity? Sooner or later the law has to be extended to cover such developments.'

'Examples?' I asked.

'Well, there was the case of the man who dug under his neighbour's boundary…'

I asked about bias and the inarticulate premise and mentioned the case of McMullin not withdrawing from hearing the appeal against my father's findings.

'Of course, he said, he should have recused himself.'

'Recused?'

'Stood aside,' he explained. 'Especially if he'd been challenged.'

I spent an hour and a half covering old ground, asking questions that I had already asked elsewhere. He mentioned Judge Kirby whom my father disliked very much, who has been described as the Australian equivalent of Woodhouse, and how my father was concerned that justice was in danger of being captured by a legal priesthood; and I was reminded again of Plato and Karl Popper, of *The Republic* and *Das Glasperlenspiel*, and I wondered if it was an eternal argument that had embroiled my father, a question of what is right in law, or what is right according to the prevailing perception of good and evil as discerned by 'reasonable' men.

Exhibit G:
The ceremonial Japanese dagger

I take it in my hand. It's from 1946, a memento of the nine months he spent in Japan serving as a member of the occupation forces. He was kicking his heels then, trying out his advocacy talents in courts martial and making quite a good job of it, by all accounts. The Italian campaign was somewhere behind him, like night lies behind the dawn, and all of them were impatient for home.

There's a small square of stainless metal protruding just beneath the hilt that releases the blade from its scabbard. I was fascinated by it as a child, by the delicate machine-work, the tiny clicking sound as the blade was released. It seemed beautiful and deadly at the same time. And I was puzzled by the texture of the material that covered the hilt and scabbard until the day Clara came by with her habitual parrot ducking around her shoulders and told me tales of snorkelling along the underwater cliffs of Stewart Island.

'I saw a fish tail sticking out from under a rock shelf, so I grabbed it,' she said. 'It was a shark. I didn't know what to do so I just held on until it thrashed itself into an adrenaline seizure. I thought it had died and I swam down and set it on the sand. After a couple of minutes it suddenly woke and swam away.'

'But,' I said, a little unbelieving, 'I have tickled a lot of trout in my time and tried to hang on to a salmon or two. It's a very difficult task, very slippery.'

'Oh, no,' she said, 'Shark skin is like sandpaper. The Japanese use it on their sword hilts.'

And I remember a few stories from that time. Just a few. They're dreamy, faint, like fading photographs. Stories of walking along the banks of a river with his friends watching for the twitching of seed heads in front of them, for snakes always have their ears to the ground. His stories of the war were always like this, misty in the detail, the actors with blank faces except for him and he is always a little taller. Not because he made himself out to be so but because, like an Egyptian drawing, he is the main character and, after all, I wasn't there. So in Japan as he hunts snakes I can see:

Fields of grass all around him burned white by the sun, the background faded to a blur and his companions wear khaki jackets just like the one in my cupboard. There is no sound, no murmur of voices, just the grass stretching ahead of them and I am watching it through his eyes, waiting for the shimmer in the grass ahead and when it comes I can see him lift his pistol and set its sights on the far bank because that is where the snake will emerge; cleverly, it has swum underwater to escape the approaching danger.

It is odd that he would hunt these creatures. After all, he had one as a pet back at the barracks. A thin crimson-mouthed grass-snake called Dave that he cherished, that he took out in the evenings to amuse his friends and which used to wind itself around the leg of the chair when he came to put it back in its shoe-box. He was always like that. There was always this duality: the hunter and the lover of nature.

They are walking again through the tall grass, my father and his faceless friends. There's a movement and he steps forward eager to see. It's a small, dark brown snake lying still amid the dry, broken summer-yellow grass. My father bends toward it like a heron arcing toward a fish. His quick right hand flies out and grabs the snake behind the head, his other hand takes its body and, grinning, the cigarette angled in the corner of his mouth, he holds it aloft for his friends to see. The snake's jaw is wide in silent anger. His friends gather around, curious. There's a small Japanese man nearby jabbering, gesticulating, his hands flying about and his nutty crinkled face filled with concern. He's tiny compared to the others, the grass comes up to his waist; the sky behind is white. They stare at him, puzzled. Then they realise what he is trying to tell them, and the men begin to stumble backwards, away from my father. The snake has wound its body around his forearm so that he can't fling it away. With only one hand free, without help, he is unable to unwind it.

And this was our currency. I did not have the wit for law and Latin and I don't remember that my father ever put a brush to canvas, but somehow I caught his interest in nature and I knew that any story from the wild would immediately command his attention.

Here is an extract from a letter I wrote from Fontainebleau in April of 1978:

> ...Barbara Strack is here for a couple of weeks. To keep her amused during her stay I have been leading her on many and varied treks into the forest. We partook of a light snack deep within the green confines last Friday to the accompaniment of spring *chanteurs* amid *les feuilles*. I was bravely sporting shorts ('*rosbif*', chime the children) and we were both walking in bare feet as we sauntered toward Moret, a small town 9 kilometres away. I was playing my flute at this stage, carelessly searching out old familiar tunes like *Frère Jacques* and Beethoven's *Fifth*. My eyeballs lay dully on the dry track stretching out before us – suddenly my hand shot out and grabbed Barb's arm in the proverbial vice-like.
>
> A few feet ahead of us, lying motionless in the sun, was a reptile *sans pieds*, as we say here. In fact a viper fresh from hibernation, its grey and black diamonds betraying its form on the monotone path. Barb uttered a number of unprintable words, she hates all kinds of worm. But never had I dreamed of such luck. As soon as I'd managed to shove my heart back down through my cardiac sphincter, I found a piece of wood with which to smack the now mobile creature behind the left ear. Delighted, I dropped him into my pack. When we got back to *chez Reant* I triumphantly pulled him out to show the residents. Never have I seen so many different shades of terror and especially as it started to writhe as I held it aloft. Annie assured me that the pearly gates would have been crowded had we not seen him in time – they are particularly dangerous at the beginning of spring. Anyway, I have his skin downstairs tacked out and salted and will send to Tim if it works out well.

I heard how he repeated this story to a friend of his, Peter Feenstra, but that he added a little spice to it by reporting that after I had removed the skin I then cooked the snake over a slow fire and ate it.

Apart from chasing snakes, Japan would have been a tedious interlude for Peter if it had not been for the legal work afforded by the reconstruction of that broken society and the opportunities provided by army protocol, a latticework of regulations for him to pit his wit against.

(Letter to his father: 1946)

There has been a bit of a crime wave here and there is a lot of business for anyone with any sort of legal qualifications. I got word the other day that I had passed Company Law, which I sat here just after we arrived, so I hope to get the degree finished this year. I have been having some fun on the Japanese trials, prosecuting Japs for all sorts of offences: black-marketing etc., also a case of white slavery. Before the war, prostitution was a recognised trade in Japan, but not so long ago, General McArthur issued an order saying that it must cease. The American Intelligence people staged a raid on Yamaguchi and copped two men who were keeping several girls in their establishment, so they were charged with disobeying the Supreme Commander's instructions. The case was defended by a Jap lawyer and you can imagine the chaos that resulted.

We have a new padre in the battalion called Murphy, drinks everyone under the table. He's new to the army. When he's trying to negotiate with one of the senior officers he always asks me to explain the correct procedure first; then he fronts up and pretends total ignorance of army affairs. In this manner he usually gets everything he asks for. We have worked some very questionable splinters between us.

With the arrival of the first draft from NZ we are getting under the obnoxious influence of the Staff Corps. I have never met a more irritating pack of bastards in my life. They all disapprove of me and a few of my friends because we call some of our men by their Christian names and occasionally have a drink with them. However, it won't go on for ever. I will be home in time to give you a hand with the spring gardening. Love, Pete.

PS Don't interpret that last comment as a promise – it was made without prejudice.

I like the story about the snake, holding it up for his friends to see as if he's holding the head of the devil himself between his thumb and forefinger. And they back away from him, his friends, just as they backed away from him when he took hold of the devil in Erebus. It all strikes me as prescient. The letter home shows also his lack of respect for authority unearned. During all his years on the bench he had little time for the ceremony that went with it, preferring to ignore the wigged parade and just get on with the job. And just as he was informal with his men he was, later, a friend to the bar, to the young lawyers who appeared before him, always approachable and prepared to offer advice. He never pretended that he was anything other than a man.

I found Major Rangi Ryan at his home on the North Shore. He'd got to know my father in the reconstructed 27th Battalion during the post-war occupation of Japan. But he'd also been nearby in northern Italy.

'He was very amusing,' said Rangi, and grinned. 'It was that dry wit of his. He and Clint Roper shared it. They had this way of talking that was like a private shorthand, anecdotes that only they'd understand. Maybe it was things to do with the law…'

I had driven across Auckland in the five o'clock traffic, an hour's journey that should have taken twenty minutes. I'd idled along motorways that my father must have watched become progressively clogged over the fifteen years he lived in that city. Fifteen years of driving down to the courts every day and then out to the open fields and wetlands in the weekends, to Ellerslie for golf and the cries of birds.

'I was in the 25th on the Senio, to the west of where your father would have been. Tough time? Well, we had to wait five days for the Poles to come up on our flank and it was a bit hot for a while until they arrived, the enemy were enfilading on our left. Every now and then we'd fling a grenade forward, of course, and that tended to discourage them.' The major is a tall, handsome man, still appearing fit and standing very straight. He had stayed with the army after the war, it had become his career.

On the coffee table in front of me he laid a soot-black album containing small black and white photographs of groups of soldiers, some clustered on tanks, some huddled in trenches, most glancing at the camera with grinning faces. These were not the boys from some American blockbuster. These were hollow faced men with corded muscles, thin and 'fit as a buck rat', as my father used to say.

'And there's Peter,' said Rangi, 'and Clint.' They're standing a little askew from the camera, two friends at ease in each other's company, caught in a flicker of light.

I asked him about Japan. 'There was not a lot to do in Yamaguchi. But we went over to the coast at one stage to watch for refugees, illegal immigrants. Apart from that there were parties, tennis, football. But you couldn't wander far.'

He told me a little about holding the winter line, the Gothic line where Kesselring had staged his formidable last resistance; and how one of Rangi's men lost a foot on a Schu-mine and another forgot to take the fuse out of a grenade while he was oiling it. 'That was very naughty,' he said with a dry grin.

And it is important to me, that expression, that comfortable cushioning of quite a frightening concept. Because I had been reading widely and in one history of the battalion it mentioned the incident, how the grenade had killed the man and severely wounded Rangi's brother. And the more I read, the further I find myself from understanding the workings of the minds of those men. I thought the more I asked the easier it would become. But it hasn't.

Exhibit H:
The Nepalese kukri

The kukri is primarily a tool for cutting wood and meat and sparking flints for fire. But in the hands of a Gurkha soldier it is also a formidable weapon, evoking shades of *The English Patient*, the scent of cordite and the chill of a winter in Namche Bazaar. But the knife in my hands did not come from the war. My father found it in some Auckland second-hand shop, I imagine, where he discovered from time to time books on art that he would send down to me. But it was Nepal as well. He had sent me there at a point when I was trying to decide whether I should go back to Art School or just pick up my brushes and start painting in the cold light of an unprotected world. When I say he sent me, I mean he had made the offer, but it's really the same thing. I couldn't have refused an adventure like that. And in the end it served me very well. When I returned from that month in the mountains I had enough material in my head to begin work on my first exhibition. It sealed my independence.

If he knew that would happen when he sent me away, I never found out. But I'm grateful, and the kukri is a reminder. But also it brings to mind the stories of the Gurkha regiment which fought alongside the New Zealanders in Italy.

'Sometimes the Italians used to try and nick provisions from the convoys driving up to the lines. It got so bad that in the end they put a Gurkha in the back of every truck. When a hand came through the canvas, whack!'

I slip the kukri from its leather case. Yak hide? Mule? Never unsheathe a kukri unless you mean to use it, I have been warned. I remember how the Sherpas used the small knives to strike flints and start fires in a tightly bound ball of yak fur, holding it in their fingers, blowing gently on it, nurturing the spark into a flame. 'They were the best,' says Bill Gates. 'The Gurkhas. They'd sneak along under the bullets and quiet any machine-gun nest. Slit their throats and not a sound.'

Ina Timms rang me one morning. 'Listen, I woke in the night,' she said. 'And I remembered Bill Gates who used to mow your father's grass when you lived on the hill. He was a contractor. He was in Italy with your father. Bill Gates. I'll give you his number. Got a pen?'

My father once referred to Ina as Lane Neave's (the law firm where she worked) most undervalued asset. 'Mind like a steel trap,' he said. 'They don't know what they've got in Ina.' And it's so. She, like my Aunt Helen, is a walking inventory.

Ali dropped me at Bill's place and left me alone with him. It's hard for people to open up when there's a crowd. The property was immaculate. Everything in its place, uncluttered amid a wide expanse of close mown lawn. Several cords of wood were piled up under an iron shelter even down to the smallest sticks that must have been thinnings. Nothing wasted. In the garage was a medium sized Fiat tractor, a Volkswagen Combie from the sixties and a sparkling Pajero from the twenty-first century.

'We're going fishing soon. We camp down at the Rakaia mouth, same spot every year. But you need the boat to get upstream, to get away from people.'

Bill's slightly smaller than average height, and his slightness would have been an advantage on the exposed ground of the Po Valley. He looks very well. 'You want to see the bees?' He showed me around. There's a stream at the bottom of the garden.

'Any freshwater crays?' I asked.

'Used to be,' he said, and shrugged. 'It doesn't run as full as it used to. Comes from a spring not far from here.' He gazed upstream but there was nothing to see. The trees had grown.

He opened the soot-black album for me and turned the pages uncertainly. 'She's getting a bit old this thing.' Some of the photographs had come adrift, the yellowing sticky tape had lost its hold. And there were the same photographs: groups of men seeming pleased to be there. Maybe just pleased enough to be away from the front line for a few days' rest. 'And there's your father,' he said, turning the book toward me for an easier view. The photo was small like the others. There were four of them. Bill to the left, someone else and then Peter, taller than the others. 'I thought that was quite good,' he said. 'I mean there with the Sphinx right behind him like that.

'It was Egypt. Just before we embarked for Italy. I don't know what happened,' he said frowning. 'Did he get commissioned or something? We lost track of each other soon after we arrived.'

I hadn't realised. They'd been split up. And I knew that I wouldn't learn much from Bill after all. Not about my father. All I would be able to ask him about were the battles and what it felt like to be there, what it was like to be a conscripted soldier. Because, like Rangi Ryan, he was only there at one end of my father's war. I needed someone from the middle of it.

'I don't like talking about it, really,' he said, gazing down at the flat back of his hands where they rested on the table.

'You used what cover you could. Stone walls. See there,' he pointed at a photograph. 'They were the best. Or a house when you could.'

'But wouldn't they be targeted?'

He spread his hands in a gesture of helplessness. 'It was winter,' he shrugged. 'And in the olive groves,' he continued, 'there were ditches. You did the best you could. We advanced behind a barrage, twenty-five yards behind the shells.'

I shook my head in disbelief. 'That's too close.' I said.

'We lost some men. Shells fell short. The rifling wears after so many thousand rounds, not their fault.'

'Why not hang back?'

He stiffened as if I'd cursed and glanced away, then back, and in a softer voice, 'You might get a bullet.'

I remembered Rangi talking about the Poles taking five days to get into position on the left of their line and how they had to try and hold the flank against enfilading fire. It was a matter of lives.

'We just wanted to get back home,' said Bill.

'And people like Upham?' I asked. 'He wanted to stay at Crete, wanted to finish the job. He used to stand up to draw fire. How does that happen?'

Bill looked down and clasped his hands. Then he gave me a very straight look. 'He must have had a lot of hate in him. You'd have to have a lot of hate. Those Hitler youth,' he said, and looked away again, shaking his head. 'They were the worst. I shot one once. The bullet creased his head, took his cap off. It should have been four inches lower.'

'It's a faceless enemy,' says Steinbeck, speaking to an American navy gunner. 'Your shells fall twenty miles away and you never have to look into the eyes of the man you kill.' (From *The Log of the Sea of Cortez*)

'They were only a couple of hundred yards away at the Senio. Sometimes we could hear them talking. The river froze on Christmas Day. Some of the blokes walked across and shook hands with them, gave them beer, cigarettes.'

'And the next day?'

'We went on shooting.'

He turned the page and indicated the image of a man in his thirties, well dressed, standing beside a shorter beautiful woman with fine, plaited hair. She is smiling straight into the camera, proud, straight backed. She holds their baby in her arms. Her husband is leaning toward her, his head tilted down a little, turned almost shyly toward us.

In the painting by Grant Woods, 'American Gothic', the grim farmer faces the viewer full on, his wife a little behind, a little turned toward him, her eyes on him, deferring. He grasps his pitchfork like it is a weapon. He is defiant. He is no man's prisoner.

On the other hand, the defiance in this small fading photograph is of a different kind.

'He was a German prisoner,' said Bill. 'Can't remember his name now. Nice bloke. We liked him, got on well. He kept in touch for a while.'

'Did you get much?' asked Ali.

'No,' I said. 'He didn't like to talk about it.'

'I can't watch these wars on television,' he had said, shaking his head. 'No one's learned a bloody thing. They should take the blokes responsible, give them a gun each, and put them in a room to sort it out among themselves.'

But as we drove away something odd occurred to me. Ina had said Bill used to come to cut the grass on our ragged piece of land on the hill. It was too much for my father, that acre and a half of rank growth swallowing up the newly planted fruit trees. He had tried a number of times to tame it with his neighbour Garth's sickle mower, a huge bone rattling contraption that threatened to turn on its operator and slice him into cutlets, but in the end he got the wiry contractor in to do the job.

If so, they must surely have shared a beer together. How could they have not, these old mates with their unique past. And yet Bill didn't know what had happened to my father after they split up in Europe. They must have talked over that beer about everything other than the war, mutually accepting the veil for reasons sacred to themselves. Discreet as the Sphinx.

'I don't like to talk about it,' he had said. And he meant it.

Exhibit I:
His battle jacket

It seems too small. It seems tailored for a boy and, of course, that's not how I remember him.

(Letter to Peter from Charles Upham)
The blokes in our age group have been the luckiest generation of all time. We had the Depression in our youth, which had the effect of planting our two feet firmly on the ground, then the war which was the greatest experience for the majority of blokes who came home again...

I dropped in on an English class at our local school a number of years ago where a friend of mine, whose father had been in Italy and whose grandfather had seen action in the Great War, was teaching a class of sixteen-year-olds. Ours is a country school and the class was quite small, perhaps seven pupils.

David had spread his grandfather's medals out upon the desk, the fettlings of antipathetic nations sifted through history's weft 'till all that's left are these: a dull, engraved swarf of brass and silver, clasps and faded ribbons. The students sat in contented semi-interest, Rob scribing arcs on the cover of his notebook, Alicia chewing gum.

'Now,' said Dave, 'can anybody tell me how the First World War began, the war to end all wars?'

There was silence. No surprise, even I'm unsure of how that blunder came to be.

'Well,' he said, 'what year was it? Anybody know?'

Nothing.

'Roughly?'

Nothing.

'All right,' he said, beginning to grin. 'Who was fighting whom?'

'Russia,' came a tentative voice, 'and ... Australia?'

'No,' said Dave, and glancing up he rolled his eyes. 'So ... let's try the Second World War. Now, what was that about? Any idea? What about you, Vanessa?'

Silence.

As I say, ours is a small country school. Nevertheless, it is possible that the events that shaped my father's generation are no longer clear in the minds of some of those who may care to read this memoir. Therefore, I feel I should sketch in a little of the background as I go. Please bear with me, I am a pupil myself.

In 1941 my father turned eighteen and enlisted as a private at Burnham Military Camp, twenty miles south of Christchurch. It is not clear how his father, Cecil, felt about it, but no parent could have been pleased to find their son preparing to go to war, especially those of the generation who had endured Gallipoli and France. Of Sir Arthur Donnelly, his mentor in law and a veteran of the Great War, it is recorded that he advised Peter that an RSA badge on the lapel could be to his advantage in his chosen profession.

Interspersed with his university studies, there followed nearly two years of training during which time he was taught the craft of warfare based on the experiences of the New Zealand Division in Africa, but when the theatre of war moved to Italy the tactics of the desert had to be revised. Eventually, on 24 September 1944, he joined 26th Battalion's advance base near Rimini on the east coast of Italy. The Germans, devoid of air defence and an equivalent of artillery, were retreating river by river and reassembling where possible to mount a stubborn defence. It has to be said that they were extraordinarily resilient in the face of certain defeat, and to hold out as long as they did was either extremely brave or simply fanatical. As we know, the fanatics were few. The rest of them, like the New Zealanders they were fighting, were just ordinary men.

The New Zealand Division was held up at the Senio River, near Faenza, for the duration of the winter. My father and his companions inhabited the stone farm houses all along the line where they were intermittently harassed by rain, snow and mud, occasional enemy patrols and the deadly bombardment of mortars and long range artillery. With the spring and the drying of the earth, the offensive began which would see the Eighth Army push through to Trieste by May. As I say, there exists no real personal account of my father's part in this drama: the best I can do is to provide a patchwork of military history woven in with anecdotes insufficiently remembered.

I would like, therefore, to pay close attention to this formative handful of years in which he is most indistinct. I want to construct in detail the context of this brief interruption in his life because I think it was the war more than anything else that shaped him. 'What I am today could be attributed to those four years in the army,' said Bill Hodge. 'It's something your father and I had in common.'

I remember being taken by my mother to my father's office in Hereford Street when I was very young and being intrigued to find a large train set laid out on the floor. My father and one of his colleagues, dressed in their habitual severe suits and ties, were on their knees, heads low to the ground. As my father pushed one of the large model carriages along the rails, the other man pulled a lever that closed a junction with a branching line. There must have been some accident down at the yards and they were trying to determine cause. It was very elaborate. I imagine my father, if following so faint a trail as his through Italy, might have gone to similar lengths, and in similar detail.

Having read the battalion history, his war records from Trentham and the few letters he wrote back to his family from overseas, I decided to visit Faenza and walk around a little, see if I could find his footprint somewhere. But more than that, I wanted briefly to breathe the air of Italy and experience something of what became for him a great love affair.

It had begun to rain just south of Bologna and it was falling quite heavily by the time I stepped off the train. As I walked away from the *stazione* in search of somewhere to stay, it began to soak into my trousers. I didn't mind. I was more comfortable wet than over the last hour where we had been squeezed shoulder to shoulder in the carriage, fourteen of us pressed into an area the size of three phone booths. Rochelle had described this to me once, how different cultures have different social spaces. In Italy, she said, social space can be as narrow as ten inches.

I have no Italian. I had nothing in Faenza but the international language and a smattering of French with which to barter for information. Nevertheless I found lodgings fairly easily and was soon settled in a room overlooking a narrow street in part of the old town. It's always this way in Europe, the old towns at the core of things like growth rings on a tree stump telling you a little of the hard times and of the good. So here in the old town were the clear stone defences within which lay much of the original architecture, while outside radiated the consequential growth, less ordered, less logical, more suggestive of individualism and less of community. And the rain came down, dripped from the shutters and turned the cobbles black. A clotted sky drifted overhead as the traffic on the main *strada*, sounding like a broken hive, mingled with the cries of passers-by and the tapping of steel heels on stone. The sound of Latin Europe seeped through everything. Until the day I walked the stopbanks of the Senio, a day of silence and distant thunder.

It was spring and it hadn't rained in northern Italy for a month. The Po River, which my father and his companions crossed in the spring of 1945 by means of pontoon bridges, was now running seven metres underground. They could have walked across it today with dust at their heels. But the Lamone, the river running against the southern wall of Faenza, was flowing nicely, albeit opaquely, and I noticed a sign designating the water quality as category C, whatever that might mean. I leaned over the railings of the bridge that connected the city with the main highway south and scrutinised the high arching brick-work beneath me. It must have been blown by the Germans in the face of the Allied advance, but I couldn't see the evidence. Not at first. The brick-work was identical from abutment to keystone, flaking, underfired clay that is common to Faenza, this ceramic capital of northern Italy. But then I noticed a star of David cut into the marble keystone and the date beneath, June, 1945. They must have worked very quickly to remake it all. The Germans were only gone by the end of April and there must have been a good deal of reconstruction to get on with, although I suppose bridges are a high priority.

I sat at the back of the cathedral a few hours later on an ancient pew that had complained loudly as I sat down, announcing my presence to the devoted handful at the front of the cathedral. The rosary was being recited, the interdiction and responses coming clearly at first and the decades blurring in a confusion of overlaying echoes, like clean breakers dissolving against the shore. Far away someone closed a door and it was like a distant cannonade. I imagine he would have come here, he and his fellow Catholics. They would have taken communion in the old way and felt the comfort of home. And when that distant door slammed did they flinch in their seats, grip the edge of the pew a little tighter? I could see a man's shoes protruding from behind the stairs to a lectern and the ferrule of his umbrella. I heard footsteps behind me, rubber soles squeaking against the ancient tiles. I saw a stained-glass window of abstract design and wondered how recently it had been commissioned. I glanced back again, the umbrella and shoes had gone.

Since the invasion of Sicily by the British, Mussolini had resigned and Italy had signed an armistice with the Allies. Immediately, Hitler ordered Kesselring to boost the defence of Italy by drawing down eleven divisions and establishing a defensive line in the north. Kesselring decided it would be better to run a line of defence further south, across the narrow waist of the peninsula between the Liri Valley on the west to the Sangro River on the east coast: the Gustav Line. Evidently there was time enough for the Allies, the American Fifth Army and Montgomery's Eighth, to take advantage of the momentary German confusion after the capitulation of Italy, by driving up the peninsula at speed to take them off balance. But due to a lack of any grand plan after the invasion at Salerno and Taranto, and an inability to supply a rapid advance, there was enough delay in the Allied camp for Kesselring to dig in on some of the best defensive ground in Europe.

Apparently, this general indecision cost the Allies dearly, for by the time the Eighth Army had made its way to the Gustav Line, an early winter had fallen over Europe and their mechanised advance ground to a halt in the mud and snow. The New Zealanders, east of the Pennines, tried for a month to punch a hole in the German line and suffered 119 casualties without any gain. When at last they withdrew and traversed around to the west, they were confronted by an even more impressive obstacle, Monte Cassino.

The town of Cassino is presided over by its monastery and the high hills on either side, and any progress up the valley was covered from all angles. It was the best possible position to defend, it was the worst to try and penetrate. Realising that it was going to be a costly encounter and wishing to minimise casualties, Freyberg ordered that the town be subjected to a heavy aerial bombardment which was to include the monastery. It was a decision that has been greatly debated ever since. While the Germans had given their word that they would not use the monastery as a defensive position, one of the Indian patrols under Freyberg's command convinced him that they were; although it appears the Germans were dug in all around the lower slopes of the building, it was actually filled with refugees from the town below. In the ensuing attack two hundred civilians sheltering in the monastery were killed.

Although Cassino was turned to rubble and almost unrecognisable as a town at all, the enemy were so well dug in that the bombing had no great effect other than to create even more defences for the Germans and a terrain that made it extremely difficult for armour to back up any of Freyberg's advancing infantry. The Maori Battalion, for example, which had won a costly fight to take the railway station at the edge of town was pushed out again by a counterattack simply because backup in the form of tanks could not get past the bomb craters or the floodwaters from the breached river and the general demolitions.

The New Zealanders again were fought to a standstill and eventually withdrawn from the fight by Freyberg who realised their casualties were becoming too high to sustain. Later the town fell to the British and Poles with help from the New Zealand artillery.

For the New Zealand Division, there was never another fight in Italy so devastating as Cassino, but the many small tragedies of which it was composed occurred again and again all the way to Trieste.

Faenza: After a mile I began the climb into the foothills, following a slow ridge that wound gradually upward between grapevines and trees which obscured the view of the town below. I paused amid some old pines for a lunch of bread, cheese and a little poisonous sausage, and as I ate I lay my back against the cobbled bark and gazed down at the valley between my feet. It looked like rich land, well irrigated, fecund, with well kept *casas*. Somewhere down there a river would be winding through the thick greenery. A cuckoo called not far away and in the distance came the occasional thump of a shotgun.

How would the Allied Forces have advanced on this ridge, I wondered? I had read somewhere that hill fighting was something they had had to adapt to. That supply was limited to mules and air-drops. Tanks here, rather than providing close backup for the troops, would be confined to the lower slopes as little more than self-propelled guns.

I needed to get higher, I wanted a clear overview of the town and beyond to the stopbanks where the 26th had fought. I brushed away the bread crumbs, shouldered my pack and continued on up the long ridge. Now and then a lizard brushed through the grass at the side of the road, sometimes a car swished by, but otherwise it was a peaceful journey wandering beneath that mottled spring sky.

I came across a very impressive villa that looked extremely aristocratic from a distance but, as I drew near, showed itself to be a decrepit invalid, disused, abandoned, but still maintaining a glorious position from which the entire region could be surveyed. It seemed to me a perfect command position for the defending army. All around it the vines ran down like thick green corduroy and a row of even pines stood sentinel along the southern boundary. But the grass grew thick at its foundations and pigeons flustered amid the broken roof tiles. Its windows were boarded and bricks sat crumbling like teeth in a skull. Still I would have liked to live there. It reminded me of my own home, the old flour mill, similarly broken and abandoned when I first found it.

Nearby a woman stood with her back to me, seemingly absorbed in her thoughts. She wore an apron. She was middle-aged, thickening, and her grey hair was tied in a loose bun. A butterfly came close and she lifted one arm to snatch at it as might a young girl. Then she put both hands to her face and stood still again. I was standing on the road, she on the other side of the fence, a line of washing between us. I called to her and she turned, startled.

'*Scusi*, do you speak English?' I asked.

She shook her head, her hands still close by her chin, her fingers curled a little. I pointed to the building. '*Bella casa*,' I said. She shook her head again and spoke to me in Italian and with both hands apart she brought them together in descending arcs as if stroking the spread wings of a dove. It was a gesture of defeat, of everything collapsing into the centre. She smiled grimly. I nodded. '*Grazie*,' I said, and walked away.

I have made many enemies in my life, most of them deserved, but I don't remember that any went so far as to try to kill me. I have no idea what it's like to have a large number of people I have never met conspire to end my life or rip my body with steel or burn it while I am still alive. I have been very frightened, mostly in the mountains, but always it has been for a short time and with the option of retreating. So I cannot imagine what it can be like to be twenty years old and in fear of losing my life day after day for two weeks at a time, off and on for years.

People just don't survive that kind of thing. Or so you would think.

When I imagine my father's war it is in terms of the small stories he told us, the briefest sketches. Like most of the returned servicemen he simply didn't discuss it.

I have read what I can about the Italian campaign in order to try and visualise the stage on which this act was set. I have tried to understand the arguments behind attacking the 'soft underbelly of Europe', I have read interviews with old soldiers and women, and I have also read Alison Parr's *Silent Casualties*, interviews with men who have lived most of their lives under the shadow of those events, pursued by nightmares they could not easily talk about; and my father certainly had nightmares. These are the years most difficult to write about given that he never really spoke of his experiences. The only stories we heard were short humorous anecdotes from which I privately formed a series of trig points and went on in my imagination to fill in the territory between. When he talked about the war at all it was to make a good story. But at either side of the frame, slightly out of view, there is tragedy.

Faenza: I thought I heard a nightingale. I heard a recording of this bird that most fascinated my father and I wondered if this was it at the side of the road somewhere in the branches above me. I shaded my eyes and peered upwards. A car came past and stopped a hundred yards farther along the road where the ground flattened out. There were a number of vehicles here where people had left them to continue on foot. It was high enough now to see the town clearly and it was a good day for walking. A man stood at the side of the road ahead of me, waiting as his wife bent to pick wildflowers. '*Buon giorno*,' he said as I passed.

'*Buon giorno*,' I answered.

A flicker of interest crossed his face. '*Englise*?'

I stopped and turned to face him. 'No,' I said. '*Nuovo Zelanda*.'

'*Nuovo Zelanda*,' he said absently to himself, and then he seemed to spark into life; 'Ah, *Nuovo Zelanda*!' he exclaimed, and started speaking rapidly in Italian amid which I heard the words '*Lino Gottica*.' I understood what he meant when he spread his arms indicating the lowlands to the east and the rugged hills that climbed away to the west. '*Lino Gottica*,' he repeated. It was Kesselring's 'Gothic Line' that he was talking about. '*Nuovo Zelanda*,' he said pointing down to the east, '*Les Anglis*.' And then pointing up to the hills, '*Les Americanos*.' He called to his wife and she hurried over to us. He explained what I was. And I explained very roughly what I was doing. He had an idea in mind, he was very excited, he beckoned me to come with him and his wife followed.

'*Parlez-vous français?*' he asked. I told him I could speak a little and at last we were able to understand each other. Apparently he wanted to take me to see a famous battle ground at the head of the Senio Valley, to a place high above the forest called Monte Batalica.

After Nine Eleven, I asked a young man at the local garage if he would care to go to Afghanistan. Possibly he had been among those pupils of David's class who seemed to have so slight a grasp of history. Kent is a good-looking man, strong and straightforward. He plays football and always sports some injury like a black eye or a split eyebrow on winter Mondays. We were drinking coffee at ten thirty and America was bombing the Taliban along with an inestimable number of old men, women and children. 'Like a shot,' he said, in answer to my question. He hunched forward and squinted down the long road. 'Yep, I'd go.'

'Up the strada,' as they used to say in Italy. 'Up the strada.' And perhaps I would have given the same answer at his age. Perhaps I would have gone too. But for what? Duty?

Perhaps duty is what we call it now because we tend to gild the frames of our most vivid experiences. But of all the interviews I've read over the last few weeks there has been one consistent answer: foremost in the minds of the men who went to war was a sense of adventure. Adventure is what drew Cecil Lewis into the airforce in 1914. *Sagittarius Rising*, his memoir of four years' flying over battle fields like the Somme, is an extraordinary work. It is a poem.

Lewis was an exceptionally intelligent man who, in due course, survived to co-found the BBC. This is the opening paragraph of his book:

I stood with Maynard Greville on the stone terrace outside the School House studies at Oundle in the spring of 1915.

'I vote we chuck all this at the end of term and join up,' said he.

'Wouldn't it be fine! – but they won't let us.'

'Why not? We're almost seventeen.'

'But old King says you can't get a commission in anything until you're eighteen.'

'Rot! What about the flying corps? They'll take you at seventeen. They want young chaps.'

'Shall we speak to Beans?'

'No, he might stop us. I vote we write to the War Office and see what happens.'

'All right. Oh, Maynard, wouldn't it be ripping!'

And of course it would be different for my father's generation. That is what they said: 'It won't be the trench warfare of the First War, that kind of war will never happen again'. I remember Kim Hill interviewing Richard Clark on television a short time before the invasion of Iraq. He was one of Bush's strategic 'thinkers'. She asked him if he thought that Iraq could turn into another Vietnam. Clark laughed chummily and flipped his hand as though dismissing an irksome fly. 'Oh, no,' he said. 'Vietnam, that was a mistake.'

Everyone supposes that next time it's going to be different. That *this time* the smart bombs will take out the evil men, this time women and children will be exempt. I was talking a few days ago with a territorial soldier about to go on tour in the Solomons. I was describing what I had read about the creeping barrage. 'Can you imagine that,' I said, 'stalking along twenty-five yards behind exploding shells.'

'Oh, that will never happen again,' he replied. 'We don't do that now.'

But war is a craft that, while fixed in theory and training, is in practice, something that must, if it is to succeed, evolve. It is not a football game governed by international conventions. Even Geneva did not prevent Captain Harris's firestorms of Hamburg and Dresden, Churchill's proposal to gas Arabic women and children in their tents, Rumsfeld's phosphorous attacks on Fallujah.

Although there was a great deal of deliberation over how and when to invade the Axis territories in Europe, once the engagement began, there was no real control over it. Things would develop and with every changing situation, the armies of both sides would have to change to survive.

(From *Italy Volume One, the Sangro to Cassino*, N.C. Phillips)

The invasion of Italy was the last of a series of *ad hoc* decisions on Mediterranean strategy. Geographical objectives had been left an open question. On the day of the Salerno landings, Churchill wrote to Roosevelt that, after the fall of Naples, 'We are, I presume, agreed to march northward up the Italian peninsula until we come up against the main German positions'. ...Lacking a long term plan when they invaded Italy, the Allies had made insufficient provision for a rapid pursuit while [the Germans] were still shaken by the Italian surrender...

Which meant the enemy was able to consolidate across the narrowest sections of the peninsula, where the high ground afforded excellent defensive positions and set the stage for my father's war.

'I can't watch the television news of Iraq,' says Bill Gates. 'It's the same old thing…'

Among enemy documents captured at Faenza, was this assessment of the New Zealand Division by the 278th German Division:

> The New Zealanders, the majority of whom volunteered for service in Europe out of a sense of adventure, are trained and led by General Freyberg, a dangerous opponent. They are specialists in night fighting. They fight on a broad front, in a way which corresponds with the German method. The New Zealanders have learned to work their way forward under heavy artillery support, close up behind their barrage, and in this way take their opponents off their guard without suffering heavy losses themselves. They are capable of fighting through difficult country without tank support.

Faenza: I have never seen more 'difficult country' in which to fight than that which surrounded Monte Batalica. It stands at two and a half thousand feet overlooking a gnarled landscape of broken hills and I cannot imagine how it could be either attacked or defended. But it was the lynch pin in the Gothic Line and it was there, in a battle to take these heights, that the American Fifth Army suffered a thousand casualties.

At the foot of the remains of a Roman tower a warrior cast in bronze lies fallen. Alongside, three bronze plaques tell the story of what occurred there more than sixty years ago. As I stood gazing down over the ragged slopes and out to the south where the hills were dissolving into the late afternoon haze, I heard my host explaining my presence to a number of people who had climbed as we had the final two kilometres from the car park to the monument. They seemed excited that a New Zealander was there and that I had come to write about it. And I remembered how my father had returned to some village with my mother, and how they had stopped for lunch and the patron and his wife had stood close by with wine and refused to let him pay for his meal. And as they drove away my father was smiling. 'I wanted you to see that,' he had said to my mother. 'How good they were to us.'

On our way back down the mountain, Roberto stopped at a small restaurant to buy ham sandwiches and a glass of wine from an unmarked bottle. 'It's Moselle,' he said, and quaffed his quickly. It was sweet and unfinished and I remembered how my father and his companions took a close interest in wine, how they pillaged what they could find and transported it in Jerry cans, inviting neighbouring sections to join them in an effort to poison each other.

Fortified, we careened down the hill, weaving through the Sunday traffic, all of us in a very good mood. From time to time, Roberto would nudge me to impart some information and at the same time turn to catch my eye, and at these moments we would leave our side of the road. At one moment I noticed a ginger Tom spring out towards us like a streak of toffee and felt a couple of thumps as he passed lifeless beneath the car. Roberto looked alarmed.

'*Il gatto*,' I explained.

'Ah,' he shrugged, a little crestfallen, '*Il gatto*.' I wanted to say that when my father's platoon was holed up on the south side of the Senio they rigged wires at about ankle height to catch the German patrols who were often sneaking over in the middle of the night. Some of the wires were attached to flares, others simply to tin cans. But there were many cats in the area and a few dogs that were often running into them and for at least six months it was open season. I wanted to explain that it was all right, that for some of us the season had never closed.

As Gordon Slatter remarks in his book, *One More River*, the sense of adventure disappeared in the middle of the first mortar attack. 'All I did from then on was keep my head down and try to survive.'

I think that accompanying this sense of adventure must be an optimism based on the conceit that you will be better equipped than the other fellow, that you will be better trained. Why would any of us take on a fight unless we believed we could win? Even the admirable Atticus Finch (*To Kill a*

Mocking Bird) confronting a lynch mob of entailed farmers had an ace up his sleeve in the form of the sturdy newspaper editor perched un-noticed in a high, open window, covering the crowd with a double-barrelled shotgun.

The initial strategy of the Americans in Europe was to deliver a hammer blow to Berlin, to hit the nucleus of the problem with a monstrous tonnage of bombs which would put an end to things right away. Perhaps the Americans in 1941 should have cast their minds back to the Somme, to the uncountable tonnes of shells delivered on the heads of the Hun during seven days of continuous artillery fire, after which, to the surprise of the English wandering towards them across no man's land, they simply popped up from the mud and continued shooting.

> (From *Sagittarius Rising*, by Cecil Lewis)
> Nothing could live under that rain of splintering steel. A whole nation was behind it. The earth had been harnessed, the coal and ore mined, the flaming metal run ... and finally here, all these vast credits of labour and capital were being blown to smithereens. It was the most effective way of destroying wealth that man had yet devised; but as a means of extermination (roughly one man for every one hundred shells) it was primitive and inefficient.

Five hundred and seventy-six tons of bombs were dropped on Cassino in three and a quarter hours, and yet, so inefficiently, that if my father had been there possibly this book would not have been written; for one in four New Zealanders became casualties during the following murderous four weeks.

Adventure? Perhaps. But I bear in mind the fact that my father went to war in 1944. One of the first furloughs of soldiers to have survived Greece and the desert campaign had refused to go back. My father must have known that things were very grim over there; the 26th Battalion alone had lost 246 men, and 511 were wounded. He must have met returned men and spoken with them. When I read his official war records I see that he enlisted with a preference for the Signal Corps. Perhaps he thought it would be a safe trade. It wasn't. When the lines of communication were broken someone had to go out and fix them. They were broken because of shelling, and the break in the wire was usually where the shells were falling.

Faenza: I walked out one morning to find the line where the 26th Battalion had spent a good deal of the winter. Now and then a spattering of rain fell across the plain but, although the clouds were building in clumps over the hills and in the north east, it was warm and the going was pleasant enough. I took a fairly direct route to the Senio following more or less the roads the troops would have taken. After about ten kilometres I reached a small group of houses and a church where the road crossed the river. Here I found a narrow, overgrown track following along the top of the southern stopbank, heading away from the sound of the occasional car and the murmur of the distant motorway.

As I said, the day was almost humid, there was a heaviness in the air. In the distance the clouds continued to build and drift to the accompaniment of rolling thunder. The stopbank was overgrown with grasses as tall as my shoulder and clumps of rushes thick as cornstalks towered overhead. There were trees growing thickly down to the river but none of them looked older than twenty years. I recalled the aerial photograph loaned to me by Rangi Ryan which showed that the river in 1945 was clear of any vegetation.

The photograph had been supplied to platoon commanders the day before the spring advance which took them across the Senio, and it is possible to pick out the farm houses. In one of these my father and his companions would have sheltered. In the photograph it is possible to see the pitting of mortar and shell bursts that mark the ground like acne. Thousands and thousands of shells had fallen amongst them during those winter months for there is hardly a patch of five square yards that has not been churned. It is a dismal thought to imagine men trying to survive in such circumstances.

After three miles I felt entirely alone. There were cuckoos in the trees and doves and something which sounded a little like a bellbird. I emerged at one moment from an overgrowth of light wood and shoulder-high grasses to find an immense field of wheat laid out before me, a field of intense green with crimson poppies running along the hollows like spatterings of blood. Until then the fields below me had been thick with vines which ran at oblique angles to the river and made a thick-leafed impenetrable cover.

But in the winter they would have been black and twisted, withered sticks of little use.

I ate my lunch and gazed out across the fields to a house three hundred yards away, to the belt of open country between it and its neighbour, and I wondered if that was where he chased the sergeant. How had they seen him? There must have been a sharp eye on the crest of the bank, perhaps right here where I was sitting; I, afraid of nothing, with no sign that anyone had ever clung desperately to this piece of earth, clawed at the ground with a trenching tool, or let their life ebb away into the dark soil. All I heard were the birds and the distant thunder.

They're in a farm house. It's thick walled, stone probably. There's straw scattered around and a bare table in the middle of the single room. It's like a stage with a minimalist set. There are men sitting around, faceless, of course. Guns lean against the wall. They're playing cards, reading, smoking. Outside there's a courtyard open to the front, open to the direction the platoon must advance eventually to the river. There are fields to the left and right. Stubble. Somewhere ahead of them there is cover, a few trees. Hedges. The Germans are just a couple of hundred yards away. There's a Tiger tank somewhere hidden in a haystack or a house. Sometimes the Germans can be seen from the top floor. My father is up there. It's cluttered and dark, but there's a window, white and clear through which he is observing the enemy line through a set of bulky binoculars that have probably been taken from a prisoner. The Germans were always so much better equipped. He's back from the window a little, back in the shadows.

Downstairs a sergeant comes into the room. He is big and blocky, he has three stripes on his battle dress. No one likes the sergeant. He's not one of them. My father has taken a watch from one of the German prisoners and left it on the kitchen table downstairs. That's all there is: a scrubbed wooden table with a watch in the centre of it. The sergeant sees the watch. 'I'll be having that,' he says, and is off out the door. Some of the boys race up to tell my father. He comes down and sets off after the sergeant across an open field. He's chasing the sergeant for the watch. There is no colour in the sky. It feels like autumn. Fifty yards ahead, oblivious to the fact that he is being followed, the blocky sergeant is making a crouching run along the vines. My father has his eye on him, determined. The Germans also have their eye on the

sergeant and suddenly there's the pop pop pop of a mortar flinging its shells into the
high white sky. My father lays flat on the ground as does the sergeant ahead of him.
Best thing is to stick where you are and hope for the best. The ground is damp, the
earth dark. When the mortars stop Peter takes a look. The sergeant has disappeared
… so has the watch.

'What do you mean, "disappeared"?' I asked.

'Gone,' he said, and spread his fingers like casting dust.

Not quite true. N.C. Phillips writes an account of picking up the pieces after a direct hit on a soldier in the desert. 'There was no body we could bury. We had to put what we could find in a bag and bury that.'

My father wrote a short story in the last year of his life called 'The Sniper'. He was in a lot of discomfort at the time and writing seemed an effective distraction. The story was submitted to a competition and although it didn't win any prizes as a literary work, it is hugely valuable nevertheless in the detail. It is said that most of us who attempt to write fiction end up writing about ourselves, and my father certainly was not a writer of fiction. He could enchantingly embroider what he observed, but he was no master of invention. Therefore, it is a fair deduction that this story described his own experience at one moment of the halted advance between the Senio and the Po rivers. Perhaps, as in Cecil Lewis's self-portrait in *Sagittarius Rising*, he was only able to talk about the things that most intimately touched him by slipping into the third person.

…Winter decided to come to Italy early that year. The baking heat vanished overnight, and cold winds and rain came racing down from the mountains and across the plains. The steady downpour driven by the wind, drenched the dry ground of summer and autumn, and turned the deep soft dust into mud. The army at last came to a halt before this strongly defended river and it became known that this would be the winter line. The army could advance no further until spring.

…The intelligence officer had issued a battalion warning that the first seventy yards of flat ground forward of the German position was heavily mined. He knew what the mines would be. There would be Schu-mines, flat wooden boxes with a hinged top, filled with explosive and a detonator which fired if weight was placed downward on the top of the box. These mines were planted just under the surface of the ground. The other mines would be S-mines. An S-mine was a round metal canister with another canister inside, the inner canister being filled with explosive and shrapnel. A thin metal stem was fitted to the top and the mine was buried with the stem visible. To the top of the stem was fitted a wire which was stretched for a few feet, about six inches, above the ground and then was secured by a small peg of wood or metal. When the wire was tripped a spring inside the mine was released and the inner canister jumped upwards and exploded about waist or head high. You could always see the wire of an S-mine in daylight, but you could never detect the presence of a Schu-mine.

…The forward elements of infantry had moved through the narrow streets and into the open countryside. His company had advanced in single file along the road in the late afternoon, and then had left the road and fanned out into a line abreast over the fields. When they reached their objective they split into groups and occupied some of the farm buildings which lay from left to right across their path three and four hundred yards from the river.

…The partly wrecked barns and houses were bleak and cold but they had one insuperable advantage. They were made of stone. Mortar and machine-gun fire could not harm the inhabitants but they had to be very careful during daylight. From their firing points on the stopbank, the German machine-gunners had a clear view of all the buildings. If they suspected a house was occupied they could notify their artillery, and their forward observers would direct the howitzer battery as it methodically destroyed the thick stone building. Half a dozen shells were usually enough.

The soldiers in the houses had packed the holes in the walls with sandbags. They used the first floor as their observation point, keeping well back from the open frames of the windows. They brewed their dixies of tea over a small, smokeless fire produced by a tin can filled with earth which had been soaked in petrol.

… About a mile this side of the town Harry had been killed. They had been moving off the road onto the muddy fields and carefully stepping across the ditch which ran alongside the road. When Harry had tried to hoist his large body from one side to the other his foot slipped in the mud and he fell. The explosion of the mine had sounded like a rifle shot and a black plume of smoke and mud flew upwards. Harry had lain still where he fell. He remembered how he felt when he went down to drag Harry's shoulders up onto the edge of the road. There was a danger that Harry might be lying on the trip wire of an S-mine and he had slipped his left hand under Harry, his fingers searching for a wire. But there was no wire. Very carefully he pulled Harry's upper body towards him until it was upright and other hands gripped the arms and pulled Harry out onto the road. Harry's battle dress trousers were in tatters below the waist. His boots were filled with blood which overflowed onto the road and trickled back down into the ditch. The air hammered and shook with the artillery barrage as a stretcher party appeared, and he and the others moved on. As they moved away across the field to catch up with the advancing line of infantry he had looked back once more at the small group huddled on the roadside, and that was the last he had ever seen of Harry. The sergeant said the next day that Harry had died on the stretcher as they carried him back.

...When the big advance began in the spring the bombs of the airforce would saturate the minefield and the stopbanks ahead of them so that only a flat, churned, ravaged strip of ground would mark where the river and its banks and its trees and the minefield had been, and the tanks would lurch and roll as they made their way forwards in clouds of dust.

...The sergeant walked to the door and pulled aside a vertical length of sacking. The chill wind was steady with an occasional shower of rain. The light was already starting to fade. The sergeant had strongly resented the early arrival of winter. In dry weather they might already be in the city of Trieste, instead of taking part in the two separate night attacks which had brought them to this position. In each attack they had laboured through the sodden ground, subdued and anxious, but sustained by the eternal human hope of life, following close behind the incessant earth-shaking roar of the artillery barrage rolling on in front of them, and here they were in this dismal place. There was a sudden gust of sleet. He went back into the room with its pungent smell of the empty stable on the other side of the wall, and as he shook the rain from his cape he picked up his mug of tea from the dirty table. Two months ago they had a platoon strength of twenty-eight, but now they numbered twelve. He had three men outside acting as lookouts from the barn and sheds, and there were two upstairs on the top floor, and he would have to replace these five in half an hour's time.

Faenza: I continued on for a couple of miles until I came to the next bridge. Here there were the usual brick abutments, but where the main structure had been blown it had been replaced with concrete beams. Beneath the bridge the river fell across a stone weir and two fishermen in waders plied the murky water. It was a very peaceful spot. An occasional vehicle came by and once a handful of voluble cyclists swished past on racing bikes. The sun came out and printed the shadow of my hand against my notepad and fell warmly against my shoulders. 'I'm a month late,' I wrote. 'By now they would have been in Trieste.'

I dropped down from the stopbank and picked up a narrow path for my homeward journey, preferring a winding and less travelled route. It was very pleasant far from the main road with vines and fruit trees and wheat-fields on either side and in the distance the hazy hills of Faenza. Once I saw a lizard leap into a hole at the side of the road. It was arse up for a while, very bright green on the underside. I grabbed the last half inch of its tail but it clung and the tail end didn't. Half a mile on I came to a church and wanting the shade, I sauntered in under the oak trees. There was a wedding in progress, flashbulbs going off inside like grenades. Two cast-iron saints stood guard on the roof, oxidising.

The cemetery lay in cool shade. I guessed there wouldn't be any New Zealanders there even though the battle must have swept around it as it moved between rivers. But I thought there might be some significant dates telling of its effect. There were not. It was an odd place. The gravestones were ornate with photographs on most of them. Huge plaques were set against the walls alongside vaults like children's playhouses in which entire families were entombed. It felt as if everyone wanted to be separate from one another, that here even in eternal slumber some deaths were better than others. All around me the faces of strangers stared accusingly, as though

I were a trespasser. They were inhuman things, none of them taken in their prime, like Hillary on the five dollar note. These last images were supposed to depict an honourable presence. But instead they are fixed for eternity, grim and unhappy, as if they'd never been children, as if they'd never laughed or loved. And I wondered in this closed, gated place which of these were the *Fascisti*.

I passed one beaten up *casa* that must have stood neglected at the side of the road for a very long time. On the facing wall were two scars that caught my interest. They were several yards apart and very similar. It looked as if someone with a blunt chisel had carved rough bowls in the wall to a depth of about six inches. And at the edges of the bowls deep scars radiated out as if some creature had drawn his steel claws across the crumbling brick. They were like bars of light radiating from the head of a saint in a medieval picture and I thought it must not have been the direct hit that worried the soldiers so much as did the pieces of metal that sprayed out on either side. It was a cruel imprint.

Someone, a female lawyer, said to him once at a bar dinner that judges were not suited to understand the ordinary man. Judges lived in a refined world, she said. A Shadowlands. But Peter had spent more than two years in huts and tents with his fellow man, sleeping in broken *case* and ditches and digging shit-holes in orchards and ruined vineyards with a trenching tool. My father said nothing in reply, he just took another glass of wine.

I glanced back at the stopbank half a mile away and recalled a story he had told when I was very young. It had meant little to me then. He said a soldier had stood on a mine. I remember in the story there was high ground ahead of them, he and his companions. And there it was, a long thirty foot wall of earth, verdent with spring now but pocked with shell holes then. They had been moving carefully through a minefield, along a narrow path they had cleared earlier. But they had been seen and had come under heavy fire. One of them had panicked and run wide. What my father didn't say was that under covering fire, he had stepped into the minefield, picked up the dying soldier and carried him out.

(Continued from 'The Sniper')

There was no art of survival in the forward areas. An infantry officer was either lucky or not, but he could shave the odds against him, even slightly, if he kept listening. He kept listening for two sounds. One was the distant firing of artillery, and the other was the nearer sound of mortars. The far away boom of a big gun would be followed in a few seconds by the sound of the shell in the air. If the troops heard the thundering high whistle overhead, then the gun was being aimed well behind them. But it was essential to detect whether the whistling sound was increasing in a crescendo, for, if so, then the shell was on its downward path and would explode near at hand. In such circumstances it was standard procedure to keep well down in a slit trench or to dive for the ground and lie flat.

...If the Germans for some reason decided to use artillery on the house in which the platoon was sheltering, the first shell would be a ranging shot falling either right or left with the path and direction of the next shell directed by a forward observer. That gave time for the men to vacate the house.

His war stories were never told simply to entertain. Something would trigger them, there was always a context. And, as I say, during the twenty years in which I was semi-conscious to his world, I have less than a dozen anecdotes, half of which were overheard.

My brother and I, for example, were playing detectives. My brother had a cap gun, I had found an old trench coat in a cupboard and I was complaining about the fact that the lining of the right pocket was torn, that things kept falling through. My father put down his paper. Thoughtfully, he took the trench coat and put it on and then he told us how one evening after a night on the town, while on respite from the front, he had been walking back to barracks by way of a lonely, empty street. In those days, he told us, the population was half starved, living on its wits, and sometimes there'd be a body in the river, someone who'd been mugged for a few *lire*. They had learned to avoid the treed edges of roads and always walked in the centre of the street. This particular night, in the middle of nowhere, a group of Italian youths suddenly appeared about thirty yards ahead and formed a line against him. Peter didn't alter his pace, he just kept walking forward, and when I imagine the scene, he has a cigarette in his teeth.

He explained that most men in the platoon had their favourite guns by that time and that he had a particular liking for the little Italian 9 millimetre Beretta with which he used to be able to keep a can moving along the ground. The Beretta was in his right hand as he walked back that night, in the torn pocket of the trench coat.

He closed the distance between himself and the gang of youths until he was about ten yards away from them, and then, flipping the coat open, he fired three shots above their heads. The street cleared almost instantly.

'Here, let me show you,' he said, reaching for the cap pistol. He took it in his right hand and slipped it into the deep pocket of the coat. Setting his face like Cagney, he flipped the coat up. The little plastic pistol caught on his trouser belt, flicked out of his grasp and spun across the room. My brother and I watched it clatter against the lino, horrified.

(From *Italy Volume One, the Sangro to Cassino*, by N.C. Phillips)

Infantry patrols are primarily the antennae of an army, feeling sensitively forward to flash signals, sometimes of danger, sometimes of opportunity, to the brain; but they serve purposes other than short-range reconnaissance. They may enable a force to grasp and hold the moral and material mastery of no man's land; they may be used to keep alive the aggressive spirit, which stagnates so easily in a war of static emplacement; they may, by swift and silent apparition, inflict casualties on the enemy, unnerve him, tire him by the need for vigilance, derange his projects or destroy dumps and installations; they may be employed to mislead him as to the direction of an imminent thrust or to force him to broaden his front; they may protect other troops on specialised missions in areas exposed or disputed; and those patrols also serve that only stand and wait, observing by eye and ear and ready to counter the patrols of the other side.

... On different nights the water varied in level from knee to neck high, but all the patrols that made the crossing found it necessary to link hands for mutual support, stretching out like the impatient souls in the vestibule of Virgil's hell 'with longing for the farther shore'.

It's black, it's all shadows and silhouettes. He is returning from a night patrol. There are three of them. They're relieved to be back. They're relaxed. They're challenged by a sentry and they reply. But one of the pickets in a slit trench who had fallen asleep wakes to the sound of voices, sees three shapes walking towards him and reacts. First he lets fly with a clip from his Thompson machine-gun that sends one bullet through the flap of my father's great-coat and then follows up by throwing them a hand-grenade. My father and his friends press themselves against the ground as they tick off the four long seconds in their minds. The grenade has fallen into a slight hollow so that when it goes off no one is harmed.

One evening a German patrol attacked the farm house. After the shooting died down my father was convinced that not all of them had escaped. He was sure that some of the enemy had taken shelter behind a haystack in the courtyard. In the morning they looked for them but couldn't find any trace of the patrol. Then someone remembered that the Italians sometimes built these stacks over bomb shelters. They found a door flat against the ground and pulled it up. The cellar was built so that when you dropped through the hatch, the tunnel ran in opposite directions, turned and then met again in the main chamber.

My father stepped down into the tunnel and after a few minutes brought out three Germans. In my mind they're wearing blue-grey tunics and their hands are clasped on their fair heads.

Again, dark, patchy, filled with silhouettes. They are returning from a patrol amid a scattering of trees. The night smells of damp pine. It can't be too dense or it would be impossible to see light between the shapes, and it is this light that saves them. My father sees the outline of a tree trunk suddenly narrow. It is twenty yards ahead of them. Its thick trunk has become just a little thinner. He signals to his men and they fall into a shell crater where they wait for a long time. Eventually one of the men suggests he was mistaken. They agree to climb out and edge forward. The moment they stand a machine pistol opens fire and my father feels the wind of a bullet passing close to his head. In the crater again they wait. Five minutes later a figure comes stalking toward them. He is heading straight for their hollow. They tense. They don't know how many men are in the enemy patrol so they hold fire.

At the last moment the German changes direction and passes by. They wait a long time. Eventually they decide to make a run for it. They each take two grenades and lob them toward the enemy cover and as the grenades burst they come out of the shell hole firing their Thompson guns. They're running through the black and grey.

It is not often in the battalion history books that the author betrays any hint of emotion. Usually they are strict accounts of strategy and the resulting advance or retreat. So I was struck by the following account of an incident at the start line near the Senio, a thousand yards to the right of my father's company:

(From the *25th Battalion History*)
Tac HQ was awaiting word when 'All hell seemed to break loose'. First came insistent hammering on the door and a sobbing voice demanding, 'Let me in, let me in!' Within a few seconds some twenty wounded, the bodies of two who had died, and as many others who could pack the house crowded the room …

These members of the 25th had been caught between the enemy and their own artillery shells falling short. At the same time one of the unstable, highly corrosive phosphorous bombs had been set off amongst them. And it reminded me of something Peter said once about those horrific little grenades; how easily they could be ignited by abrasion, and how, after an accident, they had all discretely off-loaded them into a river.

During Peter's first few days of fighting, the battalion lost twenty-one wounded and ten killed.

But nothing dramatic is ever mentioned in his letters home. He never gives any hint of what he saw or how he felt. In fact his letters are artful in what they don't say.

(Peter's letter to his family shortly after arriving in Italy)
It has been raining ever since we came here. The camp is a mixture of mud and rocks. We are in tents and great care has to be taken to prevent being flooded in the night. All the fences are built of stones, I haven't seen a wooden fence or

house yet. There are many vineyards and livestock is non-existent, much of it having been carted away by the Germans.

I went into Bari the other day. The Italians there are apparently pretty prosperous. They wear beautiful suits and shoes and seem for the most part quite unaffected by the war. Our tent is inhabited by all sorts of queer livestock. We found a snake in one of our kitbags yesterday, and centipedes, ants, lizards, mosquitoes. Also we had to get up last night and bayonet a couple of mice which were running over us as we slept.

I shall be having a little party on my birthday and I only wish Dad was present to tell, in his own inimitable way, the story of how he reared me to the supposed age of maturity. However, I shall drink a few toasts to him in *vino rosa*, or *bianco*. This little party depends, of course, on where I am at the time, but I'll have one somewhere. Give Stinker [his cat] a pat or two from me, love Pete.

Cross-referencing this letter with the battalion accounts: his company was one of two camping in sand dunes until the rain became so torrential that they bolted for houses and 'scored a shot of rum'. And as for his twenty-first birthday: on 1 November they were resting up in the village of Castelraimondo, a safe distance from the front. The weather was cold and miserable and when it was not raining it was overcast and trying to snow. There were leave parties going down to Florence and Rome and one to the university town of Perugia. I imagine that if he were celebrating his birthday, he would have been with one of these parties.

Their spirits were high enough, it seems. No one believed the Germans capable of a counter attack and the general conversation was about how long the enemy could hold out. It was presumed not long. However, the most desperate battle, the fight for the Giano Canal, was just ahead of them.

(Letter home to his family, 7 February 1945)
The weather is not bad lately, but the snow is still lying on the open country. Dan Sullivan is with us at present. There is some talk of trying to kid him to inspect our outposts on the Senio River. I need hardly say that Jerry holds both banks of the Senio River.

There is a chap in our company called Bert Stowell. He drives the OC's truck. Old Bert doesn't have to go anywhere near the front line as a rule, but when he does he comes back with some horrible stories of how close he was to getting hit. And although the shell or mortar lands half a mile away, he always insists that it was aimed at him.

Remember the chap I told you about who used to catch lizards? Well, the other day he was out on patrol and got mixed up in a bit of a shooting battle. When next seen, he was coming down the road wheeling a wheel barrow, and seated in the wheel barrow were two Germans he had wounded. Anyone else would have left them and beaten for home, but not this bloke. You get some queer types in this outfit.

This letter was most likely written from one of the farm houses on the Senio. There had been a desperate effort by 8th Platoon to push up to the stopbanks but the Germans had fought back vigorously and caused a number of casualties. When Peter talks of kidding someone to inspect the forward post it is in the darkest of humour. Since the advance from Forli late in November, the battalion had suffered 123 casualties, twenty-two killed.

(From a letter from Reg Bradley, one of my father's closest friends, to Peter's parents, 5 May 1945)

…Next I must congratulate you on Pete gaining his commission and I am, as you are, justly proud of him. I very much doubt if any chaps as young as him have gained their commission in an action zone. He is looking pretty fit and it certainly is good to see him again. As you probably know he has just returned from Rome leave and he seems to have had a good time and had a good look around.

Although he was commissioned in the field, he never spoke about it. No one knew what had occurred at the stopbank on the Senio until many years later, and I wonder now if he embedded that incident in the story of 'Harry' that he wrote about in 'The Sniper'.

Every year on the anniversary of her son's death a soldier's mother would send a card to my father. It was never discussed. But for this action he was offered either the Military Medal or a commission. He chose the latter; it meant officer training, relief from the front, a pay rise from fifteen to seventeen shillings a day and in due course, more decision making which in itself could serve to 'shave the odds'.

I read in one of his letters to a friend how, while parked up near an orchard during the war, one of his men, contrary to his instructions, wandered off into the trees to pick fruit. They heard a mine go off and looked around in time to see a boot tumbling through the air. Peter and one other man then had to inch their way into the orchard to fetch him. 'I was very disinclined to go in,' wrote Peter, 'and I was just as disinclined to come out.' In this case the soldier survived, and he goes on in the letter to describe how they met up with him again some months later in Rome where they shared a bottle of wine together. He mentioned, also, that the incident of the orchard was not referred to by the soldier. He had hoped there might have been a modicum of gratitude expressed, possibly to the extent of paying for the bottle of wine.

As I have already written, when the war in Europe ended my father was sent to Japan for ten months. Somehow, during his two years overseas, he had managed to complete papers in criminal law and contracts. In October 1946 Peter arrived home impatient to take up work again at his old office in Armagh Street under the tutelage of Sir Arthur. But, for whatever reason, he ignored his patron's advice in one respect: he never wore the RSA badge.

Faenza: I walked west along the banks of the Lamone just south of Faenza. As I left the town behind me the grass grew rank with wildflowers: daisies, poppies and sweet peas. It was spring and sometimes, on the terraces below me, there'd be an old man tending a small plot of vegetables. I passed under a bridge at one stage and noticed a rough lattice-work of timber had been erected between the girders above my head. Thin mattresses were laid across them and items of clothing; a comfortable spot in a storm. I left the river and followed a tree-lined road out into farmland, the tilled earth and wheat fields. The sun was hot and crickets burbled from the hedgerows. In the midst of all this lay the cemetery.

Before I began work on this memoir, I was asked a number of times what I thought it might be like to write about my father, if it would be an emotional journey. I hate that idea. In art it is always described in these terms: 'This exhibition has been a journey, a catharsis, a celebration...' I hate all this, I have no time for it. To my mind, an exhibition, an art work is exactly what it is, an idea to be accepted or put aside, to take or to leave.

I stepped through the shadow of the cemetery gate into bright sunlight. Before me lay four acres of mown lawn at the centre of which stood four mature lantern trees and a cenotaph. On either side of me stood ranks of clean white marble stones, each carved with the crest of a company or division and the name of a soldier. I began to walk. The breath caught in my throat as it does now to remember it. There are tears in my eyes, here, four weeks later, and it is hard to write. I had stepped into the silent presence of one thousand, one hundred and fifty-two young men, most of whom would have been the age of my daughter when they died. Two hundred and twenty-four of them are New Zealanders. I couldn't breathe. I started to choke and I began to cry. I sat in the shadow of the cenotaph and wept as wave after wave of grief overwhelmed me. And I don't understand it. I can't explain it even now.

Eventually, as the shadows began to lengthen across that vast lawn, a calm settled over me that was like an immense but pleasant tiredness and I could have stayed a long, long time.

There is a book in a small recess at the cemetery gate. It bears the names of visitors, mostly Italian, a few British and one New Zealander. They have written their names there and they have written the date of their visit. And in the column reserved for comment there is just the one word, inscribed again and again, in different hands: '*Grazie*'.

Part Two

Lago Como

Two days ago the train from Faenza had been crowded, everyone talking intimately to hand phones. The woman opposite me pressed hers to her face as if she liked the feel of it against her skin. A gypsy came on board at one of the small towns. She peered in at our booth, cast her eyes around like a switch-blade and placed a note on my knee. I couldn't read it, of course, and slipped it in my pocket to file later. She was back in a minute and held out her hand, muttering a soft, deep-throated supplication. The businessman in the corner put aside his laptop and handed her a coin. The rest ignored her. '*Grazie*', she said. Then she frowned and spoke some more, questioning us, looking from face to face. 'She wants the paper', said the businessman, looking at me. Oh, I see. I took the paper from my pocket and gave it to her. She looked full into my eyes and smiled. It was an empty thing, cold, and her eyes were sharp. '*Grazie*', she said, closing her hand around the paper in front of me as if to make a point: this is mine, and I know you. I wondered if they had been expensive to print. No, of course not. It was simply evidence: evidence that gypsies were working the train between the short stops. Fanny had warned me about the night trains and how, while the conductor locked himself into his cabin with the passports, the berths were entered one by one and the luggage searched by thieves and there was nothing to be done but lie and feign sleep. I remembered the story of Simon's mother having her bag stolen in Perugia. She remonstrated with the police sergeant for five minutes after which he shrugged, spread his hands and said, 'But lady, they also have to make a living.' The Gurkhas left in '45 and there is no one any longer keeping vigil with a kukri.

Letters

In November last year I visited Auckland and spent a week reading through Peter's letters. I reclused myself in a small cottage near my mother's apartment in Point Chevalier going through them file by file, box by box. It was a daunting process, made easier by my mother's careful editing of all his correspondence into legal, family, friends, Erebus and levels of significance. It took me five days to read it all, trying to catch his voice, the true voice; there were so many. It used to bother me when I was young, listening to him on the telephone to the farmer down the road and in the next instant to a colleague in law. Flipping from the vernacular to high English with such dexterity it seemed like fraud. And then one of our English teachers, one of the astute, pointed out that this is simply a form of communication. When Atticus Finch takes off his coat in the courtroom and rolls up his sleeves, it is not because he's hot, it's because he wants to look like one of the farmers of whom the jury is composed and to whom he must deliver an unacceptable point of view.

There are only two or three letters in which Peter lets himself off his own tight rein, for he was always guarded, and I suppose the more enfolded he became in his profession the more care he had to take and the less free he was to speak his own mind. In my opinion, the best, perhaps the most rounded of these letters was to his old friend and colleague, Garth Gould (see Appendix I, p. 239). As a child I would sit listening to these two men, understanding hardly anything of what was being said, just enjoying the sheer music of it.

It was hot and humid in Auckland. It was hot over the entire country by all accounts. I leaned over the coffee table in my confined space, turning page after page of considerations and observations jotted down between judgments over the period of his ten years on the bench. Sometimes I'd go walking to try and clear my head, to let the words settle into some kind of order. I had a phone call from Alison in the middle of it. 'How are you going?'

'It's hard,' I said. 'It's law and I don't understand it. What's up?'

'I was standing on the balcony this morning,' she said. 'The falcon flew beneath me.'

So I worked backward and forward across the traces, looking for patterns, for an inclination. And it is there, of course. He is enthusiastic at first, almost excited. 'None of the old-boy network up here,' he wrote, marvelling. 'Every man for himself.' And then he gradually becomes disillusioned, frustrated by the growing backlog of cases and a senior judiciary that was to his mind corrupting to some degree the principles of the law.

> (Letter from Peter to Rob Chambers, 1976)
> The key to all Denning's judicial utterances is that the law represents a system of adjusting the equities of opposing parties as and when they are shown to have occurred. That is not our legal system at all. It is [in Denning's view] a disguised version of executive discretion which in the last resort requires no court at all for its exercise.

His acquaintances were many. He played golf when he could and observed his beloved birds flying free over the estuary. But of the man within? His letters, unfortunately, do not reveal what drove him, what urged him to utter, 'You only have this one life, make the best of it,' while at the same time believing that 'nothing matters'.

ALBUM:
First memories

They are simple frames, flickering images as when waking from a deep sleep. I drive past Donald Place off St Albans Street quite often but rarely have I ventured there since I was five years old. I don't even know if the original house remains. I have only three memories of my father from that time; once when he took me out into the backyard where there was a low fruit tree. He wanted to show me a nest I had never noticed before. Perhaps birds built them when you turned your back or at night when the world was sleeping. My father and I stalked up on it with great care before he slowly raised his arm, reached his fingers inside and withdrew two large white eggs. I was enthralled. They were heavy. I held them in my hands for a while and turned them over and over and then when the flush of surprise had passed, they were handed to my mother and replaced in the fridge alongside the others.

The second memory is when my sister and I were sailing in a copper-mesh fire guard across the green seas of the back lawn. My father suddenly appeared on the horizon, came running toward us and leaped over the entire ship and I can see him now printed against the sky. It took my breath away.

The third is an interior shot. The house is just planes of different shades of grey to me now. And yet I see my father clearly, sitting on the edge of the bed, my mother nearby. She is standing, helpless. My father's shoulders are slumped and there are tears pouring down his face.

ALBUM:
Helen

Three years ago my uncle died, my father's sister's husband. He was a huge man, not simply in stature but in the aura of goodwill he carried with him. At first meeting his large right hand would thrust forward on a straight arm while his left snatched the cigarette from beneath a crimped eye. His face would break into a grin and his whole frame would begin to tremble with laughter as if life was the best story ever told. He was tussock and wind and lanolined sheep yard timber. He wore his hat cocked against the sun, he was the stock-agent, the farmer's best friend, and he was my father's other half. His stories were beautifully wrought portraits of the characters that lived at the frayed edges of his domain, who dwelt in the lonely folds of hills and on the other side of gates at the far ends of dusty roads.

Two weeks before he died I sat and listened to him again drawing pictures in the air: 'And George, he's so thin these days, Christ! You could draw him up your trouser leg...'

'You haven't got much time,' said Geoff Saunders. And he was right. There was so much Uncle Tim could have told me about my father but by the time I got around to asking, it was too late.

'They were driving over the peninsula once,' said my aunt. 'Tim had to call in on a client and introduced him to Peter. He didn't see anything in your father's manner to suggest that Pete had met him before, but there was something odd in the way the farmer reacted. So when they were driving away he asked Peter. And, of course, he was right. After the war there had been a number of prosecutions for war crimes. This character had appeared before your father at a court martial and, of course, the two of them recognised each other immediately. But as Tim said, you'd never have known by Peter's demeanour that they'd ever met.'

My aunt gazes at the fire, her thoughts far away. I have taken off my jacket; I am acclimatised to living in the old flour mill which ambient temperature is just a little above arctic at this time of year. I ask her about the frame in my memory where my father is sitting on the edge of the bed with his head in his hands.

'What was it?' I ask her. 'It must have been an immense tragedy, it was the only time I saw him so affected. I was about five.'

She sits back in her chair, her face pinched in thought as she shakes her head. 'It can't have been his father. He died in '64.' She clasps her hands and looks away. 'Oh!' she says, and it is though she has been struck. 'Of course. It was Sir Arthur Donnelly. It was Sir Arthur, he died of a heart attack. It was unexpected and your father was inconsolable. He adored Sir Arthur. Peter and Gordon Leggat and Brian McClelland used to visit him at his home and they'd spend whole evenings discussing the law. That was their true university,' she said. 'No one gets that kind of apprenticeship these days.'

Always there would be plates of fresh baking and a cup of tea, my father's eldest sister, the matriarch, the post around which the family washing flapped in whatever breezes were bothering us at the time. She fussed and fed us, worried for us and whipped us into line with a flick of her tongue if ever we wandered too far from her point of view. She was my father's most loyal defender and god help anyone who uttered a word against him. She was palpable as pudding on the outer, spring steel at the core. At eighty her wit is as keen as when I first crossed her.

I had spent a weekend at Diamond Harbour with Barbara. I was nineteen. I was staying with my aunt between flats and I had told her I would be somewhere else for those two days, another harbour altogether. But she is my father's sister. She discovered my deception as easily as unbuttoning a can of peas. When I returned she speared me with her iron gaze.

'If your father knew what you've been up to it would break his heart,' she said, in a very even tone. Break my father's heart? On the contrary; he would have delighted in the news that his son, despite an inability to kick, hit or catch a ball or to consume alcohol, and despite his tendency toward art and folk music, had matured, evidently, into a full-blooded heterosexual. My father would not have been broken-hearted at all, he would have been relieved.

But this morning it's different. At first there is the usual cheerful, ebullient welcome that feels like a prodigal homecoming, and the kettle is filled. 'Coffee or tea?' she asks. 'I'll just get some more wood for the fire, and you'll have some soup,' she says. It's not a question.

But as I begin to ask about her brother, a subject I have never enquired about before, she sits quite still, composed, and over the next two hours, as she turns her thoughts back along the intricate stitch-work of the years, three extraordinary events take place: the kettle boils unheard and switches itself off, the soup remains in its pan on a cold element, and the fire goes out.

'Was your father a naturalist?' I ask her. She shook her head slowly. 'So where did Peter's interest in birds come from?'

'Not Dad,' she says, continuing to consider the question. She begins to smile and I wish I could see what she sees. 'You know Peter used that garden sieve of Cecil's to catch them. He'd prop it up on its side with bread-crumbs on the grass and then hide in the bushes holding the end of a string. He was very patient. And he built an aviary for them, quite big. He'd keep the birds for a while and then let them go.'

I learned from my father the difference between a male and female chaffinch while I was still very young, and the sight of a grey warbler's nest strung on threads from a high branch with its distinctive side-entrance was like finding gold. He taught me to blow eggs and I learned to climb down from trees, or a cliff once where I'd discovered a swallow's nest, holding the precious eggs in my mouth. In a letter to my sister, describing what he had observed of a shag at the edge of the tide, he ended by saying, 'I envied that bird. He only knew the enemies which instinct, as opposed to intelligence, taught him to fear'.

'We were not wealthy, but we were not poor,' continues Helen. 'Times were hard, of course, it was hard for everybody. It was the Depression and Dad's work was not secure.

'And they were both in poor health; once they were both in hospital at the same time. Then Maureen and I were packed off to Auntie Flo and your father to his grandmother in Canon Street...'

(Letter from Peter's cousin Gratin O'Sullivan written to my mother after Peter's death)

As a child I was often sent from Dunedin to Nana Mahon's in Christchurch. Being confined to the precincts of Canon Street was not an uplifting experience – but there were my cousins. At that age Peter assumed a stature in my life that even with his passing he maintains. Where possible, I was always included in his activities, and the hours I spent on the bar of his bike left me with a permanent crease running across my seat. I can still remember the discomfort and his panting in my ear as he punched into Christchurch's nor-westers. I can remember too the frosty dank mornings when it was Peter's turn to serve mass at the Basilica. But the retained memory was really the breakfast that was waiting when we got back, and trying to unfreeze in front of the smoored fire and the redolence of sulphur and gas coming from the stove in the kitchen. Then it was off to lunch at Peter's parents', his dog, Sam, waiting and wagging. Occasionally the afternoon was spent catching eels in the races that drained the paddocks...

'I don't remember our parents going to church all that often,' my aunt continues. 'I remember seeing them kneeling by the bed praying, so I suppose they had their own belief. And we were sent to different schools, of course, your father to St Mary's. He was dux, that's how he got the scholarship to St Bede's. He couldn't have gone otherwise.' She shakes her head. 'They were awful. Can you imagine what it must have been like for him to sit there at prize-giving watching other boys going up to get the awards that should have been his? But because he was a scholarship boy he wasn't entitled, even though he topped all his exams. Did you know he came twenty-third in the proficiency list for the whole country, third in New Zealand for English? And *they* weren't even going to let him sit. Dad told them that he'd take him away and let him sit it at Boys' High, so they relented in the end. It's no wonder he had so little love for the place.

'And as the years passed, none of them could bear to acknowledge his progress in the law. Except Bishop Ashby. When your father became a QC he wrote to Peter. And later, when he was appointed to the bench. They had been in the army together. He said, "I never had a lieutenant who became a judge." Your father wrote back and said, "I never had a sergeant who became a bishop".'

And she told me of coming home after a dance, wanting to talk all about it, and finding him asleep with a book in his hand and a cigarette on his lip, still burning. She took it from him without waking him. It's a lovely image.

'Oh,' she says, returning to the present, 'you must be freezing!'

'And Sir Arthur Donnelly?' I ask.

She hesitates, 'Garth Gould,' she says, getting to her feet. 'You should ask Garth.' I nod, and temporarily close my notebook.

ALBUM:
Garth

It was overcast, a colourless winter's afternoon. Now and then desultory drops of water pattered against the windscreen and the world passed by like stains on blotting paper. As I drove past the university I noted how tall the trees had grown in the short thirty-two years since I'd been a student there, how the cars are very smart these days, and imagined that in 1946 everyone biked. A student with a car would have been an oddity. Something foolish.

Somewhere between Ilam and Riccarton I got snarled in the three o'clock kiddie traffic, SUVs everywhere drifting, bloated, slipping in beside the curb, lights blinking, mothers with tight blond hair beckoning impatiently to plastic-wrapped children with their arms stuck out like gingerbread men.

I was running late for my appointment with Garth Gould by the time I reached Halswell.

I pulled out of the fast lane into the long ribbon of lonely road we used to walk on our way back from the bus stop after school. In those days it was a mile of shingle and there was dust on our shoes. I passed two girls walking, heads bowed, one of them idly pressing numbers on a cell phone.

There were five of us back then, Janna Green and her sister, Richard Clayton and Sammy Schoellar. The air smelled of hay and it was always summer. Now and then Richard reached into his coat and drew out a twenty-two pistol to take standing shots at one of the diving magpies that dropped on us like stukas from the pine trees. The sheep lifted their heads and the birds flopped safely away through the mottled branches. That was all. Except for the buttercups in the ditch which I picked for their shiny skins.

I turned into Cashmere Road where Peter and I had stood once beside the Austin A40, a barricade to any cars that might come along while we waited and watched. At last, up on the hill, a quarter mile away, Garth came running, khaki shorts and boots, arms waving high above his head, signalling, before dropping in behind a dark outcrop. I saw the burst of smoke and dust a second before the crack of thunder that signalled the taming of another square yard of his domain. I was thrilled by it. My father grinned and flicked away his cigarette. Neither of us heard the small fist of volcanic stone pass through the blue sky in a high arc over our heads or the crack of clay tiles as it punched through the roof of the house behind us. And there, still, are the silver poplars where I used to stalk during the evening roost like the angel of death, trying to fit the black starlings into my rifle sights.

Garth, the Renaissance man of my youth, still lives on the top of the hill. The trees he planted are a palisade now preserving his privacy, but the slopes below are freckled with houses; vile sluttish things in pastel where there used to be dusty yellow broom, sienna tussock, scorched rock and quail.

'I used to come here to walk. I enjoyed it. One day I climbed through the barbed wire fence and fought my way up through the broom to the top. It was beautiful. I thought, this'll do me. Took two years of negotiations with Tom Findlay before he let me have it. Peter came up to see what I was doing and bought the land next door. Water was the main problem. But we fixed that. I built a pump-shed and bought it up from Tom's well. Council didn't like it, though. Didn't believe in septic tanks. Thought they didn't work. Quite right, they don't.'

Liz makes the tea. It is still a wonderful view, unimpeded even though the city spreads steadily towards them, a spilled basket of children's building blocks. I remember those drives to town every morning with my father, seven miles, four of which passed through lush countryside.

'It's the green belt. Some of the most arable land in Canterbury. They'll never build on it,' my father said.

But they did. They must have lost their minds.

'How did I meet Peter? Well...' Garth holds his saucer just beneath his cup, poised. He's studying the ceiling. 'It was a case I had. I was defending a Chatham Islander, a fisherman.' He took a sip of tea and then grinned. 'He had, by some account, forgotten to pay his income tax, Sam,' he said, and nodded. 'I wanted an adjournment, I wanted to look at the case a little more circumspectly than I suspected the Crown Office would allow. So I went to see the prosecutor about it and was introduced to a thin-faced young man who turned out to be Peter Mahon. I said I was seeking an adjournment. He said he wasn't about to give me one. But I had discovered along the way that there is a district court sitting in the Chathams once a year. When the case was called, Peter stood up and said to the presiding magistrate that Mr Gould wished to apply for a change of venue to the Chatham Islands. "Ha," said the magistrate, "that will be a nice change for you, Mr Mahon," at which the entire court burst into laughter.' Garth took another sip of his tea and placed his cup on the table beside us.

'And from then on we were firm friends,' he said.

'What about Sir Arthur Donnelly?' I asked. He had been Crown Prosecutor as well as my father's mentor. My father had gone to his office straight from school and when he returned from the war Sir Arthur had again taken him under his wing.

'Donnelly was a friend of my father's who'd been a surgeon commander in the navy during the war. There was a case once where my father was called as an expert witness in the defence of a woman charged with murdering her infant. My father was required to testify that he had heard of cases where a baby had been strangled at birth by its own umbilical cord. Donnelly, deciding to have a bit of fun in his cross-examination, asked my father if he had gained his experience of gynaecology in the navy. "No," he replied, "although if I came across any cord at all, it most certainly would have been naval." '

'So was Donnelly a good lawyer?'

'Well, he'd been Crown Prosecutor in Christchurch for many years and was highly regarded. He was also director of a number of public companies and the Reserve Bank, and in that capacity he was charged with the task of negotiating the lowering of the New Zealand exchange rate after the war; a task he carried out with total discretion and to everyone's satisfaction.'

A glimmer of delight passed over Garth's face and he turned a little in his chair to engage me more squarely. 'Sir Arthur and my employer at the time, Endell Wanklyn, were both directors of New Zealand Breweries which owned rather expensive premises on Moorhouse Ave. It was a site coveted by the Christchurch Tramways Company who wished to acquire it by means of the Public Works Act. They were offering the Breweries a meagre compensation and this rather upset Sir Arthur and Endell who immediately dispatched one of their law clerks each to investigate the legal position.

'Your father was one and I was the other. I remember bicycling together down to the Supreme Court library where, after some rummaging around, we located a rather withered volume on a dusty shelf in which we discovered the fact that the Tramways Corporation had no statutory power whatsoever to acquire land for bus depots; their only statutory power extended to the laying of overhead electric cables. In the end they had to pay New Zealand Breweries substantially more money than they'd expected.'

I review what I have written and lean back, easing the ache in my shoulders. It has been snowing for some time and I hadn't noticed. It falls in swirls between the poplars behind the Mill, fat white flakes against the grey bark stems blotched with yellow lichen. It is blowing under the ridge capping, and drips of water fall onto the log burner thirty feet below where they burst like distant gunfire. There is a photograph of my father and members of his platoon on skis in a forest somewhere. He said the Russians made their own deserters wear dark coats to draw the enemy fire. You remember these things. 'Snow is grey,' he said. 'The white coats they gave us were as useless as khaki.'

'As a result of the war, the middle-aged barristers who might have been expected to dominate the Christchurch legal scene did not exist. There was no "bar" as such and only one person practised as a barrister sole, and he,' said Garth with a hint of distain, 'was a retired colonial civil servant.

'A younger generation of barristers was now prominent at the bar: particularly Gordon Leggat, Brian McClelland, Peter and Clint Roper. And as the burden of Crown work continued to get more oppressive, I constantly pestered Peter to leave the firm and set himself up as a barrister sole. We discussed it frequently as the years rolled by and eventually he said he'd do it if I could find him chambers in the north end of Hereford Street. Now it so happened that I was passing number 88 Hereford Street one day and saw a closing down notice in the window. It had been a ladies dress shop, incongruously located in an ancient wooden building dating back to the last century. I went inside to inquire about the tenancy. It was available. I told Peter and the rest is history: instructions flowed in from numerous unexpected sources, not only from Canterbury but also from other provinces. You see there was a large demand from the Canterbury legal fraternity for the services of an independent legal representation...'

'Legal firms were apparently reticent about sending a client to another firm to have someone more expert in the field deal with his particular concern. They were afraid that the client might not come back. When Peter set up shop as a barrister he was able to offer immense experience in every avenue of law derived from his years in the Crown Office.'

'Leggat and McClelland and Dad used to meet with Sir Arthur in a kind of Dead Poets Society,' I said. Garth nodded. 'I had a teacher once, in my last year at school, who was a little like that. A few of us would bike round to his home after prep to discuss Jung over a glass of port and ponder questions of the heart that weren't adequately covered in the standard curriculum. Unfortunately he made a pass at one of the boys the year after I left and got thrown out. It was a pity. He was one of the best.'

Garth was grinning. 'Sir Arthur certainly was not a homosexual, Sam. He was a bachelor, and he lived with his sister in an old house on Manchester Street.'

'They were the bright young things then, McClelland and Leggat?'

'Yes, you could say that,' said Garth, and turned his glass in his hand. 'But, of course, they were ambitious.'

And I remember from the floating conversation that Brian very much wanted to be a judge. He had been doing very well as a solicitor until he took on the role of president of the Law Society after which he got so behind on his briefs that he became an embarrassment to the partners and they threw him out. Somehow he never quite caught up.

(Letter from Peter to Judge Casey)

One of my Christchurch legal friends sent me a cutting from *The Press* with the rocket you administered to McClelland's office about their delays, and if I may say so, never was a rebuke more justified. For years now Brian has hardly done a full day's work except when taking an ill-prepared jury case, and Ted will confirm how he and I spent fruitless hours practically every month, when we were in practice, trying to get Brian into the courtroom. He has got away with these inordinate delays for years, and it was certainly time he was taken to task. He has been a friend of mine for many years, but I fear that he is drifting once more, from what I hear, into the delays and difficulties which caused his expulsion from Wynn Williams and Co.

Ambition may also have served to undermine the talented Gordon Leggat. As well as taking on an inordinate amount of legal work, because he had been a great cricketer in his youth, he was in constant demand as an after dinner speaker at sporting functions which often necessitated driving vast distances at the end of the working day. But in Gordon's time it was not in vogue for young lawyers and their cousin accountants to spend their lunch hour circling Hagley Park in outsized jogging shorts. Leggat began to put on weight and eventually, at quite a young age, he contracted heart disease. But he was Weston, Ward and Lascelles' young star and they certainly did not want the bar to learn that he was dangerously ill. If it so happened that he was not available they would simply say that Gordon was suffering from a cold. My father saw through this ruse very quickly, discovering that on these occasions 'Tubby' Leggat was actually languishing in the emergency wing of Princess Margaret Hospital. From then on, whenever Gordon was off duty, Peter would say he was suffering from a spot of Lascelles' flu, a malady which eventually killed him.

ALBUM:

The Crown Office

It was my father's way to offer the law to me – the great stone column of authority which has been dragged by an adulterous, careless, negligent and half criminal humanity down the ages – as if it were a small mechanical toy which might occupy half an hour on a rainy afternoon.

(From *Voyage Around my Father* by John Mortimer)

Sir Arthur Donnelly looks to be a big man, quite plain. He reminds me a little of Garrison Keillor, or a Damon Runyon character, as he stares askance at the photographer in a picture that seems to have been taken at a race meeting. He looks a little aloof, and yet by all reports he was certainly not. He has been described as a good-fellow-well-met who would stop on a street corner and converse at length with anyone. The KBE he wore around him like an aura meant little in this respect. Probably Cecil, Peter's father, a fellow Catholic, knew Sir Arthur and introduced his son with the request that he take him on as a clerk in the Crown Office. However they were brought together, Sir Arthur liked Peter and recognised very soon that he had on his hands someone of irregular intelligence, someone with the ability to listen and understand.

My father was eighteen. Each morning, wearing a grey flannel suit and felt hat, he would bike from his father's house in Canon Street to the centre of town, park his bike at the bike stand beside the footpath, undo his bicycle clips, unclip his briefcase from his bike saddle and enter the premises of Raymond, Donnelly, 86 Hereford Street, and commence his primary duty of the day, the ritual of discussing with Sir Arthur the contents of the morning's *Press*. This daily duty of keeping oneself informed of current events was considered by Sir Arthur a necessary ingredient of any legal training. I imagine, also, that discussing what was said in print with Sir Arthur and what lay behind what was said may have led my father to quite a close understanding of the workings of the mind of his mentor. It would have been a very pleasant beginning to the day. And as time went by, it probably became clear to the other partners in the firm that Sir Arthur was taking a close interest in his law clerk, that he foresaw a bright future for the young man and he may well have been seen to be grooming him for the position one day of Crown Solicitor. This growing bond between the two men certainly did not escape the notice of the senior partner, Alan Brown, and in due course he would do what he could to undermine Donnelly's protégé.

Legal training in those days was not confined to the ivory tower. Lectures were mostly held in the evenings between five and six, six and seven, and you snatched dinner when you could.

The in-between-time was spent in research for one's employer and fulfilling the various duties that served to earn a couple of pounds a week while providing a practical experience of the legal machine. Judge Penlington:

> As a law clerk I received two pounds ten shillings and ten pence a week. That sum, with an advance from petty cash, was enough to take your girlfriend to the law ball complete with the compulsory corsage, and fortified by half a pint of cheap brandy.

'I think I moved into my first flat when I was raised to five pounds a week,' said Garth. 'It cost me one pound ten for rent and left me three pounds ten to live on... Duties? Well, there were land transfers to be organized so we'd be back and forth to the land registry office ... documents to court, documents to Inland Revenue, stamp duty, banking, office filing, indexing and, of course, insurance renewals.' He chuckled, took a sip of gin and shook his head. 'Mike Haggitt was always a little tardy with these, never quite up to date. Every time he heard a distant fire siren he'd have a minor heart attack.'

Sir Arthur's firm dealt with all levels of the profession: Raymond specialising in torts, Stringer conveyancing and Donnelly common law. Donnelly also held the Queen's Commission as prosecutor. No matter what interesting or lucrative cases may be laid before him, his first duty was always to the Crown.

'Of course,' explained Garth, 'Peter was missing out on the most interesting cases, and the most remunerative.'

'But wasn't working in the Crown Office how he came to understand the complexities of tax cases?'

'Well, of course. The Crown prosecuted on behalf of Inland Revenue.'

'Which is strange, really, when you consider that his own finances were, I don't know … so badly attended.'

'He didn't care,' said Garth.

'Didn't care?'

'He didn't care about money.'

'But it seems to have caused problems for him later on…'

'Sam,' said Garth leaning toward me a little, conferentially, 'not being interested in money always causes problems.'

Christchurch moved at a different pace in those days. There were not so many cars, of course. Tramlines radiated out from the city to all the major suburban points such as Papanui in the north, Sockburn to the west, New Brighton, and even to the giddy heights of the Takahe on Cashmere Hill.

'I was a little dubious about that one,' said Garth, with a wry smile. 'It was a heavy machine, built for the job of course. I didn't mind the trip up so much, but I didn't care to travel on it coming down. I could imagine one day the mayhem that would be caused if it ever broke loose. No, I didn't care for it.'

A few people owned cars, but entertainment didn't depend so much then on mobility. There were the races, of course, and golf, and a dance on Saturday night with Doug Caldwell's band at the Winter Gardens or The Boat House, and a bottle of gin hidden in someone's coat.

In 1976 I worked a short stint at the Fendalton Service Station. I have a vivid memory of my seventy-year-old co-worker, Owen Walker, leaning on his tyre-iron and reminiscing. 'Ah, Charlie,' he said, addressing me. 'The Winter Gardens! There's nothing in this world quite so nice as twirling round the floor with a piece of fluff in your arms.'

Everything finished on the dot of midnight in those days and then it was back home to my parents' flat with Shirley and Trevor, and Trevor on the fiddle saying to my mother, 'Come on, Smithy, give us a song,' while someone stoked up the fire. On the way home the winter fog was so thick one of them would have his head out the window watching the curb as they crawled along.

In a photograph of the day I have seen a pointsman holding back one swarm of cyclists while another swept past in a lateral direction. Suited young and old, a few women with thick skirts and hats and tied hair, and the odd car trundling along somewhere amongst it all, severely outnumbered. Everywhere was pretty well accessible by bike, tram or the few buses. During a Law Society dinner speech in 1993, Justice Penlington alluded to the Hereford Street scene.

…Annesley Harman [lawyer] owned a blue Chevrolet sedan, the pride of General Motors in 1938. The Harmans, being of a frugal nature, were in the habit of going home for lunch each day. 'But,' they argued, 'why use the Big Reds when the Big Blue is available for a fraction of the cost?' And so it was that Annesley and his four sons, all in their look-alike grey suits and grey felt hats, were making their funereal way along Hereford Street at 1.57 p.m. one day just as Peter Mahon and Cliff Perry were poised on the corner of Hereford Street and Oxford Terrace. Mahon spotted the Big Blue. He turned to Perry and in tones reminiscent of God's vice-regent, said, 'Look Cliff, there they go, The Untouchables'. A little further down the road, Brian McClelland had stepped out from a lunch with Ralph Thompson. There was the scent of *Châteauneuf-du-Pape* in the air. 'For God's sake, Ralph,' cried McClelland, 'go to ground. It's Al Capone.'

Later, when Garth and Peter became friends, they would meet for lunch most days, somewhere Peter could find 'a ham sandwich, salad and a good coffee'.

'We'd go over to Andy Todd's sometimes. Your father liked Andy, he was very keen on the trots. They got on rather well.'

'What was it about horses, Garth? It seems odd to me. He has this power-ful attraction to poetry, to Shakespeare, Dante and Keats … and yet…'

Garth considered for a moment, peering intently at a corner of the room as if drilling it for an answer. 'And Dickens, Sam, don't forget,' he said, his eyebrows up, surprised, perhaps, that I'd missed it. 'It was the human broth, you see. At the racetrack you had this fascinating brew of human nature. And apart from the subterranean element, which would have appealed to him immensely, there are also all the ingredients to weigh: the conditions of the track, the horse's form, which he would have been studying very closely, and the quality of the competition.'

'The same things he would find in any case?'

'Exactly. And of course anyone involved with the law, really has no need of fiction,' added Garth. 'The characters you come across in the course of work are themselves so varied and colourful.'

Peter's father had been very interested in the races as was Sir Arthur who had served as a steward. It was one more thing that drew the two men together. My father could be in the deepest sleep but when the muezzin tones of Dave Clarkson filtered through our house, no matter in what far room, Peter would rise and stagger blearily out, as if entranced by a Hamelin piper.

(Peter's letter to his parents from Egypt: 1944)
…Last Sunday our company went on a picnic to a place called the Delta Barrage. It is a dam across the Nile, and contains the only large area of grass, trees, etc. in these parts… We also had rides on donkeys. Eight of us had a race over a square course of about half a mile. Dad would have been proud of me if he had been there. I was well back in the field until we approached the turn for home, and as we straightened up for the 200 yard dash home I saw immediately what to do. We were on a dusty track about fifteen yards wide. There were five in front of us, about three lengths away, travelling in a bunch. They had left a gap of about four feet wide on the rails. I waited until there was about 100 yards to go and then kicked the old donk hard, at the same time giving him a slap on the neck. He started galloping so fast that I very nearly lost the stirrups and came off. As we came up behind the bunch I pulled him over towards the right and started kicking him hard. He moved past the bunch and slowly drew level with the leader, until about 10 yards from the post when

my opponent's donk started to fade a bit, with the result that I came home by a neck. There was a length and a half to the third donk, and the rest of the field were strung out well behind. One of the boys used to be a jockey and he said I won because I got my run in first. I was 3–3 on the machine, but as you know, jockeys are forbidden to back their mounts so I made nothing out of it financially. Except of course the stake money, which amounted to 16 *piastras* (3/4). During the dash through on the rails I bumped the fence with my knee and lost a bit of skin, but in the excitement never noticed it.

Album:
Murder

'Mr Mahon, I understand you were called on at short notice to conduct the prosecution for the Crown at this session,' said Mr Justice [Kenneth] Gresson when the criminal cases ended in the Supreme Court yesterday. 'There were quite a number of them and some of them not without difficulty. It should be a satisfaction to you to know that you have handled these cases composedly, competently, and conscientiously, and in keeping with the high traditions of the office of Crown Prosecutor.' (*The Press*, 1956)

Everything was going well. The law suited him. It suited his wit, it suited his sense of gamesmanship as well, for after all, he was a strategist, a card player. 'Cut it out, Samuel,' he said once when I'd been dicing the pack a little too long, 'you'll shuffle the tits off the queen.' It was an allusion to the card games played in cold stone houses as they whiled away the winter months on the Senio Line. He played cards very well.

'First time I met Peter he was appearing for us against this bloke ... well, I can't say,' said Reg, a retired tax inspector, 'and I thought gosh, we're going to lose this. Peter was hesitant, he was stammering, he seemed totally unsure of his ground. But my goodness,' he beamed, 'when the defendant got on the stand, pow!' Reg bunched his fists and brought them down, 'He jumped on him with both feet. It was all bluff, you see. He was just lying in wait.'

In 1955, during the trial of Francis John Russell, accused of being an illegal immigrant, part of Peter's examination was lovingly reported by *The Press*. It demonstrates his acute knowledge of procedure and how, when combined with his agile intellect, his performances in court would have at times been both amusing for the uninvolved spectator, and irritating for opposing counsel and judge alike.

It was illegal at that time for anyone convicted of an offence to enter New Zealand if two years had not passed since they had been released from prison. Mr Russell had 'done time' in England and arrived in New Zealand shortly after.

The following dialogue was reported in *The Press*:

Mahon: The whole matter is then a difference between your recollection and the certificate from the clerk of the Central Criminal Court, is it not?

Russell: Yes.

M: You have had previous convictions for various offences?

R: I have.

M: I will put this document to you … is [the clerk] wrong?

R: Yes. These dates should be checked by Interpol in fairness to me.

M: You want to stay in New Zealand don't you?

R: I want to stay in New Zealand very badly.

M: You have very good reasons for that haven't you? Are you not wanted by the police in Sydney on a charge of bigamy?

R: No.

M: Are you not wanted by Scotland Yard on a charge of obtaining goods valued at 3,300 pounds by false pretences?

R: Not that I know of.

At this stage, Mr Russell's lawyer, Gordon Leggat, objected on the grounds that Peter was leading his client into a position where he might incriminate himself. The magistrate agreed. He said that Peter had gone as far as he could go. But the Crown Solicitor had phrased his questions very carefully.

M: I am not asking him if he did these things. I am only asking him if he knows he is wanted by the police in other countries.

A fair point, apparently. The magistrate said he would not allow him to put any questions to Mr Russell if the answers would incriminate him. But if Peter continued to follow the form he was using then the questions would be allowed. And so Peter continued to whittle away at the credibility of the colourful accused, a character any novelist would have found hard to invent.

M: Do you know whether you are wanted by Scotland Yard?

R: Certainly not.

M: Do you know that you are wanted by the Dublin police on a charge of larceny?

R: No.

And so forth. Mr Russell was convicted and deported.

I overheard a story where Peter was asked to defend an elderly member of Fendalton's Saint Barnabas congregation against a charge of shoplifting. It was a trifling matter, but the owner of the corner dairy concerned had had enough of people making off with his merchandise without asking and was insisting on his day in court. My father had decided that he would not put his client on the stand where she could be cross-examined. Instead, he made his case by calling a number of witnesses to prove her good character. I think he called three of them, all highly regarded citizens, the second being none other than Bob Lowe, Fendalton's charismatic preacher and a popular television cricket commentator. Bob spoke glowingly of the accused and how very unlikely he thought it would be that she could take anything from anyone. When Bob finished his peroration, the Crown Prosecutor leaned toward my father and whispered, 'Any more royalty in the deck, Peter?'

My father winked. 'Just the right bower,' he said, and called the Bishop of Canterbury. His client got off, although guilty as charged, and my father made the comment: 'What would have been the point of convicting a person like that? She was elderly, she was lonely. She had picked up an item at the corner store and walked out without paying, not because she couldn't afford to pay, she simply wanted attention.' And the 'left bank' would have murmured 'Amen.'

There is a scrapbook of Peter's early cases beginning in 1947. The book is as heavy as a brace of hares, big enough for a lifetime of cuttings as if he anticipated a long and very interesting career. But although the first twenty odd pages are carefully pasted, he seems to lose interest in keeping it up to date and instead keeps notes of how cases were evolving. Of course. There was too much going on and as the cases he was involved in became more and more complex perhaps he thought it trivial to acknowledge them with simple journalistic overviews.

Some of the cases – the Mercer trial, the case of Mrs Bell and the tortured servant, and the Parker Hulme murder – are represented by several pages of newsprint. I suppose that these cases so attracted the public's attention (by day four of the Bell case there were over one hundred people jammed into the public gallery) that the papers gave them close scrutiny and their reporting is quite detailed. Eventually the album pages are blank and yellowing with clumps of paper clippings here and there ending with bits of Erebus. And Erebus, of course, was a story that required something more than just a scrapbook. Still, those early years from 1953 to 1960 give us some idea of the fabric of his world. The Crown Solicitor's office may have seemed as dusty as a phone booth from the street below, but within, for Peter, it was expanding like a Tardis.

The three very human, and therefore very public, cases mentioned above were reported in the kind of detail that has become extinct in contemporary journalism. The first case, that of forty-two-year-old Marion Mercer, involved a charge of using a vehicle as a lethal weapon; it was the first case of its kind in this country. Mrs Mercer had formed a friendship with a man half her age, a farmer called James Leslie. The romance had turned sour, however, and after a bitter argument in her car one evening, Leslie got out and set off for home on foot. After driving a short distance, Mercer turned the car around and ran him down, twice. She then got out of the car and cried, 'What have I done?' She and her passenger then took the mortally injured man in their car back to Leslie's mother's home, laid him on a bed and, apparently, did nothing. When Leslie's mother came home it was she who eventually phoned for the family doctor. Leslie was admitted to Burwood Hospital that night and died in the morning.

Mercer tried to convince the police that it was a hit and run effected by some other car. But the police found Leslie's hair on the structure of Mercer's car and enough evidence to prove she had driven over Leslie. The

Crown was asking for a verdict of murder, but the jury convicted her on the lesser charge of manslaughter with a plea for mercy.

'It was the car,' said Garth. 'They didn't like it. If it had been a pistol or an axe, yes, they'd have sent her to the gallows.'

The second case, the case of Raey Bell, would have been even more unlikely to have played out today the way it did back then, fifty-odd years ago. In the winter of 1946, a young Hamilton woman, Betty Ravenswood, was taken in by the Bell family of Kaikoura. She was fifteen and expecting a child. She had been sent away from her family for the sake of propriety, I suppose, and after all, abortion was not a legal option in those days. The child was born and immediately adopted out. The girl left the Bells' and went to work as a nurse aid at Magdalene Hospital for a year after which time she was invited back to the Bells' as a domestic servant.

At the end of three years with the Bells she was sent down to Burwood Hospital suffering from ill health. There her condition was brought to the attention of a plastic surgeon by the name of Thomas Milliken who found she bore a peculiar accumulation of injuries. The girl had cauliflower ears, one so bad it had closed up altogether. She had a deep scar at the base of her chin, a split lip that had been stitched so badly it looked as though she had been born with a cleft pallet. Her nose was flattened, she had ulcers on her shins and scars on her back. An X-ray found she had six broken ribs and a darning needle completely embedded in the small of her back.

It took ten days before she began to talk to Mr Milliken about what had happened to her. She claimed that Mrs Bell had punched her about the head, beaten her regularly with a belt and a stick, punched her hard enough to split her lip and then sewn the wound without anaesthetic. The pain in her ribs had been brought about after Mrs Bell had kicked her in the side while she was scrubbing the floor, and she could not account for the needle other than to say that Mrs Bell was in the habit of pricking her with needles if she was too slow.

When the case came to court Mrs Bell made an excellent presentation. The girl was an habitual liar, she said. She had proof. She produced several pages of confessions in which the girl had written down that she constantly told untruths. She produced letters to her from the girl thanking Mrs Bell for her kindnesses. There were also letters to an aunt saying how happy she was at the Bells'. But when Betty entered the Bells' home in 1956 she weighed twelve stone and bore no deformities or scars. When she was admitted to hospital three years later she weighed just over six stone. Almost all Mrs Bell's defence lay in the idea that boils had caused the deterioration in Betty's health. They had caused the small scars on her back, they had deformed her ears and one had burst and split her lip. My father believed not a word of it. Extract from *The Press*:

Mahon: Had anyone in the household used the surgical needle before?

Bell: No.

M: Why didn't you telephone your husband and tell him you were going to stitch the lip?

B: It was a responsibility I took on myself.

M: Your husband is a chemist and understands these things, doesn't he?

B: Yes.

M: You have never stitched anyone else?

B: No.

M: Why didn't you ask his advice?

B: I don't think he has stitched anyone himself.

M: He would call a doctor, wouldn't he?

B: Yes.

M: Why did you write a letter to Mrs Couttie the day Betty entered hospital suggesting she was mentally retarded?

B: Because she hadn't seen her for two years and would find her more childish.

M: Betty says you dictated these notes to her. You deny that?

B: Yes, I do deny it, Mr Mahon.

M: Do you know how the bloodstain came on this confession note?

B: No I do not.

M: That blotch in the writing could be either water or tear marks?

B: I would not like to say.

M: You used to force Betty to sign these confessions didn't you?

B: I did not, Mr Mahon.

M: Why did you keep them?

B: I did not keep them all.

M: There were a lot of them?

B: Yes.

A book was kept by Mrs Bell of crockery that had been broken by Betty in the time she had lived with the Bells. The cost of these breakages had been put at £181, an amount of money way beyond Betty's ability to repay. The money she was supposed to receive for her work was being deducted so that she had no financial means whatsoever. Her mother had died and her father seemed relatively unconcerned about her situation until her ill health was made known to him. When asked if he recognised his daughter when he first saw her at the hospital he said the only thing he recognised about her was her voice.

The case lasted a week and attracted a packed public gallery. On the six counts of injury the jury convicted Mrs Bell on four which seemed in light of the evidence and expert witness to be excruciatingly lenient. Mr Justice Richmond, with reluctance, sentenced her to prison for four months. Mrs Bell appealed, however, and Justice North in due course delivered the judgment on behalf of the Appeal Bench that acquitted her of all charges and she was set free.

The third case, the Parker Hulme murder, was perhaps the most widely known. (It was reported in *Time* magazine at the time, and was made into a feature film under the title *Heavenly Creatures*, in 1994.)

Again it was not as complex as many of the other puzzles put before my father, especially cases to do with commerce and tax; but this was one that exhibited a twist of human nature so rare that everyone stopped to pay attention. There was never any doubt as to what had happened nor who had committed the crime. The doubt lay in the detail and the detail was whether or not the two girls knew that what they had done was wrong in law or whether it was wrong by common standards. The difficulty for my father was trying to guess at how a jury or judge might decide this. In preparation for the case he seems to have unearthed conflicting previous judgments in similar cases in England and Australia, and having laid them out, argues for one over the others. He knew the only defence was to argue insanity. He had read the girls' diaries and statements and it was exactly what he would have argued himself if he had been defending them. But his duty lay with the Crown and not the girls.

Among his letters and papers there is this one exceptional file on the case: sheets of almost transparent paper, typed and handwritten. Included are copies of evidence and cross-examination by both sides, and his familiar horizontal hand in blue ink as he takes notes during the trial. And it is possible to see his mind at work in the rare crossings-out. It reminds me of the verses at the beginning of a book of Browning's poems which are copied from his pencilled original. There is very little adjustment, it is as if the poem left his mind almost completely formed. Almost.

Unlike the other two cases mentioned, Peter was assisting, apparently, Alan Brown. The Parker Hulme case had come at a difficult time for my father. Sir Arthur Donnelly, the man who had exerted, perhaps, the most influence on his life, had died suddenly a month before. My mother was at home with two children, and needed a good deal of his attention. But my father discovered he was having to do most of the work for the trial, covering for the fact that Alan Brown was rapidly losing his mind. Halfway through the trial Brown had to withdraw from the case and shortly afterwards was admitted to Sunnyside Hospital.

'There was the time,' said Garth, 'that Alan threw all the office letters into the Avon River! Peter tried to get the Law Council to intervene, to do something about Alan. But they wouldn't. Eventually Alan's sister, I think, came over from England and had him committed.'

Pauline Parker was sixteen years old and her friend Juliet Hulme fifteen and a half when they devised a plan to kill Pauline's mother. Pauline and Juliet had formed a friendship that excluded almost everyone else. They had both been affected by ill health, Pauline by osteomyelitis and Juliet by tuberculosis, to the extent that they had slipped out of step with their peers. Both had become introverted and taken refuge in writing, a vehicle by which they extended their shared fantasy world. According to a police witness: '…the correspondence toward the latter stage became extravagant and grandiose, full of murder, violence and bloodshed…'

The crisis in their relationship came when Juliet's father decided to return to England and take his daughter with him. The girls had become inseparable. Both girls had sold their horses to try and raise money for Pauline to travel with Juliet and her father as far as South Africa, but while Juliet's parents didn't mind the friendship so much, it was Pauline's mother and step-father who, in the girls' minds, seemed to provide the impediment. The mother especially did not approve of her daughter spending so much time with Juliet at her parents' house in Ilam. As the friendship grew deeper, Mrs Parker noticed her daughter was losing weight and was becoming progressively withdrawn. With the date of the Hulme's departure drawing near, the girls decided to kill Pauline's mother.

(From Pauline's diary)

…she is most unreasonable. I heard [mother] making insulting remarks about Mrs Hulme while I was ringing Deborah [Juliet] this afternoon. I was livid. I am very glad because the Hulmes sympathise with me and it is nice to realise that adults realise what mother is. Dr Hulme is going to do something about it I think. Why could not mother die? Dozens of people are dying all the time. Thousands, so why not mother and father too? Life is very hard. This evening Mr and Mrs Campbell have come. I had a pleasant bath…

Mother went out this afternoon so Deborah and I bathed for some time. However, I felt thoroughly depressed afterwards and even quite seriously considered committing suicide. Life seemed so much not worth the living and death such an easy way out. Anger against mother boiled up inside me as it is she who is one of the main obstacles in my path. Suddenly a means of ridding myself of this obstacle occurred to me. If she were to die…

We rose very early this morning at eight and messed around for a little while waiting for Gopsy* to paint Deborah. While he did this, I tidied the room and messed about a little. Afterwards we discussed our plans for moidering mother and made them a little clearer. Peculiarly enough I have no qualms of conscience. Is it peculiar that we are so mad? I was picked up at 2 p.m. and we went out to see Rosemary. I have been very sweet and good. I have worked in a little of our plan…

What Pauline meant by being very sweet and good is that she made herself unusually pleasant around her mother so that she would be pleased to agree with the girls' request for a special outing to Victoria Park on the Port Hills overlooking Christchurch.

(From Juliet's diary)
The day of the happy event. 22 Tuesday. I am writing a little of this up on the morning before the death. I felt very excited and the-night-before-christmassy last night. I did not have pleasant dreams though. I am about to rise.

The park has many walks and at that time of the week there were very few people about. At about midday the three called in at the tea rooms for ice-cream before continuing on down a secluded track. About two hundred yards further on, Juliet dropped a small pink stone on the ground and called Mrs Parker's attention to it. As the woman bent to pick it up from the track, Pauline took a half-brick from her purse that was wrapped in the foot of a stocking and hit her mother across the head with it; that one blow was not enough to kill the woman. It took a great deal more than that. The girls then, blood spattered, ran to the kiosk where they informed the proprietor that the mother had slipped and banged her head on a rock. Their story never really took hold and by the end of that evening it was

---

* 'Gopsy' must have been none other than Rudolph Gopas who attempted to teach me painting at Art School in the seventies. He was a crazy man himself by then, in my opinion; I remember him stalking about the studio with his head buried in Hesse pausing to look up from time to time to insult a student, usually female, reduce her to tears and then continue his reading. As a young refugee from Lithuania, he had kept body together, even if his soul was elsewhere, by painting portraits of Fendalton's cherubic children. He was a good portraitist and in great demand. I wonder if the painting of Juliet Hulme still exists. It would be a thing indeed to look into that young and quite beautiful face, to study the eyes, and consider that within two days the girl sitting so composedly for Rudi would be committing one of the most infamous crimes in New Zealand's history.

obvious to the police that the girls had killed Pauline's mother.

The defence could only be one of insanity and it was my father's job to construct a case to prove the opposite, as in paragraph eight of the opening address to the jury:

> There is another request I have to make of you. The dead woman is the mother of one of the accused – the girl Parker – and was brutally done to death and as far as one can see had done nothing to deserve her awful fate. On the other hand the two accused who are now occupying the centre of the stage and have played the important parts in this tragedy are in a very difficult and distressing position and the result of this trial may have the most direful consequences for them. Gentlemen, [the jury was all male] I do not ask you to try and forget about these matters altogether. You may pity the dead woman and be incensed against these young persons in the dock, or you may feel pity for the two accused in the dreadful situation they find themselves today. These things have nothing to do with this trial at all. Sentiment and emotionalism have no part in British justice. Your duty as you have sworn to perform it is to deal with the case on the facts and not allow your judgment to be swayed by feelings either for the dead woman or for the two accused in the dock. All you are concerned about is to decide whether or not the two accused killed the unfortunate Mrs Parker and whether or not they intended to do so.

There are sixteen pages to this opening address. It contains these curious final words:

> The intention of the prosecution is that this plainly was a coldly, callously planned and premeditated murder committed by two highly intelligent but precocious and dirty-minded little girls. I will now call the witnesses.

Curious, I would say, because after the lovely legalese employed for all fifteen previous pages, it slips at the end into the vernacular. Although Alan Brown would undoubtedly have delivered this opening address it sounds very much to me like Peter's voice. It was not unusual for a junior to do much of the work in a case of this nature; and given that Brown was on the verge of mental collapse even before the trial began, it is not improbable that Peter may have written it for him. If this indeed was the case, then it makes sense that the address be summed up in common language, that the final paragraph was crafted to stick; just as, twenty-five years later, a similar closing paragraph was crafted to stick in the minds of those who would read the report on Erebus.

Peter certainly wanted the jury to think that these were not special girls, even though their intelligence had been alluded to. He was concerned that the jury might afford them special treatment. One witness described Juliet Hulme as having an intelligence quotient of 170 plus and went on to say, 'I have been told that she is one in a million'.

Peter has drawn his pen through these lines and replaced them with his own hand: '…she is said to have a high intelligence quotient.'

Presumably, Peter did not want the jury to think there were only three other people in the country as clever as Juliet. It might have persuaded them to be lenient, just as the Renaissance cardinals had been with the murderer Cellini.

Within the Parker Hulme file, there are three pages of hand written notes where Peter seemed to be looking at commonwealth cases concerning defences of insanity which depended on the interpretation of 'insane'. I'm not sure whom he was writing this for: himself or Alan Brown. The conclusions he came to certainly did not help his case. I can only suppose he wanted to look at the issue from the defence's point of view. He wrote:

Construction of s.43 (2) of the Crimes Act 1908: The question is what meaning is to be attached to the word 'wrong'. Does it mean 'legally wrong' or has it the general meaning of 'legal or moral wrong'? s.43 was first argued in 1952 in *R. v Windle* before the Court of Criminal Appeal [England]. It was argued that the word 'wrong' was to be construed in the general sense, meaning 'evil' as opposed to 'good', without any specific legal connotation. The court held, however, that the word 'wrong' meant 'legally wrong' and nothing else.

The judgment of Lord Goddard [presiding over that appeal] goes on to say: 'It would be impracticable for a tribunal to have to adjudicate on whether the community thought that a particular act was right or wrong.'

...this ruling is a binding authority in England. In 1952, shortly after the Windle decision, the High Court of Australia had to consider the same point and came to the opposite conclusion. The case for appeal argued that the judge in the Windle case had erred in directing the jury that the defendant's defence of insanity could only succeed if he could establish that he did not know his act was legally wrong. In short, the Australian judge had followed *R. v Windle* and it was argued in appeal that the Windle decision was wrong. The High Court agreed with this view. They ruled that the appellant could not understand the nature and quality of his act, and if he did, he did not know that the act was wrong, because he could not distinguish good from evil.

Lord Goddard's reasons for his interpretation were based on the impracticabilty of a court of law being compelled to estimate the community's conception of good and evil. ...However, is it not for the jury to consider that question? Is not that a very appropriate question for a jury?

He finishes his research by saying that there was no direct authority in New Zealand on this matter and where there existed two conflicting decisions in the commonwealth it was usual form to follow the English ruling in preference to that of the colonial one. But although it seemed clear that the Supreme Court should follow the Windle decision, there was no actual compulsion for it to do so. He concluded that the majority of legal opinion preferred the Australian decision where it regarded the word 'wrong' as meaning 'legal or moral wrong'.

Consequently, Peter would have known that the prosecution's case would have been hard to make. The girls seemed nutty as gnats. He would have to show they were cold-bloodedly aware of what they were doing, that they had murdered Pauline's mother, not out of passion or impulse, but as the only clear way to suit their own ends. In a loose hand, in characteristic blue ink, he has written:

SANITY

State or quality of being sane.

Soundness or health of mind.

(*Webster's Dictionary*)

RATIONAL

Having the faculty of reasoning; endowed with reason. Exercising one's reason in a proper manner; having sound judgment; sensible; sane.
(*Shorter Oxford English Dictionary*)

Terrence Gresson, defending Pauline, suggested that the question of sanity was a medical one to be answered by experts. He produced two such experts, Drs Medlicott and Bennet, who stated that the girls were suffering from paranoia associated with *folie à deux*, or communicated insanity. This insanity was accelerated by their homosexual relationship. They knew what they were doing, the experts said, but were unable to form any rational view of the rightness of what they were doing. Gresson said that while a defence of insanity was often discounted by juries as a last resort, it could not be so in this case where it was based on medical evidence of the highest order. 'The condition of paranoia and *folie à deux* takes away any legal responsibility,' he said. And he had taken note of the prosecution's closing words, countering them in this way: 'These girls are not "ordinary, dirty-minded little girls". They are mentally sick and their preoccupation with sexual matters is a symptom of their decreased mental condition.'

On the prosecution's side of the case were the senior medical advisor to Auckland Mental Hospital, and the medical advisor to Sunnyside Hospital and its superintendent, all swearing that, in their long experience and association with thousands of patients, they had 'never known of any two insane persons combining to commit a crime'.

I have not been able to find the prosecution's closing address; possibly it reiterated the opening address since the defence hadn't presented anything unexpected. But before Judge Adams began his summing up, he saw Hulme's junior counsel, Brian McClelland, and my father in his chambers to advise them that he did not intend to put the insanity defence to the jury.

This contradicted my father's sense of due process and he replied that if Adams didn't put the insanity plea to the jury he would 'feel obliged to seek leave to withdraw from the case'. It was a stand described by many of the legal fraternity as one of integrity and courage. For my father, this decision would have been an intolerable shifting of the chess pieces after a game well played.

Adams relented, the full defence was put before the jury, and the girls were duly convicted and separated after all; Hulme to Mt Eden and Parker to Arohata Prison. Not very much is known of what happened to Pauline after she was released, but when the story was made into a film by Peter Jackson, there was a pulse of renewed interest and Juliet Hulme was discovered to be living in England where she had made a very good career for herself as a writer of crime novels.

ALBUM:

Cadenza

Garth glanced at his watch. 'I'd better be moving,' he said, 'we're playing bridge at six.' He stood up. 'But, look, I have something for you, Sam.' He darted from the room with quick determination as if he had just remembered a lit fuse somewhere. I followed him outside and across the lawn to a small shed. It was constructed of concrete block and although the years had rendered it grey and it was flecked now with lichen and sinking into a froth of leaves, I could smell still the acrid scent of new cement. I could see Garth in his khaki shorts, a lick of black hair across his temple, grinning out of a photograph in which the sky has faded to an egg-shell blue. He's holding a shovel in his hands beside a heap of gravel and a gaping concrete mixer.

Inside the shed we found a large music system with speakers. 'We've had the living room redesigned, Sam. This is all too big for it now. Going to buy something a little more compact. You'll find the tapes don't work very well but most of it's still good and there's a CD player with it. Come on, give me a hand here.'

It's all installed now in this cavernous Mill and I have to say again that the speakers of the seventies just can't be matched by today's compact systems. Garth has bequeathed us also a heavy stack of vinyl which we will make our way through over the next month or so, selecting favourites and especially the cadenzas from violin concertos. It's extraordinary for me to find them all so lovingly cared for, hardly a scratch. When I listen to my own thirty-threes, it's like gazing at a beautiful landscape through a nest of barbed wire. And I write all this for a reason, I write it because it demonstrates something about my father and friendship.

Twenty-five years ago, Garth came to visit me at my cottage in the hills, a few miles inland from here. He had come to shoot a few hares with his young son, Peter, and when he arrived I was hacking away at the fiddle, chasing some evasive Irish jig around the cat gut in a very inexpert way. He said, 'I didn't know you played.'

'Most people say I don't,' I replied, and hastily put the instrument back in the shadows.

'You must come by one day when you're in town, and I'll play you some Heifetz,' he said. I did call in. He sat me down in a deep chair, set a disc on the turntable and lowered the stylus onto the beginning of a violin cadenza. Garth sat a little apart, folded his hands in his lap and appeared to go to sleep. When the piece finished he leapt up, removed the disc and replaced it with another. With each piece he knew exactly where the cadenza lay. I was enchanted. After a while the door opened and his wife wheeled in a trolley laden with coffee and cake. Garth opened his eyes, glanced at her, nodded and then closed his eyes again. She left the room as soundlessly as she had entered. Two hours later I was drinking another cup of coffee with my father. I told him about the visit with Garth and that exquisite hour with the violin. 'I had no idea Garth was interested in music,' I said.

'Neither did I,' said my father.

Album:
The station master's daughter

How did my parents meet? I should answer this in the way my mother would, after all it's her story. Whatever I ask my mother I am always replied to in narrative form; it is always a story which starts a long way from the subject and takes its time getting there. 'Mum, why do you do this?'

'Do what?' She's genuinely puzzled.

'Well, you always give me so much more than just the facts.'

She shrugs. She's unrepentant. 'I can't help it,' she says. 'My mother would make assumptions if I didn't fill in all the details. It became a habit.'

'So far as I can recollect, you have not mentioned in any letter so far that you have listened entranced to the lilting song of a nightingale,' wrote my father in one of his letters to Fontainebleau. *'There should be a few nightingales in your area...'*

It was a moonless night in the Dardanelles. The sea was unusually calm as 'Tiny' Freyberg slipped into the water and began his swim to the Gallipoli Peninsula. Those lonely two miles took him an hour and a quarter and who knows what was going through his mind all that time. There were mines, of course, several Allied ships were already lying at the bottom, and the beaches themselves might well have been salted with explosives awaiting the first boot of invasion. But no one observed the lone swimmer as he rose amid the phosphorescent surf to set his pale feet against the black sand. No one saw this one man, armed with a revolver, standing between millions of tons of coiled steel. I imagine it was a silence to remember.

It was night time also fourteen hundred miles away in France where Stanley Smith, twenty-one, lay in his great-coat, given up on living, simply hoping for sleep. For seven days the barrage had rolled along the front building toward the crescendo of Boiselle where five tons of TNT, secreted beneath the German redoubts, blew a column of dirt four thousand feet into the July sky. Cecil Lewis saw it all as doggedly he flew the line taking photographs. He was two miles away when it went off and his machine surged a moment under the shock of it. But he flew on anyway, completing his stock of film, flying and reloading the camera at the same time. Sometimes, when he glanced ahead, he saw the crow flutter, that thing, that black shape he could never quite get into focus. It was the glimpse of a shell that had reached its apogee and was pausing momentarily before starting down on its way to the enemy lines. It was evening and all along the salient the guns like diamonds flickered at the edge of night, thirty thousand tons of steel falling down on thirty thousand tons of flesh. And when at last the silence came the Allies climbed from trenches all along the Somme and wandered out on no man's land to face an undefeated enemy.

'Was it really like that?' asked the station master's daughter, having read to him a memoir she had picked up at the library. Stanley Smith had listened unremarking to my mother's voice, he had listened and had set his mind along the weary track of yesterday, and as she turned her face to his he sat silent still. But he nodded, and she saw along the creases of his dear, kind face, beneath the lenses of his glasses, a dampening as if in those fond valleys now at last the tide was coming in.

'Come on, we're late,' said Marie, wheeling her bike through the gate. The door opened and Mrs Smith called after them, 'Don't stay too long with Mrs Scott,' she said. She was wearing an apron and her hands were dusted in flour. 'You'll be back by lunch you two.'

The girls set off up the country lane, away from the sounds of the river, away from the freezing works, the paper mill, the railyard and the rolling stock; that constant drift and clash of dull iron and red coach-work.

It was summer, there were skylarks hovering over the fields and buttercups in the ditches. The road was dusty and their tyres crunched the stones. The country air was thick with the scent of life. They stopped at the gate and walked their bikes between the tall trees that concealed the homestead. Marie knocked on the front door and then stepped back.

'She's been quite withdrawn since Dougal was killed.' Girdle scones fresh from the oven lay on a white plate. Steam drifted.

'Stanley was the only one of his brothers to go away, you know.'

'Your husband?'

Mrs Smith nodded. 'He didn't like it when Dougal went, and now he's dead in Canada and she's got Laurie fighting in Italy. I don't know how she sleeps.'

'I don't imagine she does.'

Mrs Scott made tea for the girls and served it in the finest china. When they were finished she asked, 'And what will you sing for me today, Margarita?'

'What would you like, Mrs Scott?'

The lady clasped her hands across her midriff, drew in a deep breath and gazed out the window to where the heavy flowers hung their heads. 'What would I like,' she intoned, and released the breath from her body. 'I would like…' she tilted her head on one side. 'Perhaps the *Ave Maria*?'

And then afterward, Mrs Scott led the girls out into the garden to show them the primroses and jonquils planted between the trees in pools of milky light and cool shadow. It was a redress of sorts. Defiantly, she could litter her world with violent, perennial colour. The child would leave, of course, but she would come again next week; the garden would collapse into winter and be reborn with the spring. This she could do, this she could attend to. But her brightest flower, its face forever turned to the sun, was lost in Canada, and no spring would ever bring him back to her.

As the girls rode away they stood on their pedals and felt the wind against their faces. Behind them the lady walked slowly up the wide lawn, her back turned to the world, her thoughts trickling through memories like fingers through the feathered heads of flowers.

The slow train from Palmerston to Dunedin stopped at every village along the way. It was a long journey for Margarita on a Saturday morning, but it meant an hour with Mr Johnston, her singing teacher. Afterwards, she would climb the hill to the weather-board house where her two maiden aunts stood sentry duty at the gates of civilization. There she would stay the night before returning to Palmerston on the morning train. Sensing something a little untamed about the young niece, Stanley's two sisters paid strict attention to her informal education. 'And what do you propose to do when you leave school, Margarita?'

'I'd like to travel, Aunty Nell.'

'Travel? Yes, of course. But how will you afford it? What do you expect to do for a living? You know, although your voice is an exceptional gift, it can only ever be used for the pleasure of others. It won't make you an income.' And they were right. Donald Munro, also a pupil of Johnston's had made it as far as Covent Garden, but in the end, in order to secure a dependable income, came home to teach and to form New Zealand's first opera company.

'Well, I had thought about being a nurse.'

'Oh no, Margarita. That won't do,' declared the proprietorial aunt. 'Wiping bottoms is hardly something to be recommended as a career for anyone, let alone you.'

'You could do a lot worse than training as a hairdresser with Mr Johns. We know Mr Johns quite well, and we shall ask him if he is taking on apprentices. Yes,' continued Aunt Lucy, 'Mr Johns will do very nicely.'

My mother's immediate future determined, the aunts took her to a picture show that evening and as they stood for the national anthem two young men in the row in front of them, astonishingly, remained in their seats. Aunt Nell prodded one of them firmly with her umbrella. 'If you don't like this country, young man, you can leave it,' she said.

The staff car pulled up at the edge of the road in a pall of dust. My father snapped to attention and executed a pert salute. 'Tiny' Freyberg had survived the Dardanelles and various other reckless adventures to find himself, at the time he met my father, a full General and leading the New Zealand 2nd Division in Italy. He addressed himself to the young officer standing at attention by the side of the road. 'Those your men, lieutenant?' Down the bank my father's platoon were busy plucking peaches from an ancient orchard and stuffing what they couldn't eat down their tunics.

'Yes, sir,' answered my father.

'Thieving bunch of bastards,' muttered the General and then curtly ordered his driver to push on. It is said that when crossing a piece of Tuscany well-known to be within range of the German mortars the General ordered his driver to stop and shut off the engine, so that he could listen to the song of a nightingale. His driver and the two other occupants hunched low in their seats while they awaited whichever came first: the order to proceed or oblivion.

In 1945 an early winter storm laid the lower east Canterbury coast under snow. The war in Italy was coming to an end. Lieutenant Mahon had been transferred to the 27th Battalion in Naples where soon it would be sailing for Japan. Peter was disappointed. They were all hungry for home. Laurie Scott, on the other hand, had been furloughed at last and his ship duly arrived in Lyttelton some time in July, where the many wounded were put on trains to take them to the homes they hadn't seen for two years.

> *Tracking down the coast where the south wind chatters, there's a white cloud scattered like a broken breath; there's a fire in a fist of sand-cast iron and soot peppers down across the white linen flanks; there are judder bar bridges spanning the rivers where the green water curdles round the white-capped banks.*
>
> *Every man stares as the rails slide by and it sounds like a hundred gasps of death; and every man is thinking of a river somewhere, of a hundred lost friends and summer on the other side, somewhere on the other side … are girls in pink dresses, terra cotta cottages, barrels full of wine and a multitude of crosses; in every homesick heart there's a subtle fond remembering.*

Laurie leans against the sill and stares out across the flat country, the wide featureless paddocks with the stark clean mountains on the horizon. The sky in Italy was yellow he thinks. Like an oil painting, like an old photograph. The train rocks them like a cradle, these boys coming home; khaki clad, cigarettes leaning from slack mouths, a quick grin of anticipation, a twitch of sorrow, a memory gathering dust, a confusion of loyalties. The train slides down the countryside like a tear.

Stanley Smith takes out his watch and checks the hour. He takes down his frock coat and his wife helps him into it and every time it reminds him of his great-coat and the mud of 1918. But there are eight brass buttons down the front and they shine brightly in the wan light and as he places the station master's cap on his head he turns back to my mother. 'Would you like to come?'

They wait at the edge of the platform, father and daughter, the old soldier standing square-shouldered as if on parade, gazing up the northern line. He is wearing those same round wire-rimmed lenses through which he watched his friends fall one by one.

All the long journey people had cheered their passing, waving along the lines, at road crossings and bridges. There were bands and bagpipes, and food on trestles at every stop and steaming pots of tea. And now as the train slid into Palmerston Laurie's journey had at last come to an end. He took his kit down from the rack and waited while a nurse led a young soldier down the aisle. Although blinded and with both hands destroyed, he was cheerful to be going home. Laurie stared out the window. A young man with one leg limped across the platform and was swept into the arms of his wife who had slipped through the cordon. Amid the tide of khaki he caught sight of the station master. 'Mr Smith,' he called, 'I remember you from Mataura.'

Stanley grinned up at him. 'Good to see you safely home, Laurie.'

'And is this the young girl who used to sing for my mother?'

Stanley glanced at Margarita and nodded. Laurie grinned.

'Would you sing for the boys, Margarita?' he asked. 'I know they'd like it.'

The staff sister could not understand the delay. She came bustling up the grey platform, white linen streaming behind her like a locomotive. 'Station master, why aren't we on our way? I have sick men here who need to be in hospital...' But it was no good. The train wasn't going anywhere, not until my mother had been taken to all the cars.

You did not say if you have heard a nightingale yet … there should be some in your area.

Margarita, your voice can only ever be used for the pleasure of others.

Two years later my mother finished her apprenticeship to Mr Johns and embarked on her first year of nursing. Mrs Brown was now the matron of Dunedin Hospital. She had been with the Voluntary Aid Detachment during the war and taken care of Freyberg when he was wounded. She was a straight note played without embellishment or grace. She had heard that her newest charge possessed a remarkable voice and when it was announced that the lady Freyberg was to pay a visit to the hospital, matron took my mother aside, led her to the new hall and bade her sing so that she could make her own evaluation. 'Very good, nurse Smith,' she said, at the end of the audition. 'Lady Freyberg will be coming here on Friday. I would like you to sing for the assembly.'

At other times she was asked by one of the house surgeons to sing for the patients. I see her in my mind, her dark hair mid-length and wavy, bespectacled, attractive, following along with every directive, her hands demurely clasped behind her back, singing for the broken-hearted. I don't feel she was ever entirely the captain of her soul nor the mistress of her fate. 'I want to travel,' she said, and no one seemed to be listening.

She sings seldom now, well, at least I haven't heard her in a long time. But I remember in chapel when I was young this voice beside me suddenly unleashed to fill the air from vestry to font, from chancel to sarking. It was like someone letting loose a rainbow indoors. It seemed improper. And always there were those curious faces turning, captivated, and I was embarrassed and wished she wouldn't.

My father had been home from the war for four years before he met my mother. She was in Christchurch. She went to a dinner to make up the numbers. She wasn't well and didn't want to be there. Neither did he. He accompanied her back to her flat and a week later rang to ask if he could visit. She said yes, and he did. They became engaged. 'But you must travel,' he said, and she did. She went to Australia as she had planned, met up with her Palmerston friend Marie Hutton, the girl who had accompanied her on those bicycle trips to sing for Mrs Scott: and then, after all, she returned to marry the law clerk in the firm Raymond Donnelly. My mother's spring had come to an end and my father was commencing a career that would absorb him almost to vanishing, in much the same way as the Glass Bead game absorbed Joseph Knecht.*

If ever there was a time to see the man clearly, caught between his old family and the new one of his making, between someone else's war and the career he had chosen, I imagine it would have been then.

---

* See Appendix II p. 244

ALBUM:

Fulton Avenue

The cottage at Donald Place, which my father had purchased with his war gratuity, was sold. The home next to Garth was being built and in the meantime we shifted to a rented house in Fulton Avenue, still about the same distance from Hereford Street, but with a little bit more room. I don't remember very much about it. I remember fishing in the nearby river and falling in, drinking from the gutter on the way to school to impress a number of small friends, and trying to learn the lyrics of *My Old Man's a Dustman*. I remember setting fire to a box of twenty-two ammunition just to see what would happen and helping my father weed the vegetable patch which was overgrown with stinging nettles; he told me they were dock leaves. And I distinctly recall that on my way home from school one day an older boy took me into some trees and showed me his penis. I didn't think there was anything particularly remarkable about it but when he insisted on inspecting mine I took to my heels and told my mother. She laughed and gave me a hug. 'If it ever happens again,' she said, 'you just tell him your father's a policeman.'

I frowned up at her. 'Really,' I said. 'Is that true?'

'Sort of,' she said. But that was enough for me. She had removed my worry as easily as if it had been a splinter.

My father came and went from work and the seasons turned around him. I remember him waking us in the morning to see what patterns the frost had made on the windows overnight, and I knew that he sometimes embellished those natural designs a little for our entertainment, just as he would embellish stories from time to time. It was with the same intent that he had taken hens eggs and created a nest in the apricot tree out of lawn clippings. There was magic in it, but it was never a lie. It was a kind of creative non-fiction.

So I learned to ride a bike at Fulton Avenue, weaving my way across the lawn; I changed schools; and I asked Helen Somers for her hand in marriage. Her father, a future Appeal Court judge who would one day find against my father in the Erebus case, lived at the end of our road with his wife Louise and various offspring. One day I found an electric eggbeater in our rubbish can at the gate. I was fascinated by it and took it to the Somers's house where Helen and I managed to get it going. It worked beautifully as far as I was concerned, and very soon we had flour and water spitting all around the Somers's kitchen. Louise caught us, uttered a number of loud complaints and returned the beater to the trash and me to my mother. The next day I biked down the road with a ring I had fashioned out of copper and gave it to Helen. Our engagement was called off, however, by an elderly aunt. 'I think we can do a little better than Sammy Mahon,' she advised. Many years and a couple of disengagements later, the aunt was heard to declare at some dinner party that perhaps Sammy Mahon might not have been such a bad idea after all.

ALBUM:
Halswell

I can't remember the year or how old I was; but most probably it coincided with the time my best friend Bill coerced his sister Penny to parachute off the garage roof using a large black umbrella. His mother was furious. Bill ignored her, and lacking further sisters, he strapped the umbrella to himself and tried again.

I was thinking of Penny as, entirely uncoerced, I stood at the top of the clay cliff at the bottom of the drive trying to will myself over the edge. I had stacked a number of cardboard boxes at the foot of the cliff and covered them with an old mattress from the garage. I had seen it on television, how the stunt men fell from water towers onto constructions of this sort, turning in a slow half-somersault to land on their backs just off camera.

The wind was blowing from the west as usual and there would have been loess in the air, that fine yellow river dust that had softened the volcanic slopes of the Port Hills for centuries until disturbed by subdivision. I think of that home now in the reduced form of a child's drawing. Soft crayon, simple lines. One round hill with a wedge taken out of it on which sits a small brick house with a corrugated iron roof. My mother is permanently framed in the kitchen window. My father's car is on the drive, a round Austin of some description, and my father is halfway between the car and the house, either leaving or arriving. He is wearing a grey coat and hat, and he has a briefcase in his right hand. In his left is the perpetual cigarette, his wrist slightly turned away from his body. Behind him there's a garage with a piano, above that a little bit of hill, a rusty wire fence with flecks of wool snagged in the barbs, and a single pine tree with a magpie in it. And, as I say, I'm standing at the bottom of the drive, at the top of the cliff, waiting for courage to lift me out into thin air.

I've seen a picture of my father and his school mates, arms folded, shoulder to shoulder posing for a photograph. One of them holds a football, another a shield. My father seems very much part of it all, part of a team, something

I will never know. A child always understands what its parent longs for in him even if it is never said. My father longed for me to be a sportsman, to be one of a team. And I never was. Worse than that, I never wanted to be. For my birthday he bought me a canvas punching bag and hung it from the low branch of the pine so that I could practice tackling. I dived at the thing all holidays working the turfs loose with my trailing heels until the ground was turned to dust and my chin raw from the linen. Dust, pine cones, dry white pine sticks, the smell of resin and the creaking rope. But it didn't help.

I would stand in that most lonely of places on the field dreading the long kick from the enemy and the ball sailing over all the other heads until there was just me and it and god help me if I missed the mark.

And then it was summer; those interminable Saturdays standing in the outfield waiting for something to happen, and when it did my mind was somewhere else of course. Sometimes a ball from another team playing back to back with ours would fall like a grenade against the hard dirt beside me, smouldering red leather, and I would wince and wonder what exactly was the point of wasting my youth like this, waiting for some cretin with a stick to split my skull. I had other things to do.

There would have been wind. Beyond the road the hill fell away further to the wheat field where every summer a harvester came and worked its way outside in, diminishing the yellow crop to one tiny island. Then we would wait on our bellies, watching with hawk eyes for the hares at last to break cover and run from the thrashing blades.

I gazed back down again at the mattress. If I make myself tip, I told myself, beyond the point of no return, then I would just have to make the best of it. And that's what I did. Once I had gone too far there was no fear any more, just a quiet, intense focus in doing the thing as best as I could.

I was very pleased with myself as I rolled across the clay and realised that for the most part I was still intact. No one spoke about it although it must have been obvious that I had sprained my ankle. I wonder what my father said to my mother. 'What's the boy done?'

I imagine my mother concentrating on laying the table. 'Oh,' she would say as an aside, ' I think he jumped off the cliff today.' But cliff-jumping was not in the school curriculum and it's not considered a team sport even in these permissive days, so I suppose it is hard to remark on.

Nevertheless, if I had been him, I would have been a little concerned. I might have said something.

ALBUM:

The bay and iconoclasm

Like many New Zealand families, we were drawn to the sea every summer. Maybe it was part of a culture that is lost now, I'm not sure. These days I go to the river instead. There is a little bay on Banks Peninsula called Wainui, situated on the flank of one of its two volcanoes and in those days it was fairly remote from the commotion of contemporary living. The roads to the bay were mostly shingle and there was a scattering of houses, a few holiday homes and a little shop that served the farmers in that far flung arm of the peninsula. There were tangles of native bush in the valleys and graveyards of totara stumps on the high ridges; proud, tall, stiff spikes combing a sky where the clouds were whiter and the sky bluer than ever since. There were cod and flounders and there were butterfish drifting under the kelp at the edge of the rocky isthmus where the sea sucked and belched and reached up to us as we skipped from ledge to ledge, sticks wound with string in our hands, rusty hooks and dried meat.

When I was seventeen, a year before my father accepted the judgeship in Auckland, my mother bought a small bach tucked away up a green valley. As you drove by the property you almost missed it: its narrow, iron gateway was cramped with evergreens. There were trees all around and wood pigeons hung upside down eating the laburnum leaves. And at the foot of the lawn a stream ran past over green boulders. It was a place hidden from the world and it would have been lovely to keep it. But my father's appointment to the bench in Auckland meant we had to slough off a lot of what we loved.

I was trying to sleep one night and not able to because of my father's famous snore. It was remarkable. My mother suggests it was caused by his own father's determination that as a schoolboy Peter should learn to box. Who knows. It was pattern snoring of the first order; beginning softly, like the breathing of a child, and then passing through deeper and wider chasms of reverberation until with a start he would wake himself for a split second, turn over and begin again. In that brief respite I would try to slip under the cover of somnolence. But the moments were not long enough on the night in question. So in desperation I created them artificially by flinging a paperback across the open living space to smack against the wall of my parents' room. The sound would stop instantly and all would be silent, for a while. And then the routine would begin again. Whack, another book. There were eight paperbacks stacked on the wicker chair, and when, exasperated and drunk with insomnia I discovered all my ammunition spent, I threw the chair. This time the entire family woke. 'Wassat?' enquired my father.

'It's your son,' said my mother, who somehow had been sleeping peacefully at his side. 'He's gone mad.'

'You were snoring!' I shouted. 'I couldn't sleep.'

'No, you weren't,' said my mother to my father, bolstering her diagnosis.

So I leaped out of bed, packed my clothes and stalked from the house. It was two in the morning. A mile or so beyond the bay I found a pleasant field and settled down among the daisies with my jersey as a pillow. I was just drifting into blessed unconsciousness when I heard a nasal snuffling in my ear. I sat bolt upright. It was a hedgehog.

The sun woke me early while the bellbirds were still ringing in the gum trees. It was very pleasant. I walked all the way to Little River where I'd left my Morris Eight. I climbed in and drove it back the way I'd come and was in Wainui in time for a late breakfast. No one said anything. And that was how it was. We'd have some massive flare up, get it out like a lanced boil and then continue as if nothing had happened.

There was a boat one morning moored out in the bay. A mysterious white yacht. It was hot and we went down to the beach to swim. My father stood at the edge of the tide and stared out for a long time to where the boat lay far off turning lazily in the breeze. He swam well. He dived, and when his head broke the surface he shook the water from his eyes as if taking a bearing on his target, and then began his stylish, methodical overarm, heading in a straight line out to sea. I stood on the sand and watched in admiration and dread as he grew smaller and smaller until I could hardly see him among the undulations of water. And then at last I could just make him out, hauling himself up the side of the yacht being greeted by those on board. I was awed and I was afraid. To me the water was an enemy and yet he had gone out into it in a straight line and survived.

One holiday lunchtime when I was five and we were staying with the station master and his wife we took the winding track down to a beach below their house to spend a lazy afternoon at the edge of the water. While my father and sister were out among the waves I was left to guard the wicker basket lunch. But the tide came quickly in and I moved the basket to a rock. Soon I was on the rock myself, the skeins of lathered water creeping around its base, gurgling and whispering my name. I was terrified and as in a dream my father and my sister would not come back.

We were fishing in Wainui Bay near the deep rock shelf where the butterfish came to feed on kelp when the anchor got lodged between some rocks. No amount of pulling could break it loose. I looked into the water; bars of sunlight drove down into its depths between the matted kelp, drifting and flopping with the rise and fall of the swell. The boat creaked and strained against its tether and I was sure we would have to cut it loose. My father threw away his cigarette and took off his shirt. Then to my dismay he slipped over the edge of the boat and disappeared beneath the water, down into that freckled sunlight, following the rope to the bottom. I couldn't bear it. He was brave: he was made of cast iron.

But it was at the bay that I discovered the first evidence of rust. We were camping up in the thick bush. I had taken my new air-rifle and gone hunting for birds, for anything that moved, actually. Sliding through an undergrowth which was tangled with passion vines and supplejack, I caught a movement in the foliage above me, a fractured silhouette against the sky. I aimed at its throat and fired and it fell, a lump of feathers blue and green and white with a crimson bead against its chest. A few minutes later I burst from the trees and held it aloft for my father's praise. 'Christ,' he said, 'you'll have us all in prison. Here,' and he took it from me and tucked it underneath some newspapers in the boot of the car. At least he wasn't going to let the kereru go to waste. An hour later my sister and I were standing on top of a knoll overlooking the campsite a hundred yards away. I pointed out a couple of fat native pigeons sitting together on the branch of a dead beech tree jutting out from the canopy below us. 'It was one of those,' I said. And just as I spoke we heard a crack and a piece of bark flicked away from between the birds, startling them into the air. I darted into the bush, down the slope, over a creek, hurdled a fence at the side of the road, dived into the bush and out again in time to see my father slipping my air-rifle back into the car.

A year later we were packing to leave when my father realised we had forgotten that the net was still out, set near the headland. We would have to retrieve it. The sky was overcast and a heavy southerly swell pounded the beach. As I held our dinghy against the sand, he climbed unsteadily into the stern which was immediately dragged around by the receding water to face the incoming waves. Before I could do anything about it, one of them crashed square against the boat and burst in a white shawl of crocheted spume that wrapped itself lovingly around his shoulders. Both his knuckled hands gripped the sides of the boat and, although his lips were pressed together against the butt of his extinguished cigarette, that one word, the forbidden word, slipped out like a fart into the chill air; and my world shifted irrecoverably. I was amazed, it didn't seem possible. I said nothing. I jumped in quickly before anything else could happen and took the oars. I did the best I could to help with the net and getting back to shore and made myself busy lest there be a silence in which the matter of the word be mentioned. I had a certain amount of reconstructing to do first.

And that is what we do, I guess: spend our lives reconstructing the models that suited our parents, reshaping the world a little or a lot to fit our unique shape. And in the process it costs a little love.

ALBUM:
Folks on the hill

'They were peculiar, some of them,' said Russell, the quiet pipe-smoking neighbour who taught me to work wood. 'I remember we were summoned to the Commander's for a neighbourly get-together and your father saying, "Christ, I'd have to have a couple of gins under my belt before facing a frolick on the fo'c'sle."

'And when I met that teacher of yours, Tommy Tothill, for the first time, he said to me, "So are you a professor or a lawyer?" I told him I worked in hardware. He didn't know what to say.'

On the way to Faenza I called in on Simon Schoellar. He lives in the apex of a valley in the Swiss Alps and carves the wooden beams of houses with hunting scenes and the traditional decorative patterns of his adopted country. Klosters is a longbow's shot from Halswell and the childhood we shared, but he was a witness and I wanted to hunt around a little across those old fields.

I found him in his workshop, legs braced, his broad bulk bent over a fine chisel, the blade big as a thumb nail with a scalpel's edge. 'You bastard,' he said, looking up at me with his familiar crooked grin. 'You could have called you know.'

'How do you remember Dad?' I asked. We were sitting with coffee outside surrounded by the stones he has dragged up from the river and the heavy wooden beams that have been fashioned by his broad callused hands.

'He was very clever. But I don't know if he ever felt part of the crowd up there on the hill. My mother was eccentric,' he added as if by way of an excuse.

'She was wonderful,' I said. 'She was the life of the party. Her creativity made living in the sticks bearable.'

As I have mentioned, we lived on a hill for the better part of my childhood, surrounded by wilderness. It was my father's unconscious gift to me. I could come home from school, throw off my drab uniform, take the rifle from the cupboard and lose myself in the quiet valleys that ran up to the crest of the old volcano behind us. I had traps in the pine forest. I had secret ponds and companionable stones. I had horse mushrooms and flights of geese in the autumn. I had silence. I had summer flies crawling on my skin, harriers in the sky and the wind in my face: waiting for something to happen.

At first, when I was too young to go alone, he would accompany me, dressed in a heavy great-coat and balaclava. We would search the evening hills for the hunched forms of hares or the whir of a duck. And then, one remarkable day, he allowed me to go alone. 'Remember the fences,' he said, 'and always imagine the gun's loaded.'

A mile away the old stone quarry hung like a black rag, reverberating from time to time, shaking the ground. The concrete pad on which the house stood cracked. My mother worried that the pipes would start to leak. There were hay bales piled in the paddocks in the height of summer and when it rained I made a nest there, safe, breathing the fragrance of crushed fields. Beyond the quarry a cluster of houses marked the end of the road where a number of families lived connected I suppose by us, their children. And somewhere up there, Simon would be designing some intriguing new implement of destruction.

He rang Garth one day and asked him if he could borrow some blasting fuse. He was thirteen. Garth rang his mother. 'Simon's just asked me for some blasting fuse. I thought I should pass that by you first, Joan.'

'Yes, Garth. Well, that's quite all right by me.'

'But, Joan, if he wants to borrow blasting fuse then probably he has every intention of blowing something up.'

'Well of course, Garth. But, for goodness' sake, he's just trying to express himself…'

Garth handed over the blasting fuse without another word.

I wonder now if we were in training for some future war, like kittens learning to hunt. After all, our grandfathers had been given the Somme and Gallipoli; our fathers Crete, the desert and Italy. So, naturally, we assumed they'd find one for us too, and we were all secretly nervous. Already the war in Vietnam had claimed some vague older brothers.

I suppose it is not surprising that the more memorable parts of our holidays were spent hunting each other with air-rifles and homemade bombs. Simon especially was my mentor. I see him now sitting in the shade of a cabbage tree working away at the stock of a crossbow; polishing the wood it seemed for hours. He was fifteen, his hair falling in a thick fringe over his eyebrows as he worked. While the rest of us fought and swam, Simon patiently honed his blades and mixed explosives in the garage.

I remember creeping up on one of our huts in which I had convinced my brother to make an heroic last stand. He was young and trusted me quite unreasonably. We had armed him with an air-rifle and strapped an old steel helmet on his blond head. We were also armed, but with grenades made from aluminium pipe filled with potassium chlorate and sugar and were creeping through the unmown grass.

'KCIO-3,' says the chemist, peering at us over the rim of his glasses. 'What would you be wanting potassium chlorate for then?'

'Tanning possum skins,' we say. It is the usual answer.

'Hmm,' says the chemist, raising his chin. 'Not making any bombs then?'

'Oh no, sir.'

'Right then, boys,' he says, wandering off to the back shelves. 'But you just be careful.'

We crept to the bank, close as we dared considering my brother's excellent aim, and rolled on our sides to light the ends of Garth's blasting fuse. The bombs fell short and blew divots of grass from the ground and we heard the satisfactory sound of torn metal whirring through the air above our heads.

The sun shines over those days and the larks sing from their invisible height as they look down on us children where we lie on our backs in the open fields, grinning. The possibilities are limitless.

He was an uncompromising adversary, my father. I never saw him back down from anything. I knew very well the lines of demarcation and I knew that if I crossed them I'd be punished. Life at home was very much like school in that respect. I spent most of my time keeping out of his way. And yes, I broke his rules often, but I never lied to him nor he to me and that was an extraordinary thing. Like two strangers on a bus, both heading in the same direction, sharing the same close space, we could only ever guess at the workings of each other's thoughts. Yet between us there lay an unspoken respect. One day my mother summoned me to his room. He was ill; I think he'd slipped a disc and was spending some time resting. I didn't know why I'd been summoned, just that: 'Your father wants you.' There was urgency in my mother's voice and it made me very uneasy. He was propped up on pillows with a brace around his neck. He held the phone in his right hand.

'Have you been anywhere near Professor Robertson's bird nests?' he asked, without any preliminaries. I couldn't speak for a moment. Nests? Professor Robertson? I hadn't met the man. I'd seen him at a distance when I took my gun off over the hills. His house was about two hundred yards away across the paddocks but I had never had reason to go near it.

'His daughters say you've been taking eggs from his nests. Is that true?' I was overwhelmed. This was a first. I had committed many crimes in my life, some I would have been very proud to have confessed to, but never before had I been accused of something I hadn't done. I shook my head. I couldn't speak. Tears came to my eyes. I was about to protest when my father raised his hand. I swallowed my words. He lifted the phone and spoke to the professor. 'My son tells me he hasn't been near your nests. If he says he hasn't then that's good enough for me.'

I left the room amazed. Why was my word good enough for him? How had I earned it? And all these years later all I can think is that I never lied to him, and he knew it.

Simon clasped his hands behind his head and tilted back in his chair. 'Perugia was his idea,' he said. Simon's parents had gone to Italy for two years to study at the international university, the 'university of strangers'. 'Your father must have been there during the war and fallen in love with the place.' I thought of Castelraimondo and his birthday leave.

There's a wooden duck on the sideboard. A piece that Simon carved for himself. With my father and myself Simon shares this strange dichotomy of the hunter and the lover of nature. The duck is perfect; it's alive, the head especially shaped to accommodate a knot in the wood so that it becomes an eye. The curled tail feathers have been individually crafted and then spliced into the grain with an invisible join. This is a piece my father would have adored. I could imagine him leaning forward, his arms straight, hands braced against his knees, his lower jaw slightly pulled back, creases around his eyes as they gauged it. It would have made him smile.

I remembered a painting I'd done of a skylark dead in its nest. It was something I had found in the paddock, a still life. 'When will you paint something live, Samuel?' he asked. 'A skylark hovering in the air, perhaps?'

'When they learn to sit still,' I replied.

Simon and I sat in silence for a while, the sound of the river behind us. I was thinking about him and the parallels with his own father, also an émigré. 'Did I tell you about the falcon?' I asked, finally.

He nodded. 'It's not unusual,' he said. 'Just accept it. It's like the night my father died. I woke at about three in the morning and sat bolt upright. I woke Franzi. I was rigid. "I've got to ring home," I said. "Something's happened." So I did. I rang the hospital. A nurse answered and then the line went dead. I rang again and this time I got Mum. "Simon," she said, "your father just died".' He gazed at me across the table and shrugged. I said nothing. 'You don't need to let go of your falcon,' he said.

Album:
Waikari

'It did him a world of good. He looks so much better,' said my mother, on my father's return from a five-day visit with me. I don't remember much about it except that it was summer, that it was hot, and that it was my first year in the country living on my own. It was the year of the disaster although Erebus had not yet happened. Captain Collins had everything to live for and so did we. The fields all around me were thick with the blossoming yield of rape, the sky was a constant cornflower blue and there's a perpetual skylark nailed to that summer of 1979. It was the year I made a mattress out of grass clippings, kept a pet hawk on the front lawn, flew my first rocket, learned to horse-ride and, of course, it was the year I met Caroline.

My father stepped off the bus, picked up his case and golf clubs, and set out to walk the two miles to my cottage on the rise beyond the village. It was hot, as I said, and after a few hundred yards he deposited his luggage behind someone's neatly clipped hedge and carried on for most of the distance until, just out of town, a curious farmer pulled over to give him a lift. My father looked nothing like a farmer, even when he tried. Even on those days he joined Garth in one of his weekend stunts of blowing boulders or cutting down massive pines or laying concrete. He always looked like he had stepped out of an office with just the tie removed: like Jimmy Stewart – in my mind – striding across the Scottish moors in *The Thirty-nine Steps*. So of course the farmer was curious. It's a small town, and even though these days it has lost a lot of its family feeling, strangers still stand out. The farmer dropped his grey-haired charge at the artist's front gate and drove on, curiouser still.

My mailbox in those days had a piece of wood fixed to it with the name Butzenshortz painted across it, because that is what I always wore. The postmaster thought it was German and had me pegged as some kind of intellectual.

Those few days were simply time out for my father. He read and he smoked and he cat-napped in the middle of the day which I remembered from when I was ten years old and we were hunting in the Waiau hills with Clint Roper. I wonder now if that too came from the war. Sentry duty in the night, bombings at any time and sleep whenever and wherever you could find it.

I owned very little in those days. Just an easel, a few paintings, a number of rifles and an old Honda 350. I took my father one afternoon up to Hawarden's nine-hole golf course. He sat on the pillion, black shoes a little dusty on the rear pegs, the cuffs of his trousers rising up to his shins above short black socks and wearing a spare helmet with a broken chin-strap. His golf bag with its few clubs rested along the fuel tank and jutted forward over the handle bars. The warm summer washed around us, birds lifted from the seal and the tall dry grass leaned with us as we passed.

I left him there, he, promising to find his own way home, me, a little nonplussed. As I swung away I glanced back and watched him walking toward the clubhouse, bag over his shoulder, a self-sufficient man, and I felt a little envious. I have always tried to avoid people, I have always found them difficult. Peter was indifferent, I think. He seemed comfortable in anyone's company.

Another son would have offered to accompany him around the course. I couldn't. For one thing, I found golf particularly tedious, and for another, these farmers among whom he would be chipping balls, are the natural antonyms of art. When I first arrived in North Canterbury, the usual remarks would go something like: 'Oh, so you're a painter, eh? Well, I've got a woolshed that needs painting, mate, ha ha.' Or, 'An artist, eh? Bullshit-artist most likely, ha ha.' You got tired of it pretty quickly.

But sure enough, as the sun was slipping behind the limeworks, turning the thistledown into bright stars, a pick-up truck dropped him off at the gate. Apparently, he had spent a very satisfying afternoon with my bucolic landlord.

Probably we had hare stew that night, possibly garnished with horse mushrooms from below the pines. The next day he decided he'd quite like to make an expedition down to the Great Northern, the old weather-board hotel he had passed on his way up from the bus. I didn't drink at all then although there's often a cold beer in the fridge these days, and I had never set foot in the pub even for fish and chips. Why would anyone want fish and chips when the river bed was crawling with rabbits and a bullet cost four cents. It didn't add up.

'I'll drive you down,' I said.

'No, I can do it,' he replied. 'How do the gears go?'

I was astonished. 'You can drive this thing?'

'Of course. I used to ride dispatch in the war. An Army Indian. You never forget.'

So I ran him through the gears and warned him about the light shingle at the foot of the hill, and that was that; for the first time in thirty years my father threw his leg over a motorbike and gunned the engine. He wobbled off down the driveway toeing the gear lever as he went and it made a disconcerting sight indeed. My father on a motorbike, my motorbike, wearing a white string singlet, khaki shorts, short socks, black shoes and my old mountain mule pack across his shoulders in which to place anything he found at the hotel worth his finding. As soon as he slipped out of view I grabbed a ladder and climbed on the roof to watch. My stomach was tying itself in all kinds of knots as he approached the treacherous shingle corner at the bottom of Limeworks Road, and it was with relief and growing anxiety that I saw him bend easily into the corner and head for the village. The anxiety grew from the fact that if, indeed, he made it all the way without falling or striking an immovable object, he still had to run the odds of colliding with Constable Gear who might not take a liberal view of a judge of the High Court driving a motorbike with his licence thirty years out of date.

I watched my father until he was out of sight and then slid down the roof to the ladder and the safety of firm ground. I sat in the kitchen and waited. I could do nothing else. About an hour later I heard the familiar, uneven sound of the Honda making its way back to me. He curved it in beside the garage and brought it to an uncertain halt.

I was amazed to see him in one piece. We sat at the kitchen table, the doors and windows open to relieve the heat. I poured myself a cup of tea and he poured himself something from his recent purchase.

'How'd it go?' I asked, interested. 'Did you have any trouble parking the thing?' It was a very heavy bike and if the peg didn't come the whole way down it would yaw and collapse onto the ground and refuse to get up again without a great deal of trouble.

'No problem,' he said.

'Anyone there?' I asked, wondering if any of the few people I knew about town had seen him and already alerted the constable.

'There were three jokers at the bar,' he said. 'When I walked in they went quiet. I sat down and asked for a beer. The bartender was drying glasses. The others were just looking at their drinks and saying nothing. We sat there for a few minutes in silence. Then the bartender asked if I was just passing through. I took a slow, meditative sip from my glass and then I said, "Maybe".' He grinned. 'I think at that point one of the boys might have glanced my way.'

Peter often saw great theatre in ordinary things, in the commonplace. John Burn, lawyer and avid letter writer, points out that this was one of the reasons he made such an entertaining correspondent. My father admired greatly those thinly drawn sketches of Hemingway's where he could catch the tension of a situation in just a few clipped sentences. The scene at the Great Northern may not have been reported with strict accuracy by my father, but it was beautiful in the telling.

(Letter to Janet 12 February, 1980)

Dear Janet, I spent three or four days with Sam at Waikari and I must say it was an interesting though Spartan existence. Only one meal a day is served. For breakfast, if you so desire, is a piece of toast and half a tomato, the other half being served for lunch. The one meal is a casserole consisting of either hare or rabbit fillets, sometimes both, cooked with potatoes, onions, mushrooms and carrots, together with other ingredients of like nature, the entire contents of the casserole having been shot or grown in the near vicinity. I must say this is a most succulent repast, especially when you have been starving for twenty-four hours. The steaming dinner plates are then carried outside and the dinner is eaten at 8.15 p.m. on a hillside overlooking a valley several miles wide, while the evening sun gilds the distant hills like Bo Derek's toenails, and all the air a solemn stillness holds. The remnants of the pastoral casserole (there aren't many) are then nonchalantly tossed on to the grass and a peaceful cup of tea is imbibed indoors. Even after three days I was getting thinner and my eyes were clear and alert and vigilant, and Mother had half a mind to send me back there until I was fully rehabilitated in mind and body. The guest room, if I may describe it, had a mattress resting on the floor, and the wire touched the floorboards. But I got used to it. All you can hear is the song of the thrush commencing his evening recital, or the lark his morning orison, or the clip clop of horse hooves as Philippa arrives for morning tea...

Bill Gates standing at extreme left with Peter Mahon second from right, Egypt, 1944.

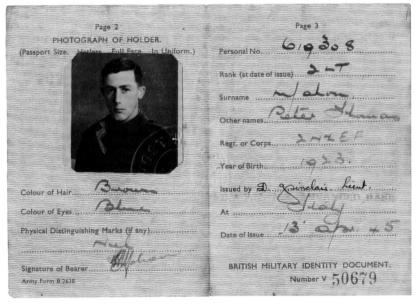

Peter Mahon's military identity document, 1945.

Senio River, Italy, 1945. (Aerial photo taken the day before the Allied advance.)

Senio River, May 2007. (Google Earth)

Clint Roper, Italy, 1945.

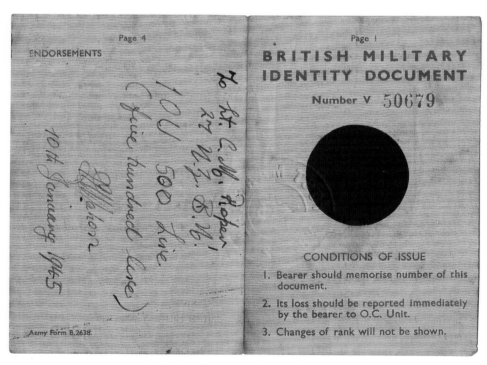

IOU written on the back of Peter Mahon's military identity document.

From left: Rangi Ryan, unknown, Clint Roper, and Peter Mahon, Italy 1945.

Stanley Smith, the station master, fishing off the Otago coast.

Peter and his Army Indian motorbike, 1944.

Peter, a one-finger typist, photographed at his parents' home, c. 1947.

A 2008 portrait of Peter Mahon painted by the author.

The author's mother, Margarita Mahon (née Smith), striding out, early 1950s.

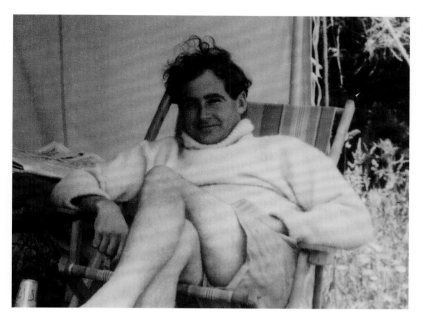

Garth Gould, c. 1957.

Mr P. T. Mahon, who is assisting the Crown Prosecutor at
the trial.

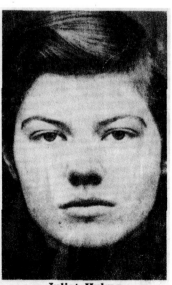

Juliet Hulme

Peter Mahon at the time of the Parker Hulme trial, 1954.

Pauline Yvonne Parker (left) and Juliet Marion Hulme, 1954.

166.

JUNE 1954

19 SATURDAY
170—195

We practically frantic with excitement today but we weren't late for the day was a novelty itself. His notice is not a new one but his time it is a dif- ferent p and which we intend carrying out. We have worked it out carefully and are both thrilled by the idea. Naturally we feel a trifle nervous but the pleasure of anticipation is great. I shall not write the plan down here as Deborah is writing it up when we carry it out (I hope) We spent last night and day before having a happy time adventure and very exciting day. We also stamped a few extra pictures and now we are off to town to sleep. We breakfasted in town this morning.

Page from Pauline Parker's diary, 1954.

Justice Peter Mahon at the bench.

The author and his hawk, Waikari, 1980.

Peter Mahon with Charlie Upham, and his wife Molly, c.1984.

The author's portrait of Owen Woodhouse: pencil and conté, 1987.

Peter Bromhead cartoon from the *Auckland Star*, 27 January, 1982.

Bronze of Peter Mahon (2007) held at the Auckland University Law Library.

Portrait of Peter Mahon taken before publication of *Verdict on Erebus*, 1984.
(George Weigel & Son)

Album:
Upland Road

From the time my parents moved to Auckland I lost close track of them. The few times I visited I was uneasy. The city bothered me. The earth was the wrong colour for a start, and there were exotic smells exuding from the stalls along 'K' Road. The streets curved around hills where the roads of Christchurch lay in a right-angled grid making it impossible not to know exactly where you were. In Auckland I was forever getting lost, heading for Newmarket on the motorway at one moment and then being flung down to the harbour the next, like a marble on a giant pinball machine.

Their house stood on a ridge in Remuera, not too distant from the courts. It was a two-storied weather-board villa with a balcony from which my brother could take pot shots at me with his air-pistol across a generous stretch of lawn. There was always a cat, a Labrador once with no personality whatsoever, and a baby grand that my sister played very well. Evenings would find us all at different corners of the building busy at our own enterprises so that when my mother came to serve dinner she would call to us in an operatic contralto that filled the hallways and stairs just as it had once filled small churches: 'Pe-ter, Ja-net, Tim-o-thy, Sam-u-el!' To which we would all reply, separately and in differing keys, 'Com-ming!' I heard Garrison Keillor describe once how his mother would call up the hill to her children in exactly the same way, calling them to dinner from their civil war games where they had dragged old logs together for cannons. It was what he called 'my mother's evening song'. Shortly after Peter died my mother came to stay a few days with me in the country. It was dinner-time and I came down from the workshop to the cottage to find her standing staring at the hills, tears in her eyes, her hands clenched at her waist. 'I was about to call his name,' she said.

Two of my close friends came to visit while I was staying at Upland Road. School had finished forever and we were about to head off in different directions. It was exciting and terrible and I invited them to come for dinner. I cleared it with my mother and asked if we could have our meal separately. When Chris and Marg arrived I led them through to the living room where the fire was blazing. My mother had set out a bottle of port and a few glasses which I thought was very considerate of her. We sat and talked like ancients and it felt good. I heard my father come home and willed him not to interrupt us. He didn't. After an hour my mother slid open the door to the dining room and announced that dinner was served. We went through and sat down. Chris noticed there were only three places set at the table. He looked a little confused. 'What about your parents…?'

'Oh, they've already eaten,' I lied. He looked surprised. It was still quite early. They glanced at each other and then took up their implements and joined me as I enthusiastically began to deconstruct another of my mother's culinary masterpieces.

At this point, the door quietly opened and a tall, sombre figure appeared. My father was wearing a dark suit and a bow tie. Over his left forearm was draped a white linen serviette while in his right hand he held an uncorked bottle of wine. He oiled over to Marg, stooped, and enquired whether she would care to accompany her beef-steak with the house claret. 'A fine little number this … or so I am told,' he said, pouring a little into her glass. I stared at him, coldly, my cheeks burning. He poured wine for us all and then left as discreetly as he had come.

For Christmas Day my mother always wanted something special, something I suppose that she might have remembered from her own childhood. The only Christmas dinner I remember at Upland Road was one in which we were all, for different reasons, in unseasonable spirits. My little brother was complaining in bitter terms that he was going to miss the soccer game down the road in which he would have been the star performer; I was thinking of spending time with a friend who happened to be passing through and wondering how soon I could make my escape; my sister had her own preoccupations; and my father's mind was on the imminent game at Middlemore.

I think my mother would have liked Christmas dinner to resemble Norman Rockwell's painting of an American Thanksgiving dinner, everyone smiling beneficence at each other across mountains of food. But as we sat in our paper party hats, my brother keeping my mother occupied with a lively fusillade of discontent, the rest of us drifting with our own mutinous thoughts, I guess we would have more accurately resembled a Giles cartoon, reluctant celebrants sketched in black and grey. When the first course was dispensed with my father lit a thin cigar. My sister, arch and secretarial turned to him: 'Father, it is not considered polite to smoke between courses.' Peter projected a thin stream of smoke toward the ceiling, placed his cigar on the rim of a small cake plate and got to his feet. I thought he was going to make a speech. He didn't. He said absolutely nothing. Instead he skipped nimbly around the table, tapping my sister and my mother lightly on the breasts as he passed, and then resumed his seat and the offending cigar. My mother stared at my sister. My sister stared at my mother. I grinned thinking that at last he had lost his mind and that soon I would be feeding him with a spoon. My mother found her voice: 'Peter, what on earth was that about?' He had been contemplating the ceiling. He turned his attention then to his cigar and turned it slightly in his fingers.

'That?' he said. 'That, Mother, was the titter that ran round the crowd.'

Part Three

Lago Como

I sit alone and review what I have written during the last twenty-four hours, my scrawl almost indecipherable in the faint light.

> ...You look for perfection in all things, you hope for something outstanding. The words of people of all the world are here, inscribed on broad steel plates, a memorial to the time of my father and his companions. But for the most part it is an egoist gesturing. I move from one to one looking for something more, something from the heart.
>
> High above me the Como monasteries are turning yellow and red in the afternoon light, a mile away a fountain plays silently and pigeons gather at my feet.
>
> Then suddenly the world is dumb, even the sound of my pencil scraping across my notepad is lost, because here at last is something real; just like the glimpse of a Catholic Christ hanging in an alleyway of Faenza or the scent of a cigar in the street smelling of my childhood and of burning autumn leaves.
>
> 'In the name of all the Jews of Europe,' it reads, '...if the sky were paper and all the seas ink, it wouldn't be enough to describe my suffering and the things I see around me... I say goodbye to you all, I am crying...' Chaim, fourteen, Pustkow Camp.

Sitting at the edge of the lake I watch the people pass. As the heat drains from the day, the joggers come to display themselves like plumed birds. None of them looks like a runner, they look like their bodies have taken them by surprise. Here comes a pot-bellied American and two youths a little embarrassed. Then a little man with a moustache, wrists limp, fingers pointed downward like paws, legs too plump for his body, too much arm movement. Some are permanently wired as if afraid of the sound of their own blood. A girl comes past, red top, black pants, breasts too large, arms pumping up and down, small steps ... but as she passes the boys she reaches out a hand and they touch palms. Quite cool.

Ah, at last, a man in a pink shirt riding upright on a single-speed bike, a child on the bar and one on the carrier. Something authentic, something Italian. Something close to my idea of Eddie Izzard riding a Vespa, glasses pushed back in his hair, and as he passes a lovely girl he mutters, '*Ciao, baby*'.

There's a blonde woman in a knee-length pink dress waltzing with her baby and laughing. Her husband laughs as well, photographing them. Out in the bay there are fishermen in row boats. Far off some youths begin making a fuss and in a minute the *carabinieri* arrive from two directions and whisk them away. The light is fading, the couple are sober now, the man wheeling the child sedately and the girl, thoughtful, a little apart, elegantly smoking a cigarette.

The sky has a nor-west look, clouds like slivers of wood. Swifts are feeding their young, darting up behind the clock face in the *piazza*; after all, it's spring. For his age, the man at the hotel seemed old. His mother stood behind him, tall and thin with orange hair. Two Romanians were arguing the toss, he argued back, hands extended, smiling: 'This is the way it is,' he said, 'everything in town is booked up, take it or leave it'. The mother gazed at me over their heads and dragged her thumb slowly across her throat, grinning.

At seven thirty the town's awake, at least the working part of it, coming and going from the train station. A boy breaks open a pile of newspapers, there's an urgency in the stride of the passers-by, faces grey, set to face a working day. There's a cool wind coming down the lake from the north and the fountain isn't playing this morning. Tackita tackita of small wheels being dragged across old cobbles. The sun comes over the hill, it's eight o'clock.

It wouldn't have been this noisy for him: scooters doing wheel stands, buses, the common drone of cars bumper to bumper at five; old town, new faith, the constant rosary. And during a Hail Mary, graceless, I skip across between a couple of beads. I want to ask them what they do here, what work there is. I stood in Hereford Street one day, outside the spectacle dispensers which was once his office, and watched with the same curiosity. Sometimes I have felt like a tourist in my own town.

Looking for the old Italy, walking amongst the new: a slot machine in the corner, chips in bags, cooler for the drinks, bright plastic colours and some lugubrious internationalist like Stefan Eicher on the radio. The waitress is making ham sandwiches, wrapping them in plastic for the lunchtime clientele. '*Arrivo, presto, pronto, prego, ciao*', she says. Old man, grey hair, leans over the paper, standing, stroking his chin, reading of the incremental changes. The black water laps. Some of it was here for my father.

After Erebus

In 1984, forty-eight eminent New Zealanders petitioned Prime Minister David Lange to award Peter a knighthood. Included were the present Governor-General, Anand Satyanand, the present Chief Justice, Sian Elias, a director of post graduate legal studies, a professor of law, the dean of the University of Otago Law Faculty and a former minister of justice with the Labour government, Martyn Finlay.

When you consider that Lange was able to knight an insubstantial man such as Kerry Burke, described in Lange's autobiography as 'useless in cabinet and eased out to the great relief of nearly all...' and yet was entirely unmoved to honour a man who, apart from his years of dedication to the Crown had, by his findings on the Royal Commission, performed a service of international significance, you have to suspect something in the State had gone rotten. It is not credible that the united opinion of forty-eight persons of such exceptional standing in the community, and in law, should be ignored; there could not have been an appointment which would have pleased the public more. There must have been a hidden impediment, something extraordinarily inflexible. So what was it?

It is autumn. Alison is away in Golden Bay for a few days and I have fallen into old familiar patterns. I took my father's book down from the shelf last night, dusted it off and began to work my way through it again. I finished at five in the morning with the faintest light discernible behind the eastern hills. It was cold and I should have been tired but I wasn't. My head was full of words and the Mill huge and hollow. I put one of Garth's vinyl discs on his machine, poured myself another cup of tea, and settled back into my old chair with my down jacket pulled around me.

'I can understand your fondness for this hour of the day,' wrote Peter. 'It is a curious thing that the hour before dawn brings with it the lowest ebb in the tide of human emotion. The mind becomes overshadowed with sombre reflections. With no expectation of favour or reward we fare on our long fool's errand to the grave. Then comes the first pale streak in the eastern sky, and hope stirs once more. With every passing minute the darkness recedes, a distant thrush begins its overture and the veil of melancholy dissolves in the morning light.'

Maria Callas sings her aria from *L'elisir d'amore* in the guise of Adina. She is saying 'goodbye'. And I play that track over and over, and although I don't understand a single word I hear, it doesn't matter. Her voice is raw, pure, broken and perfect. And overall I'm aware of Callas, that she's in the room. And in that far off, reduced child's picture of our house on the hill, I can see my mother at the kitchen bench with tears running down her face.

There are true voices, like true art and true wine, but they are rare in this world, especially in these times of imitation. My father's voice is all around me, in piles of paper, in books, letters, in my memory, on tapes and in thin transparent sheets of type and yellowing notepads with his hand expressed in a flat undulation of blue ink. It is a firm, clear, unhalting hand. His voice changes like a diamond presenting different colours as it turns its facets to the light. But no matter how the tones may change, or the intensity, it is the same diamond, the same stone, and it loves the light.

There is a minor mystery here, a question that I feel has never been fully answered. Why did he leave the judiciary after Erebus? Why did he walk away from them, his detractors? The public and the press were always on his side as, it appears, were most of his colleagues. In a very short space of time he had assumed folk hero status in this country. So why did he not play his enemies as he had always played them, and stayed?

His primary stated reason was that the minority finding of the Court of Appeal had implied he was not competent as a judge and made his position untenable. The court as a whole had reversed his order for costs against the company, Air New Zealand, a punitive finding he had made against it for wasting the hearing's time and for lying to him. The Appeal judges said he had no basis for that finding.

And yet it is one of a judge's basic roles to evaluate the credibility of evidence based on the demeanour of the witness. Apart from measuring the evidence, he had measured the men who stood in the dock before him, just as they had been measured by everyone else in the courtroom as well as many members of the public who watched parts of the inquiry in the subsequent documentary film footage.

(Letter from Peter to James Buckley QC)

All the navigation witnesses were persistently cross-examined before the Royal Commission on the basis that a 27 mile shift in the destination waypoint was known to the Navigation Section to have occurred in 1978, and that the evidence to the contrary was so improbable as to be without credibility. In this respect the demeanour of these navigation witnesses was all important. My own questions to them were very obviously based upon my reluctance to accept that such a long catalogue of mistakes could possibly have occurred and have been committed by this group of people. The mere recital of all the mistakes by counsel and by myself gave the airline every opportunity to call whatever further witnesses they had in order to verify the occurrence of this apparently improbable sequence of errors. I again emphasise that it was not merely the evidence given but the way in which it was given by Hewitt, Amies, Johnson and Kealey which led me to reject what they had to say, and once I had rejected the thesis of all the cumulative mistakes then I had no alternative but to express the view that there had been a combined attempt by the Navigation Section to deceive the Royal Commission...

Woodhouse's judgment goes further than the majority judgment by holding that the Mahon report breached the rules of natural justice:

A suggestion of an organised conspiracy to perjure is different from the possibility commonly faced by individual witnesses that their evidence may be disbelieved. Grave findings of concerted misconduct in connection with the inquiry ought not to be made without being specifically raised at the inquiry. Once the thesis of such a conspiracy had emerged in the Commissioner's thinking as something upon which he might report, he would have had power, if that question were indeed reasonably incidental to his terms of reference, to reconvene the hearing if necessary so that the alleged conspirators could be fairly confronted with the allegation.

All these considerations suggest that the Commission was bound by the broad requirements of natural justice. These included a reasonable opportunity of meeting the unformulated allegation of organised deception and concealment that was apparently passing through the Commission's mind.

...we do not overlook the fact that this court [Appeal] is making an assessment in isolation from the *viva voce* evidence given at open hearing of the inquiry. But the present issue is simply whether the affected officers were or were not deprived of the advantage of answering unformulated charges. In such a situation the advantage of actually hearing and seeing a witness is hardly a relevant consideration.

But the law that my father was relying on had been partly argued, ironically enough, by Lord Denning. It relates to the difference between an investigation, such as a Royal Commission, and a trial.

If these [conclusions by the inspectors of the Dept of Trade and Industry] are such as to be critical to any of the witnesses, they have to open the inquiry, recall those witnesses, and put to them the criticisms which they are disposed to make. What will be the response of those witnesses? They will at once want to refute the tentative conclusions by calling other witnesses, or by asking for further investigations.

In short, the inquiry will develop into a series of minor trials... that would hold up the inquiry indefinitely. After hearing the evidence, the inspectors have to come to their conclusions. These need not be tentative in the least ... they should be made with courage and frankness.

In 1980 a commission was set up to enquire into the conviction of Arthur Allan Thomas for the Crewe murders. During the hearings the commissioner, Judge Taylor, made it clear that he did not believe the evidence being presented to him by the police, who then appealed for review on a question of bias. In an interview with the *New Zealand Listener*, Peter put the following argument:

It is said I should have warned the group of witnesses that I believed I had heard a concerted false tale about altitude and navigation. That I should have given each witness the chance to testify again to see if they could talk me out of this view. I would have thought that would be evidence of bias. You see, the case hadn't finished. This is what Judge Taylor was doing. Taylor said [to the police witness], 'You're a liar'. So they [the police] immediately went to the High Court to try to stop the hearing on the grounds of bias.

Law academic, Stuart Macfarlane, comments in *The Erebus Papers*:

A careful comparison of the decisions of the Court of Appeal in the Erebus and Thomas cases will be found highly illuminating. The irony brought home is that Mr Justice Mahon's scrupulous attempts to be fair to the parties and witnesses before him by steadfastly avoiding any semblance of bias enabled the Court of Appeal to hold that he had breached the rules of natural justice through not making clear to the Air New Zealand witnesses that he disbelieved them.

Although my father believed that as chairman of an inquiry he was obliged to keep his opinions concerning credibility to himself, he said that he did speak to counsel for the airline, David Williams, in his chambers and warned him about the deteriorating level of credible evidence. He also warned the airline obliquely through his discussions with Mr Martin in London. (Refer *Verdict on Erebus,* page 186.)

Professor J.F. Northey in the publication *Recent Law,* (1982) dissects the Appeal judgments and finds that:

The Court of Appeal [the minority and majority judgments] was agreed on only one issue; the invalidity of the award of costs of $150,000 against Air New Zealand Ltd. The court found that the Commission had no power to make that award and quashed it. ... There can be little doubt that in future there will be only modest enthusiasm on the part of the judiciary (and others) to accept appointments as a Commission of Enquiry. There can also be no doubt that Mahon J. carried out his difficult task in an entirely satisfactory manner. He more than satisfied the demanding standards required of a Judge sitting as a Commissioner. He presented a report that is not only acclaimed as a fine piece of scientific and legal analysis but was also seen as embodying enviable and elegant prose.

Had he merely observed that he did not believe witnesses X,Y, and Z, and left it at that, the Court of Appeal would probably not have bothered with the proceedings.

In an informal discussion with my sister, Janet, Professor Michael Taggart commented that by the time of the Erebus Royal Commission there was a huge wave of change occurring in administrative law and that Peter was unfortunately riding on the wrong side of it in respect of the 'fair hearing' branch of natural justice. When she asked how anyone could have known that they were acting in breach of the rules at that time, Mike remarked that unlike legislation, common law is retrospective. And at that point he offered Janet a quote from the English jurist/philosopher Jeremy Bentham who once referred to the concept of 'natural rights' as 'nonsense upon stilts':

Do you know how they make [the common law]? Just as a man makes laws for his dog. When your dog does anything you want to break him of, you wait until he does it and then beat him. This is the way you make law for your dog, and this is the way judges make laws for you and me.

In Peter's letters he explains very clearly his reasons for leaving the bench. But I think there was more to it; to put it simply, I think he was bored.

When he accepted the appointment to the judiciary, he thought he would be joining a collegiate. But clearly he found a great deal of the judicial work tedious, work that was not as taxing as he had encountered as a lawyer. He wrote to a friend in 1979: 'The great majority of my time – nearly 70 per cent – has been taken up for the last three or four years hearing banco cases, and the content of those cases is most wholly trivial.'

The job of judging can be likened a little to that of a football referee, one who knows the rules and applies them as he observes the game. But Peter had been a player himself, not an observer. He had been very nimble and he had played in all positions. But unlike an athlete who reaches his prime at thirty and then deteriorates, that had not happened to him. Among his letters there are odd references that appear to give credibility to the idea that he was restless, that he was contemplating a change before Erebus came along. And if he had remained on the bench what chance would there have been that anything as challenging would ever come his way again? He wrote to his friend Justice Somers in 1980:

> This Royal Commission on the aircraft disaster is proceeding at a slow dogged pace, for by this time there have emerged some areas of fact which are the subject of obdurate dispute... this is certainly the hardest work I have ever done since I was appointed to the bench.

And therefore, we must presume, the most enjoyable.

Many lawyers regard the bench as a step up in their career, but just as Garth pointed out that Peter had little interest in money, neither did he have any time for the position or pomp that went along with being a judge. On the plus side of the argument was the fact that his judicial position gave him security and a pension. The work shouldn't have been too demanding and there would have been plenty of time off for golf. But the work, as it turned out, was unreasonably heavy due to a lack of judges and the Chief Judge's seeming inability to manage the lists.

> (Extract from Peter's letter to George Barton)
>
> ...he [the Chief Judge] always insisted there should be no more Judges in Auckland than in Wellington, despite the fact that Auckland and Hamilton between them did slightly more than one half of the total Supreme Court work in New Zealand, and it was this factor that began the huge accumulation of arrears with which we are at present struggling.

Yes, he managed to find time for afternoon golf by carefully rearranging his cases, but he was always making that time up in the evenings writing reserve judgments. At one stage, Peter was working something near to sixty hours a week.

The job, in short, did not suit him as it suited many of his colleagues, and I think he may well have considered alternatives long before the Erebus Inquiry. In one letter he writes about pulling up stakes and moving to Perth where my sister was living. He spoke of the remuneration as a law lecturer at an Australian university where he would have received roughly the same salary as that of a judge in New Zealand but working half the hours. So what kept him here? It is possible that if Erebus had not intervened he might have made up his mind and gone to spend his last years teaching those who were still capable of learning, picking up a little consultancy work, and in his spare time doing what he secretly longed to do: to write.

When he resigned from the bench he gave up the security of a full pension, ironically something he had worked very hard for on behalf of his fellow judges, and on his return to Christchurch he needed some kind of work to supplement his meagre means.

But first he was obliged to prepare the Royal Commission's case for an appeal to the Privy Council against the Court of Appeal's finding.

Many members of the public had been outraged by the Appeal Court's view that there was no evidence of the fact that my father had been lied to. One man in particular, Mr Pridmore, who had lost his wife in the Erebus tragedy, offered to raise funds for an appeal to London. My father turned down this offer on the grounds that it was the Crown's obligation to fund an appeal to the Privy Council since it was in the Crown's name that the Commission had been established. Once the appeal was granted it took many weeks to prepare the case which had to be directed through an English QC, and then, because of his deteriorating health, Peter could not attend the appeal himself. My mother went in his place.

I wonder if, as the case drew near, he ever brought to mind the warning given to him by Sir Michael Myers many years earlier:

(Letter from Peter to David Williams)

I was interested to read counsel's opinion as to the appeal in Coleman v Myers, although it bears a dismal similarity to other documents of that kind, emanating from the Inns of Court, which I have read in days gone by. The counsel whose opinion is sought hands the documents to a reluctant junior in his chambers and eventually they produce an opinion in guarded terms which usually is not worth reading. In my one and only conversation out of court with Sir Michael Myers, he told me that if I was ever engaged in a case in which an appeal to the Privy Council was being considered, I was to avoid English counsel at all costs. He said they never sufficiently mastered the case to be able to give a satisfactory opinion, and if briefed for an appeal, did not trouble to read the brief until the day before, and were indifferent as to the result because they had nothing to gain from incurring the respect or displeasure of colonial solicitors, being only concerned to retain the goodwill of the English firms who briefed their English cases.

The Privy Council upheld the findings of the commission that the airline had been at fault and that the pilots could in no way be held to blame; but it favoured Woodhouse's opinion that there was no probative evidence for Peter's finding that he had been lied to, and agreed to quash the punitive costs. The airline immediately took this to be an entire vindication of it's position, and broke out the champagne.

There had been a lecturing job advertised at Canterbury University for which Peter applied and at the same time a position at Lincoln College had been newly established and needed to be filled. As I have already mentioned, the job at Canterbury was re-advertised without any reply to his application. The position at Lincoln was very certain for a while, and then at the last minute it was allocated to Andrew Wright, the husband of Ruth Richardson, finance minister in the Muldoon government. Reluctantly, in order to make ends meet, Peter took out a practising certificate so that he could give legal opinions, a move that attracted a certain amount of criticism from some of the senior judges. But he had little choice.

And now, as one prospect after another seemed to come to nothing, his health began to deteriorate further. A 'mild' heart attack he had suffered in Auckland in 1975 had been a lot more serious than anyone suspected and he was beginning to suffer the first symptoms of cardiomyopathy.

But at last he was writing. He was writing *Verdict on Erebus*, and we saw in him a new vigour, that creative energy that anyone who puts chisel to stone or paint to canvas experiences. That mysterious thing he had encountered in the Uffizi so long ago, that had puzzled him and worked against all logic and for which there seemed no name, had come alive in him. It emanates from the creation of something original. He was constructing and deconstructing sentences in a way he had never done before, and where once he had written creatively in order to entertain, this time it was serious.

'They tell me that you should set a regime,' he said. 'Start writing at ten in the morning and finish at three, aiming for a thousand well-crafted words. That's how Hemingway did it.' Good luck, I thought. My own conviction was that you worked when the muse struck. And if it was two in the morning, well, so be it. But Peter did it his way and it worked. I was puzzled. I tried it myself. I sat at the easel one morning at ten and waited. At first I didn't feel like painting at all. However, I picked up my brush and started to dabble, and by and by it came. And it came, I think, because I had placed myself in the creative context.

The book took him three months to write and was hugely successful. The first edition sold out within a week and went immediately into reprint. There were 20,000 copies sold all told, and it won the New Zealand Book Award for Non-fiction in 1985.

The book of his letters to his children and close friends, *Dear Sam*, was no less popular and it is certain that he would have taken the experiences of his life and writings and crafted them into further volumes if his health had allowed.

(Peter wrote to George Barton)
One of these days, when I retire upon the handsome pension at present available under the Superannuation Act, I might be constrained to write a

short record of my life and times, and may reluctantly be compelled to allude to the history of the tenure of office of the late C.J.[Dick Wild], although naturally I would exclude the bits about using office for his own advantage and for the advantage of one or two select friends.

He should have come to Lake Como to write, but it was too late. He returned to Auckland instead, and took up a parttime lecturing post at the university. He liked it enough. He liked the young minds and the old friends, because after all Auckland, possibly without his knowing it, had become his home.

Last month, with a couple of friends from the music school across the road from the Waterloo Quadrant, we man-handled a tall plinth into the University of Auckland Law Library and placed on it the bronze head of Justice Peter Mahon. It seems a long way from where it was cast here in our foundry, but I was taught that sculpture should not only have form and something to say, it should also have context. Ironically, he looks very much at home there among the 'bohemians' of the 'left bank'.

Narcissus and Goldmund

(From Sian Elias to Peter, 28 January, 1982)

I have now read the judgments of the Court of Appeal and share your disgust at a system which would mete out such treatment. Quite apart from the result, the way in which it was achieved was greatly discourteous ... It really seems to me to be time for someone to undertake a legal and political appraisal of the Court of Appeal. In particular the stress on 'pragmatism' and the reluctance to articulate principle are trends which could bear some critical examination.

I am really writing to let you know the great sense of loss I feel in your resignation. That feeling is, as you must know, one that is shared by virtually all practising law. We are quite stunned to think of the bench being deprived of you. I really cannot think whose judgments we shall now read for pleasure...

So I suppose it is time to take a closer look at the relationship between Peter and Owen Woodhouse, the man who seemed to cast a shadow over every judgment of Peter's that was likely to go to appeal. I should point out that I cannot see that I will be able to present Owen in any way other than through Peter's eyes, and a monocular view is never the clearest, even where my father's opinions are backed up by other voices.

Perhaps it was Owen's precidential finding under the Matrimonial Property Act that property should be divided fifty-fifty that finally tipped the balance. It annoyed my father. He saw it as a grand display of social engineering without due consideration for detail: a case of *Pragmatism v Principle.*

Owen, working on the basis of fair play, aware that women in situations of divorce were often left stranded and without adequate means, proposed to change the law to their advantage. The new Act deemed that both partners of a broken marriage, a marriage that had lasted over two years, were entitled to an equal share of the property. It was an honest attempt to address an evident social inequity. My father thought the Act was badly constructed, and when he said so, his words were reported all across the commonwealth, not only because his views were the first to challenge the new law, but because, as usual, he had fun doing so:

(Peter's letter to Garth Gould, 1978)

It is a good thing that Denis Cotterill went to his grave unaware of the impact of the Matrimonial Property Act upon the assets of his wealthy farming clients. I have been dealing with one such claim this week, and there is another for hearing tomorrow. No doubt you have given this statute anxious consideration.

The broad effect of it in a farming case is that the wife is entitled to half the value of the homestead and domestic chattels, and unless the contributions to the marriage partnership, not the assets, have been clearly unequal, she also gets half of the land, livestock, plant and buildings in each of the cases at present under consideration, the wife is claiming about $100,000. Each farmer is already in debt to the stock company for his March income tax, and is making large mortgage interest payments. Assuming that a claim for $100,000 succeeded, I suppose the farmer could borrow another $20,000 for a down payment and then pay the wife interest on $80,000 for several years pending repayment of the balance. The interest on $100,000 being non-deductible, he has to earn about $20,000 per annum to pay interest on this debt alone, quite apart from his interest payable to his mortgagee. I will send you a copy of the judgment on the first one, which is a characteristic case of its kind.

A wife who becomes bored with country life is certainly placed in a favourable position. After a few halcyon years of show-jumping and jet-boating on the river, she leaves for the city with the children and lodges a claim for half the farm even if her contributions, as defined by s.18, only entitle her to a third of the equity in the sheep station, she still obtains a substantial amount with which to entice a new lover and take him on a world trip. In the judgment which I will send, the handsome forty-year-old wife will receive a sum sufficient to ensure a swarm of devoted admirers from whom she can select one whose youth and tested sexual prowess will lead her into a second springtime. While they are sunbathing at Biarritz the unfortunate husband will be staving off creditors, and will probably end up selling the farm. After paying off the mortgagee and stock company, and finding $40,000 in tax for the difference between standard value and market value, he may have enough left to buy a corner dairy.

The actual judgment was not quite so decorative, but nearly; it sums up in this way:

> If the respondent in the present case finds in the end that he cannot meet the heavy capital liability imposed by this judgment, and that his farm must be sold, either by him or his mortgagee, with the consequent destruction of an enterprise to which he has devoted the whole of his working life, then I can only repeat that this is a consequence directed by Parliament, not by me.

Owen Woodhouse must have been livid, and neither would Sir Geoffrey Palmer have been terribly pleased. (Palmer was Attorney General under Lange and had probably worked with Owen in constructing the Accident Compensation Commission. Woodhouse was Palmer's Arthur Donnelly and Palmer was the kind of academic lawyer for whom my father had very little time.) These humourless men who saw themselves perhaps as the masters of law rather than its servants seem devoid of the one essential ingredient of humanity; a sense of the ridiculous. Geoffrey Palmer's interviews with Kim Hill on constitutional law are masterpieces of pedagogic certainty. To me, they resemble sermons from a lectern, rising to crescendos of religious fervour, delivered to a room presumably filled with small children. My father's sense of irony and his facility with language would have sounded in the ears of men such as these as something akin to contempt. Voltaire, who employed his wit similarly to remorselessly tease the wigged aristocracy, was beaten for it by hired thugs. Did they in more subtle ways conspire to punish my father?

I have read hundreds of Peter's letters, and among them I have prised the following excerpts written in the late seventies and eighties. They represent a creeping dislike of Woodhouse, somewhat similar to rust:

(To Judge Somers)

Woodhouse will leap and gesticulate like a landed trout when he sees that I gave someone 16 years, but I could see no alternative. Suppose that a defendant committed a robbery, then a week later a rape. I think you have to add the sentences together. I enclose a note of my observations on sentence, so that you can defend me against Roper and Casey.

(To Lloyd Brown QC)

After a lot of wavering between Somers and McMullin, the latter has been selected for the Court of Appeal. As Holland says, one of the really notable lightweights. Still, he has cultivated Woodhouse with great assiduity, and has dined and wined everyone who matters, rather like Beattie. Unremitting industry really does bring success. I asked Ron [Chief Judge Ron Davidson] how it was that Somers was not selected. He said that McLay [Attorney General] had preferred McMullin, but Somers had been told that he would be appointed to replace Richmond towards the end of next year.

The internecine wrangling, so I gather, was as follows: Richmond and Cooke wanted Somers, and Woodhouse wanted McMullin. Woodhouse distrusts Ted's [Somers] legal ability which would be inclined to throw cold water on Owen's adventurous ideas. Woodhouse apprised McMullin some months ago of how matters stood, and they got Speight in as a member of the supporters' club and Speight leaned on McLay. Richmond and Cooke kept pressing for Somers, however, and when Ron was appealed to, he cleverly said he would leave it to the minister to decide. Of course the minister could not care less, and eventually succumbed to the Woodhouse approach. Ron told me himself that he had stood apart, and merely waited the outcome of the dispute.

I suppose this demonstrates the really awful thing about Ron, which is that he simply doesn't care. Even as ex-officio head of the Court of Appeal, he was content to let it all drift by. He has abdicated to executive judges the administration of all court business, and now he allows the Court of Appeal, itself, to select its members, which is very wrong…

When Somers was eventually appointed to the Court of Appeal my father wrote to Burn:

I am waiting daily for the first report of a hostile confrontation between Somers and Woodhouse in the Court of Appeal when the latter attempts to decide some legal question upon a social justice basis. I should imagine the conflict cannot be too long delayed.

Going back to your letter of 15 March, I was interested to hear your account of arguing matrimonial property cases in front of Woody, and I can follow his broad view that everything should be half each. Taking a broad view is a convenient substitute for thought.

(To lawyer David Williams)
The Court of Appeal decisions in criminal appeals have left the Crown Law Office in a state of chaotic bewilderment. Their main trouble, Richardson apart, is conceit. No reasoned legal decision by a primary Judge is, in their opinion, ever right. If the appeal is dismissed it is generally for different reasons. Every appeal is approached, so a number of counsel have told me, on the basis that the Judge is prima facie wrong. Yet there you have Richmond and Woodhouse, from whom no one would ever have asked for an opinion when they were at the bar, and Cooke, whose main forte was getting the facts wrong in every case in which he was engaged, and submitting that each decision against him was wrongly decided. Davison considers that the Court of Appeal will remain unsatisfactory until Richmond and Woodhouse have retired, in about two years time. But I think Richardson is first class. He gave a judgment the other day which I think is a *tour de force*. I enclose a copy...

His criticism, of course, came to a head over Woodhouse's minority, damaging opinion against my father when Air New Zealand took the commission's findings to appeal. He replies here to a supportive letter from Sir Brian Todd then chair and managing director of Todd Petroleum Mining Co.:

Neither I nor my colleagues are ever very much concerned about a reversal by the Court of Appeal. Sometimes we think that the appellant Judges are right, sometimes we think they are wrong. And in the day when Sir Alfred

North and Sir Alexander Turner were predominant on that court, we all had great confidence in them. But with the accession of Sir Owen Woodhouse, everything changed. He is not, and has never been, a lawyer and owed his appointment to Dick Wild who was a life-long crony. Woodhouse is in truth a cracker-barrel philosopher who has never read anything in his life, and whose rare appearances in court where he practised in Napier were distinguished by fumbling ineptitude. Still, in the company of good lawyers on the Court of Appeal, he has managed to get by with many of his eccentricities submerged by the pressure exerted by his colleagues. Recently, however, with two or three of his colleagues being people without much moral fibre, he has been getting his way and some extraordinary decisions have been handed down.

In the Erebus matter he made up his mind long before the hearing that he was going to attack my report. His own omniscience, aided by a remarkable intuition to which he frequently alludes, told him that the aircraft had been flying in cloud and the crew did not know where they were. On the very last day of the appeal hearing he posed a rhetorical question: 'How could the crew have flown directly into the mountain when it was right there in front of them?' At this juncture, counsel for the Attorney General despondently sat down. As for McMullin, his position was graphically revealed in *Truth*. The young lawyer who briefed the false evidence was virtually living at the McMullin residence both before and during the inquiry, and McMullin's insistence on sitting on the case, despite objection by the Pilots' Association, is almost unbelievable. And those are the two Judges who attacked me in a manner described by the Auckland Law Society president as 'vindictive'. It was the content of their joint judgment which decided me to resign. Their judgment is nothing more than a disguised approbation of the Chippindale Report, and in reality reflects the attitude of the management of Air New Zealand, each such opinion being quite outside their jurisdiction.

Anyway, I have made my effective protest and I have the whole of the country's legal profession, as I see it, behind me.

I should have no difficulty in getting a part-time lecturing job at Canterbury University, and there is a probability that when they advertise for a third professor in law some time this year, I will get the job if I apply. Combined with my pension I could get by quite well. Also this job would not start until mid-year which gives me time to write the book...

Pedagogy

No one ever got a word of sense out of a school master! If they knew anything
they'd be out doing it. That'll be your misfortune for the next ten years. To be
constantly rubbing up against second rate minds.

(From *Voyage Around My Father* by John Mortimer)

Andy Denis called in one evening unexpectedly; since we only see each
other about twice a year it was a visit well-timed. I had been pondering why
Peter wasn't offered the job at Canterbury and I thought that, of all people,
Andy might have known the answer.

At sixty, Andy's fit as a flea with the handsome, chiselled features of a
Tibetan monk. He has a mannerism of lowering his head slightly when he
speaks which gives him a deferential air, almost as if he is about to press
his palms together for the 'Om mani padme hum', but I think this is a
postural habit of his developed from years of plunging through untracked
West Coast bush and running marathons. He ran two in one day once.

Andy studied law at Canterbury, did a masters at Harvard and finished
up with a PhD from Cambridge in Icelandic law: the medieval precursor
of our British system.

'*Domr*, Sam,' he says, enjoying the resonant sound of Icelandic in his
throat. 'It translates as "Doom". You remember the "Doomsday book",
the judgment book? Doom, Judgment. That's what it was until the French
came along and introduced the idea of a court with all the gowns and wigs,
and yet all this pomp and ceremony emanated from thirty-six refugees from
Norway sitting in a circle in an empty paddock.'

Andy had lectured at Canterbury in family law as well as torts, and
Woodhouse's sense of social justice had had a powerful effect on both
subjects. 'There were some really awful things done under the old system,
Sam,' he said. 'A woman who had spent ten years bringing up four children
could be thrown out because her husband wanted to dart off with someone
else, and she could quite easily end up with no house and no means of

income. Woodhouse put an end to all that. And the ACC put an end to a system of litigation from which lawyers were the primary beneficiaries.'

As I say, Andy's an academic, and I imagine my father would have placed him firmly on the left bank, but I'm sure Peter would have enjoyed discussing the origins of the legal system within which he moved as agilely as Andy moves through thick scrub.

'Your father wrote a marvellous essay once,' he said, with a grin that forced the tight skin of his skull into deep crevices, reminding me of stone etched by mountain winds. ' "Issue estoppel and the negligent motorist," ' he said.

'The what?'

'He took two cases with opposing judgments which apparently couldn't be reconciled. But he did it!' He waved his hand in the air as if dispersing sandflies. 'I can't remember the details now, but it was a masterful piece of mental gymnastics. It was before ACC came into effect, you know, when everyone was suing everybody else and blame was apportioned. When you're a student you want to pick holes in judgments, prove you're clever.' He shook his head. 'I think there were some of your father's that I couldn't agree with, but "Issue estoppel and the negligent motorist"...' He grinned again, 'It was brilliant.' Then he prodded the air. 'Professor Burrows. If you want to know why your father wasn't invited into the faculty you should talk with him. He's a very honest man, Sam. He'll tell you what you need to know.' I wrote down his name.

Alison came in with a cup of tea. Andy was only pausing on his way down to Christchurch from Nelson and was expected somewhere for dinner. He is always like that, always in a rush, and his visits are models of high-speed transactions of information. 'I'm pretty sure we had one once,' he said as he stood to go.

'Had what?'

'A retired judge ... was it Haslam? Can't remember. Anyway, I thought he was a bit of a dodderer, couldn't understand really why he was there. But your father,' and he grinned again. 'No, he would have been good. Talk to Burrows. Big brick house at the end of... He's somewhere near Kilmarnock Street, I think...'

He wasn't. The retired professor had been hunted up for the Law Commission and was living in Wellington. He was waiting for me when I stepped out of the lift on the nineteenth floor of the Intercontinental. His office is one of a number of open-plan cubicles looking out across Wellington Harbour. The day was overcast, the water far below us grey and sluggish.

There were six subjects I wanted to discuss with John: Lord Denning, social engineering, recusement, Dick Wild, my father's resignation and why he didn't get the job at Canterbury. And Andy was right; the professor was very clear and helpful in every respect, except the last. And simply because, although he had been part of the law faculty at the time, he hadn't been a member of the appointments panel. But he suspected Peter might not have possessed enough academic depth for the job. When I told him that my father had not even received a reply to his application, he was astonished.

'Andy suggested that the faculty might have been afraid of him,' I said. 'That to have someone amongst them who had been dispensing law in the real world might have made them uncomfortable.' The professor pressed his fingers to his chin, considered the idea, and then shook his head. 'I wouldn't think so,' he said.

'I would have thought they'd have been delighted to have him,' said George Barton, two hours later in reply to the same question. George had taken over the complex tax case my father had been working on for the Europa Company, dragged it back to the Privy Council, and won. He is one of the most astute lawyers in the country. 'And as for any lack of academic background …well, he'd published quite a lot… and you have to remember that he lectured in torts at Canterbury in the fifties…'

'And they had employed Haslam,' I said, remembering at the same time Andy's summation of that judge's talents.

'Haslam,' said George, leaning forward in his chair, 'was generally regarded as a disgrace to the bench.'

The professor had given me an hour and a half of his time and it was well past midday when I rose to leave. He had given me names of the few still living who might have been part of the appointments committee in '84 and he had underlined much of what I already knew. As we walked back to the lift I noticed that although most of the office had departed for lunch, one person still remained at his computer. I tapped lightly on his door. The head prefect turned and offered me his famous smile. 'Did you get my letter?' I asked.

'Yes,' he said. It had been about a week since I had written to Geoffrey Palmer asking for his version of why an honour for my father had been blocked by the Labour Government. It just didn't make sense. As Jim Anderton had said, it would have been to their advantage to honour a man who had stood up to Muldoon. It would have been a healthy political move. Even as recently as 2006 the United Nations had referred to the Erebus Report as being significant to world aeronautical safety. So why was nothing done? I had asked the question widely and the whisper came back from a number of directions to the effect that if Mahon had been knighted, Woodhouse would have resigned in protest. In my letter to Palmer I pointed out that the evidence suggested it was he, in fact, who had blocked the honour. And now, as I sat in front of him the question hung between us in the air.

Palmer is a little heavier than I remember, the hair a little less untamed. I wondered if he still had the pipe somewhere, a reminder of a more relaxed, permissive era. He had been prime minister, once, for a short time, playing Percy Alleline to Roger Douglas's Haydon:* a wooden figurehead on a sinking ship from which the pirates, unobserved, were busily extracting all the gold. In the rough and tumble of the real world he had failed to protect us and he knew it. So he took his knighthood and an armful of books, shut himself in the ivory tower, and as far as I'm concerned, never came down.

---

* John le Carré's, *Tinker Tailor Soldier Spy*, presented to the world the character of Smiley, whom my father loved deeply. The story is based on the penetration of MI5 by Kim Philby during the Cold War. Philby was discovered but escaped to Russia. Haydon, le Carré's version of Philby, is not so lucky. Smiley, the wise old owl of the British Secret Service, tracks Haydon down by painstakingly working back and forth across innumerable dusty files looking for sequence, obfuscation and intent. It was Smiley's methodology my father's unravelling of Erebus most resembled and when a film was eventually made about the air disaster, Alec Guinness, who played the part of Smiley for the BBC, was the man first considered to take my father's part.

'Do you think you might find time to reply?' I asked.

He shrugged, and glanced to one side as if my letter were lying somewhere close at hand. 'Well, I've only had it two or three days,' he said.

It was not an answer. We both knew that. We sat in silence for a moment. 'Is there anything you can tell me now?' I asked.

A few empty seconds followed during which his smile disappeared, his eyes dulled and his face assumed the personability of cardboard. His voice dropped into a hollow at the back of his throat; you will remember it from the interviews with Kim Hill. 'I've had to take advice from the Cabinet Office,' he growled.

We stared at each other for what seemed a long time. Perhaps as long as it takes to press the butt against the shoulder, feel the curve of oiled walnut against the cheek and take a careful lead on an incoming duck. I smiled. 'Right then,' I said, getting to my feet. 'I should go.' And I left him to his work, sitting in the same chair once occupied by his mentor, Sir Owen Woodhouse.

As I waited for the lift to take me back down to the grey day, I recalled a remark of the concert pianist, Diedre Irons; 'Much of what you need to say, lies in the pause between notes.'

(Excerpt from the *Dominion Post*, February 2008)
Sir Geoffrey Palmer who was Minister of Justice and Deputy Prime Minister at the time, seemed particularly disdainful to the idea of knighting Justice Mahon and he remains so to this day.

'Justice Mahon was a very eminent New Zealander and he did a lot of good things, but [the Erebus Report] wasn't one of them,' Sir Geoffrey said caustically.

My father had lectured in torts at university in the fifties to earn a few pounds more. In those days, although times were hard, most of the returned servicemen were given jobs out of a sense of debt, but they were not always paid well and the excuse given was that they were four years out of touch. However my father may have felt about teaching, his classes were very popular, the lecture theatre was always full. And when I read the letters he wrote to his protégés and students I could not help but feel that he would have been an invaluable asset to any university.

Like all children I wanted to bring him gifts. All of us did. When we found someone clever we'd want to bring them together. But it was impossible. I engineered once an invitation to dinner with a lawyer friend of mine whose wit I was sure he'd enjoy. But my father fell asleep between the first and the second course and I was highly embarrassed.

I would have liked the opportunity to bring him together with Chris. But my father died long before I met him; long before that lonely, snow-drenched night from which I stepped into a room full of strangers and was introduced in halting English to his daughter Fanny.

I hadn't seen her father for eight years, and then suddenly, three weeks ago, on my way home from Italy, I was standing again where I had stood then, on a small path above a slope of rank spring grass and wild flowers gazing down at the little hut beside the lake of Halwill. He was indistinct from that distance, moving about with the paraphernalia of lunch. Wisps of smoke lifted from his fire into the still air, dissolving in the cotton woods like rice paper on the tongue.

The seed heads brushed against my jacket, Chris turned and grinned and I held him as I would have wanted to hold my father, art and science in my arms in equal balance, a rare thing. Chris had made me a microscope once from household scraps: a piece of tin, a wooden shingle and a bead of glass. It took him fifteen minutes.

We sat at a table in the sun, Fanny, Marian, André and I, with peach wine, bread and bratwurst between us, and Chris talked about the green flash at sunset and refraction. 'Ah, but this is just information,' he said, waving his hand. 'And that is the problem with education nowadays. We place such emphasis on information and teach nothing of wisdom. Information without wisdom is like holding a bunch of arrows with no bow to shoot them.'

Marian poured the pink wine into tall glasses. 'Oh, but this is really beautiful,' he said, referring to something other than the wine, the 'really' bridging all other ideas. 'You know those soap bubbles, when they are really old, really thin, how they look red? And how is it?' he said, inviting an answer, expecting none. Pointing his finger in the air and grinning like an elf, he continued, 'The blue gets trapped. You see, the skin of the bubble becomes just as thick as the wavelength of blue light which enters and is cancelled out by its own reflection, see here…' and as he draws on a piece of cardboard the crickets chirp, the clouds drift and the shadows of the trees lengthen and move slowly from right to left, unusually for me.

I walked in on my father once to explain the rather exciting news that studentships were being offered at university on the condition that you agreed to teach for two years at the end of your degree. 'They would pay for Art School,' I said.

He put down his pen and removed his glasses. 'Samuel,' he said, with a wounded, baleful look, 'Don't be a teacher.' And that was all. It was the first time he had made a firm statement about any decision in my life. I didn't argue. The thought disappeared from my mind and never returned.

I sat with Fanny and five of her colleagues on a second floor balcony of the *Bezirkschule* while we had lunch. We had been assembling sets for the school play. One of the teachers was arguing about something to do with costumes and it was offending the Brechtian ideal. We sat at a circular table, Jurg's hands expressive, the Swiss German knitting them together in thick uncarded strands. I caught Fanny's eye. She smiled and rolled her eyes. I turned away. Down in the courtyard an old woman carrying two heavy plastic bags was walking a straight line toward her apartment. She had paused for breath. She was as bent as a question mark, her arms straight down beside her, her fists two black dots. It was as if she were asking, 'Why?' and answering herself, 'Because! Because!' The teachers sat in a circle staring inward, dealing with that which is known, while the greatest question lay outside, walking a straight line. Why? Because!

For the really important questions no amount of pedagogy can prepare us. 'Don't be a teacher,' my father had said, afraid perhaps that all questioning might end there.

And, still, I would have liked to have brought him Chris.

When I was thirteen I was very unsure of my place among my fellow students. I felt odd and incapable. I complained to my mother and she comforted me by repeating what my father had said to her once: that school is an inadequate model of life. That those who excel within its walls often wilt later in the brighter light of the wide world. 'You will be surprised,' he said, 'to find those whom you never previously noticed emerge from the shadows and do extraordinary things.' But perhaps his obvious low regard for the profession might simply have reflected his peculiar treatment at the hands of the Catholic fathers; for hadn't he himself been confined by teachers to the shadows?

The dependability of betrayal

He told me once about walking on Cashmere Hill and seeing Clint come by on the other side of the road. Clint saw him, and then looked away.

(George Barton)

I have mentioned before in this memoir that I believe friendship to be a less dependable commodity than betrayal.

It could be said that applying this jaundiced view to every situation is a form of emotional insurance. I think it's just sensible. And by maintaining this perspective you might think that for me the world appears a particularly drab place. Not at all. It means, simply, that I expect very little from my fellow man, so that when confronted by unencumbered kindness, it is all that much sweeter an experience. But above all, when you expect nothing, you can never be let down.

My father knew all about human frailty. He may not have displayed it in some of the cases he tried for the Crown, but that would have been because the Crown required him to take that position, evidenced in his 'instructions' to the jury during the Parker Hulme case:

> ...You may pity the dead woman ... you may feel pity for the two accused... Sentiment and emotionalism have no part in British justice.

But he was a man overflowing with sentiment. When not at 'the office' or writing reserve judgments, or playing golf at Middlemore, he could be found in his study leafing through volumes of verse, soaking his thoughts in the most frail of human precepts. He understood the human condition very well and it must have bothered him greatly when the temple on which he founded his faith was taken over, no matter how temporarily, by what he clearly considered the high priests of mediocrity. I would suppose, therefore, that if he were betrayed it was because he allowed it.

Again, among so many others of his silent teachers, he had read, and understood, Shakespeare. With that most eloquent map of the human heart in his grasp, how could he ever have been surprised by the Iagos within his profession? There was also the character of Smiley, so close an impersonation of himself, betrayed by Haydon, betrayed by the priesthood of his own very select temple. These are writings he admired and loved because they so mirrored life as it is, not life as we want it to be.

Compassion? At the height of his battle with Muldoon there appeared in the press an interview with Sir Rochford Hughes, technical assistant to the Erebus Inquiry, in which he enumerated points where he thought the judge had erred. Peter was rung by a journalist to ask if he had a rebuttal. He certainly had. Peter recounted how counsel for ALPA (Airline Pilots' Association) had approached him asking that he take only peripheral note of Sir Rochford, given that his experience of flying emanated from the war when navigating involved the pilot peering from the cockpit and searching the ground for familiar landmarks. The reporter conveyed all this to Sir Rochford at which point he became quite upset and explained to the reporter that he hadn't wanted to say anything in the first place. Muldoon, he said, had put him up to it. Again the reporter came back to Peter. Peter, feeling for Sir Rochford, understanding his position, told the reporter to let it go. Despite all this, there appears in my father's files a very sensitive letter from Sir Rochford, written just as the storm clouds were brewing. It offers Peter his support and friendship. It is a noble document.

My father wrote a number of letters to Judge Somers during the early days of the Erebus case. But as the investigation progressed, any mention of the commission vanished. But here is an early extract:

(15 July 1980)
The more the evidence proceeds the more the plot thickens, and the more the possibility grows that I may have to issue something like a formal citation of the US Navy whose radar controller failed to warn the DC10 aircraft that it was not visible upon his screen. This aspect of the matter has been adroitly avoided by the Chief Inspector in his report. Did someone tell him to leave the Americans out of it? I am going to ask him this question in due course, and I

may find myself compelled to call for the files of the Civil Aviation Division.

I understand that in this type of proceeding I am not only entitled but required to descend into the dust of the arena, and so far there is certainly plenty of dust.

Ironically, Ted, with whom he had shared these first misgivings, sat alongside Woodhouse on the Appeal benches as they reviewed Peter's findings. Ted could not go along with Woodhouse entirely and took the side of the majority judgment. Peter could forgive Ted for that, understanding the man if not his judgment. But when Peter resigned it must have hurt Ted terribly to think that in some way, no matter how minor, he had been responsible. It was clear from his letters that the two men had once been good friends, and yet, when my parents subsequently returned to Christchurch, they never again crossed paths, even though Ted's home was a handful of miles from town.

Not so distant, on the other hand, was the home of Clinton Roper.

Passing over some photographs among my mother's files, I found Peter's identity paper from the war. On the back, in pencil, is scrawled the following:

To Lt C.M. Roper 27 NZ Bt.
IOU 500 lire.
P.T. Mahon 10/Jan/1945

It was written some time while the New Zealand forces were waiting out the winter on the Senio River. I assume the two men were on leave, possibly in Rome, because Clint was in the 27th Battalion and my father the 26th.

'Clint was tall and good looking,' my mother recalls. 'He was a joker. He was fun. Left to themselves they would have been great mates forever…'

Peter described an incident when three of them were trying to obtain lodgings at the officers' club in Rome after Trieste. When they were questioned by a military policeman at the door, Clint stepped forward and addressed the sergeant: 'We three are members of a court martial,' he said.

And then, indicating my father: 'This is the prosecuting officer…' He then turned to the man on his right, 'And this is counsel for the defence.' Then, drawing himself up to his full height and standing to attention, he added: 'And I, sir, am the accused.'

It would have been deeply hurtful to Peter, the absence of Clint Roper when he most needed him. After Erebus, when Peter was hovering in purgatory, uncertain of his future, Clint was coming and going from Christchurch regularly, and yet never once crossed my father's doorstep. Watching from a great distance, I found it inconceivable that these two men should have lost each other in the dust of the appeal battle. After all, they hadn't lost each other in Italy.

Let me back up a little here and explain the depth of this relationship, because it is very important, even if it may seem a little insensitive to put it under so bright a light. I should say here that I don't think my father would approve of my doing so.

In a previous chapter I described how Major Rangi Ryan turned the pages of the soot-black album letting history flicker under the light of a new century, and amongst those frames was one in which my father and Clint stand side by side, hands in their pockets staring at the camera. It is not a posed shot. They are relaxed in each other's company, a couple of friends it is clear. 'There,' says Rangi, 'you can see it already in his face, that shadow.' And he was right. On the ship home from Yamaguchi, it was suggested that Clint be confined for the duration of the voyage, so fearful were the medical officers that he would injure himself in some way. My father would not hear of it, would not allow his friend to be locked away like an animal, like someone insane. So he took care of Clint himself. I don't know in what way, perhaps just dedicating the long hours to him. Again, as in the photograph, it may have only required the silence of an unquestioning companionship. Who knows, and to whom do we go for witness?

Clint arrived home physically intact, but was put into hospital where he was attended to by people well accustomed to returned soldiers suffering invisible wounds. Clint was not insane, he was just unhappy. When eventually he became engaged to the nurse who had been caring for him, he invited my father to be best man at the wedding. My father agreed, of course, and mentioned it to Sir Arthur. Sir Arthur took him aside and imparted the news that a case was being constructed by the Crown against a member of the fiancée's family. Peter, on no account, should attend the wedding, and on no account must Clint know why. It was a difficult situation for Peter. He had to let down his friend, avoid the wedding and come up with a credible excuse. *

'Joan never understood, of course,' said my mother. 'I'm sure she never forgave Peter.'

When Clint was on his feet again, and looking around for something to do, my father suggested the law. He thought it would suit him well. And so it did. He started as a law clerk in a Wellington office and, in time, transferred to the Crown Solicitor's Office in Greymouth. Eventually he came back over the hill to Young and Hunter and in a few years was invited to join Peter; the old soldiers were fighting side by side once again, only this time the *strada* was Hereford Street. When my father resigned as Crown Prosecutor, he recommended Clint for the job against Sir Richard Wild's preferred choice of Bob Edgely. My father advised Dick that although Bob was a competent lawyer, it would be an unpopular appointment given that he fought with everyone, inside and outside the courtroom. So Clint took my father's place, and in due course was elevated to the bench, and from that time possibly the two men drifted into different orbits.

But when my father could have done with the simple warmth of companionship, of 'a speechless human understanding', Clint was not there. On the occasion of Clint's knighthood he was interviewed by the press. He mentioned my father five times in relation to Peter's influence on his career. Perhaps, by then, he felt it was safe enough to declare the association.

---

* See Appendix III p. 246

Clint

I'm ten. We've driven for an interminable time, too many hours immobile for a kid longing for the promised adventure of hunting deer with my father's famous friend. And this is Clinton Roper, at last. A man I never knew except through the oil-paper window through which I view, still, the short stories of my father's life. Major Ryan turns the page of yet another album of fading black and white photographs, the sticking tape yellowing and giving way altogether. 'There's your father,' he says. 'And that's Clint beside him.' And I see a man slightly taller than my father staring back at me, the forage cap set askew like all the others. But I can't see his eyes.

I had heard somewhere in the floating conversation that he'd received a Dear John letter from home and gone to pieces. Is that probable? To have been through fire for so long, to have seen so much real hurt, how could a man collapse over a lost romance. Unless it was the one thing holding him together all that time. Perhaps this girl had been the sticking tape from all the photographs of his life failing at last.

We drive along a dusty farm track, the car rocking on its springs as turkeys fluster aside like washing ladies, sticking out their heads and skipping through a slack wire fence. We pull up outside an old weather-board, derelict house. There's Clint's car already, a long dusty Holden with its boot up. He steps out from the dark interior onto the sun-bleached porch and grins. My father and he shake hands and my father flicks the ash from his cigarette. Clint's son is older than I am: perhaps fifteen already. Learned, adult. We're introduced. There's not much to say, I'm ten: I'm simply awaiting orders.

The house thrills me. There's dry goat shit scattered about the floor like paper marbles and faded floral wall paper peels from the match lining. It's shadowy indoors and cool. Outside the sun beats down from a white-hot sky and sets the fields humming. My room is empty except for a wire bed and a mattress with faded ticking. In one high corner a wasps' nest, abandoned, blooms like a paper lantern left over from some lost Christmas. I spread my sleeping bag on the bed and lie down, testing the kinks, staring at the ceiling with its lonely dead light bulb dangling on the end of a braided flex. Summer flies are turning around it in an eternal vortex. I lie on my side and stare at the open window where the grass, the hot, white grass, reaches up from the sill, tall with thin seed-heads like starved wheat. A plum tree spreads its bruised leaves and a length of fencing wire, stained brown with rust, reaches right across the frame, an improvised washing line, I suppose. I am suddenly aware of the crickets drumming and the endless buzz of field flies and it seems the hills are swelling in the midday heat. They're alive, I feel. They are filled with secrets. They are drawing me like the Serengeti Plain drew Hemingway.

The two men set up camp-stretchers in what was once a comfortable living room. Above the fireplace there's an ornate mantle on which stands a platoon of cartridges of all makes, remnants of past battles. I'm entranced. I hold them and feel the cool brass, copper, waxed paper and smell for the first time the scent of cordite that has been the concomitant of death for at least a century. It is the subtle incense of a higher confirmation, a graduation of sorts, a casting off of childhood.

We're walking along a farm track. Clay-baked by the summer, winding upward toward the bush-clad hills. We've been walking for hours. John and I together, my father and Clint ahead, both wearing khaki shorts, shirts with dark sweatbands under the arms, boots and grey socks and rifles slung across their shoulders and there is an easy companionship there ahead of me that I can see with my young, uncritical eye, and I imagine they walked beside each other like this the whole length of Italy. Two men with matching intellects sharing wit and irony, perhaps even the silence of those rarest of friendships where nothing needs to be said. They're walking at ease and in rhythm like climbers striding out the miles of a riverbed before the first escarpment, the march to Trieste not so long ago for both of them. And I wonder now if anything so etched in the fabric of memory could ever have been 'long ago'.

We sit at the edge of the track leaning our backs against the turned turfs. In the distance a dead tree stands out from the scrub with the dry hill rising above it. There's a magpie perched on a top branch. It's as big as a bluebottle from here. John reaches across me and takes the rifle. He pumps the action and a shell slides into the black breech. I can smell the oil from where I sit and I watch him as he tucks the butt under his cheek and frowns along the sight. It's noon and there's a slight heat haze rising from the barrel so that the ridge beyond it is quivering. Clint and my father lean forward, interested, their wrists on their knees, cigarettes dripping smoke. My father creases his eyes against the light. The rifle doesn't move at all, but there's a crack like a dry stick splintering and far away, across the valley, the magpie lays its head on its shoulder and drops like a rag from the tree. My father grins, his face creased with pleasure. Clint puts the cigarette to his mouth and, expressionless, John passes the gun back to me. Nothing is said, but in my small opinion he has now taken his place among the demi-gods and I will never leave his side.

An hour later as we approach the crest of a slow hill, John touches my arm gently and stops in his tracks. The two men have fallen to the ground ahead of us and unslung their guns. We can't see what they see. We can only watch them foreshortened, grey as the earth on which they lie, feet spread for balance, shoulders hunched. There are two slightly spaced explosions and we are racing toward them. Down the other side, across a ferned creek, within the shaded hem of the beech forest, lies a doe brown and white, quivering with departing life.

The guts steam in the fern as the deer is dressed and then its length tethered to a pole. The journey home is long and hard, three hours, and I share the weight of it. There's the promise of the skin at the end of it all. But I'm not tall and by the time we reach home the fur has worn where it dragged a little against the ground. John skins it anyway and rolls it up like a mat with a little salt to keep it green and in the evening takes me out with him to look for rabbits in the dusky light. He doesn't say much. I ask all the questions. He is my seer, my wise old man of the hills. And half a lifetime later, one lonely night, he takes the same gun, lays his head on his shoulder, and this quiet, beautiful boy falls asleep forever.

Part Four

Lago Como

Where would he have stayed? Here in this hotel? There, with a better view of the lake? Or further round perhaps, a little removed from the crush of the tourist crowd.

The day was hot and even though it was still mid-morning the sun burned and I found myself leaning in to the shadows as I walked. After a mile or so the road came to an end. Above me there were trees and a small track zigzagging upward. I climbed to a road. There was no walking path that I could see so I just clung to the verge, what little there was, and suffered the nearness of the passing traffic. The tunnels were the worst, the amplified clamour and the vertiginous coming and going of shapes without horizon or context.

Eventually I came to a small village, an accumulation of houses clinging to the side of the mountain through which a footpath led, and where sometimes the houses were so close I could reach out and touch both sides at the same time. Here and there they joined overhead. The cool stone shadow was welcome after walking so long in the bright midday. Now and then I passed groups lunching in walled courtyards; they didn't seem to notice me. I came to a stone stairway leading straight up from the village toward the trees, every step a foot above the last. Sweat stung my eyes and my shirt stuck to my back. Lizards skittered away where they had lain invisible on mottled stones. There were moss and ferns on either side of me and finally, out of breath I stopped, unslung my pack and took out my lunch of bread, cheese and water. The sky was a throbbing powder blue and the trees ticked with fibrillous life. Maybe here, maybe this village. He might have found a room here where it is quieter, a sanctuary from us, somewhere he could order his memories and set them down in paragraphs and chapters.

> *I'm sitting in the shade of trees a thousand feet above Como. It's the end of the affair, I suppose, my father's love for Italy. It's complex and simple – complex because we lose count of the hammer blows that shape us, and simple in that we are always happiest where we are not. I've come to know that of him at least. There was a restlessness in him, not so much of body as of mind. My father was travelling somewhere, changing trains, changing language, and there was never time for the rest of us to catch up. He's been gone now for twenty years.*

In the middle of my writing a voice interrupted me. An old character wandered out of the trees. I was surprised, old characters had no right being this high, especially old characters with white hair, a paunch and a pair of sécateurs. He greeted me and we proceeded to have a lively conversation during which he told me that the large villa on the far shore was owned by a *politico*. It was called *Villa d'Este*, he said. He pointed to the far-off-crimped snow ridges of Switzerland and Monte Rosa. '*A destra*, Yugoslavia,' he said. We talked for some time. He owned a house in the trees that I could not see, and a swimming pool. We might have recognised a handful of syllables among the words we were sharing but not much more.

'*Arrivederci*,' I said at last, turning to go. '*Grazie.*'

'*Prego*,' he replied.

A few hundred feet higher I came to a small Catholic shrine where the track levelled out and led off in the direction from which I'd come. It was peaceful, finally, to be among the trees where the air was still and cool with a lush undergrowth unlike the forests of Aarau and Fontainebleau. To a large extent it had been left to itself, the old logs melding into the forest floor to nurse the new growth. After a couple of hours I passed over a small creek where a stream fell between large square stones like remnants of a castle. Here there was a glade of ferns and a froth of wildflowers blue and white and a chill breeze accompanying the water as it fell toward the lake. This was as peaceful a moment as on the stopbanks of the Senio and I paused to savour it. But I wondered at the same time why I hadn't seen any wildlife along the way. There had been no sign of human passage; no footprints, none of the usual stray cigarette butts or shreds of plastic. Just one rusted cartridge case, very old. And the caterpillars were hatching from their cocoons in the trees, hanging on thin strands of silk along the path so that I was constantly wiping them aside like spiderwebs. No one had been here for a long time. So where were the animals, the squirrels at least? Always there'd been a red squirrel ducking behind a tree in Fontainebleau. I wondered if it was simply that my thoughts were turned inward and that my head was full of noise, full of the assembling words which would find their way into my notebook at day's end. So I made a conscious effort to engage my hunter's eye, and a hundred yards later I saw my snake coiled to one side of the track.

I thought it was a toad. Well, it was, but at first sight it seemed the toad was emerging from a snake skin like a fist from a stocking, that the toad had been feasting on the rotted remains of a dead snake. This is not so fanciful. I saw a possum lying at the side of the road once still twitching with life. When I stopped the car to take a closer look I saw that the possum had been dead a long time. It was twitching because a ferret had climbed inside the corpse to feed on what remained. The toad flopped out of the snake skin onto the path and sat there slimy and dazed, its legs moving like it was drunk. Meanwhile, the wide mouth of the snake quickly closed, the jaws engaged themselves, and a black tongue flickered from a beautiful heart-shaped head. In one smooth convulsion it turned and slid under some large rocks. I studied the toad. He was about as appealing as mud. I had found one with Fanny once and she had warned me about the poisonous slime adhering to the skin of some toads. I prodded him with a stick and then rolled him into the undergrowth.

The snake was still visible beneath his rock, coiled like a fist. I should have left him alone, I was about to, but then I remembered Dave, my father's Japanese grass snake. How then could I just walk on by? What would he have done? I found another stick, thinner and longer this time, and gently I began to probe under the rock, trying to find a way of enticing him out. Eventually I worked the tip of his tail into the open, enough to get a good grip between my thumb and forefinger.

I suppose all manner of cataclysms could have occurred around and behind me at that moment and I wouldn't have noticed. I doubt if I blinked. I doubt if I had ever been more focused on anything before in my life as I gently eased that gorgeous creature from his lair. Slowly he came, gradually releasing his hold until there he was suddenly free and beginning to coil. I let him go in the middle of the track and he immediately tied himself in a thick green knot, his black tongue sniffing the air trying to discern what manner of creature was tormenting him. I used the stick again to find the middle of his body and lifted him. He draped himself evenly over both sides and I was able to lay him down in a straight line this time. He lay unmoving as I let the stick run lightly down the length of his back and remained immobile as I studied him as closely as I dared. It was almost as if he were playing dead. All the life seemed to have gone out of him. I turned him over and saw the large pale scales of his belly. His back and head were a brown-green colour, burnt umber, sienna, yellow ochre and cobalt blue, an Italian palette. At another time, of another age, I might have put him in my pack and taken him as a present to Fanny at least. Or sent his skin to my brother. But I'm older now, and he was a lovely thing. I lifted him off the track and set him down in the green-grey ferns.

Half an hour later I was drinking a cold beer on the heights of Brunate, overlooking Como and the valleys to the west which are riddled now with terra cotta. There have been so many letters I have wanted to write; so many adventures I wanted to share if only in the telling. I know he would have enjoyed this one. I sipped the chill unnamed ferment and smiled. From where I sat I could see a long way south, to the flat plains across which the Eighth Army had clawed its way so laboriously, so painfully, toward the Po River.

Liberalism, reactionism,
and the inarticulate premise

*Mr Justice Holmes, one of the great American judges, drew attention long ago
to the attitude of a judge being conditioned by the subconscious attitudes of
the mind. He referred to this phenomenon as the 'inarticulate premise' of the
man on the bench.*

(From *Dear Sam* by Peter Mahon)

My father, I think, liked to see himself as a liberal while playing the part of
a Victorian reactionary. I think his philosophies were eclectic, and I suspect
he dwelt in a private no man's land, caught between extreme points of view.
However, because most of us prefer identity to possessing no definition
at all, in the end I think he adopted an undeclared conservative stance, a
position of logic and order from which he could hold the world in clear
focus. After all, he was a marksman. 'It is better to have a closed mind,' I
heard him say, 'than to have no convictions at all.' I think by this statement
he was impugning the socialist ideologues who tended to weigh everything
in an unending search for social justice, and their vacillations annoyed the
hell out of him.

Alistair Cooke once made a comparison between the two presidents
Carter and Reagan. He said Reagan's worth lay in the fact that he could
make a decision, and if it was wrong, then everyone soon found out. Carter
on the other hand would stand at the crossroads weighing up whether to
go left or right, trying to make the most ethical judgment. He was like a
centipede, he said, with all its legs moving in opposing directions, going
nowhere. I think my father tended towards Cooke's point of view.

I have often wondered how it was that we were split like so many
New Zealand families over the question of the Springbok tour. My father
was obviously a very intelligent man and the facts of the case are clear in
retrospect: sanctions against the Botha regime were very effective; sanctions
including the sporting boycott. But effective or not, we were reacting to a

democratic plea from a subjugated people not to play around with their oppressor. A farmer friend of mine called in the other day with Mandela's biography in his hand. 'Have you read this thing?' he asked. 'My god, it's brilliant. What an amazing man…'

On my table at that very moment was a copy of Nicky Hager's *The Hollow Men*, the book that had recently forced the resignation of the reactionary leader of the opposition. 'Listen,' I said, 'you lend me your book and I'll lend you mine.'

Brian stared at the cover and winced. 'Sam, I can't think of any reason why I would possibly want to read that thing,' he said, staring at it as if it were excrescence.

'Well, Brian,' I sighed, 'don't leave it another twenty years before you do.'

And the odd thing is that when we were marching against apartheid, Brian would have been exactly the kind of good old boy who flung eggs and tinnies at us as we walked up the street.

Sometimes, all it takes to destroy prejudice is to ask a question, or read a book. Information on what was happening in South Africa was accessible to anyone who cared to find out. My father didn't care to find out.

Years later I remember Jim Bolger putting his arm around Mandela when he came here for a visit. Jim had been a high -ranking member of a government that was happy enough to let him rot in jail. So why the blind spot? The inarticulate premise, perhaps? Because it has to be remembered that during the war in Italy Peter was fighting side by side with the South Africans. They met each other on leave, they played football against each other, they depended for their lives on each other. How could these people possibly be regarded as fascists. 'Why, we were fighting against fascism together in 1945.' And yet my father had seen at first hand the brutality of the white masters toward the blacks when he had visited South Africa in the sixties. He had seen it and dismissed it as an aberration. I suppose most of us find it hard to accept a change of view, that is until circumstances compel us to confront the facts.

It was just so with Erebus. When my father read the first reports of the plane going down in Antarctica his immediate presumption was that the pilot was at fault. The pilot always is, surely, just like the captain of a ship. I still meet people who believe the captain of the doomed aircraft must have been responsible. But these are people who have never read my father's report and probably never will. It would disturb the shape of their world too much to do so. I have found it also with Lynley Hood's controversial book about the Christchurch Civic Creche. I have met a number of highly educated people who refuse to read her analysis of the case and the only deduction I can come to is that they are afraid, that it is not just a single truth that will be altered, but all the structures to which that truth adheres. After all, concepts don't exist unattached to some larger belief system: apples are either attached to a tree or they lie on the ground. One doesn't expect to find them floating in the air.

My father didn't care to look closely at the African situation, and I suppose he was not required to. But if it had come before him as a case in law, if he had been asked by Desmond Tutu to sit on a commission, would he have taken a different view?

Here is a section from one of his judgments where he upholds a police appeal against a lower court dismissal. A charge of disturbing the peace had been brought against a 'protester' outside a sporting venue where a South African team was playing during the '81 tour:

The argument of the respondent which succeeded at the hearing proceeded upon the allegation of unlawful arrest by which his individual freedom of speech and movement was impeded or restrained. It may be worth noting, in passing, that the concept of freedom is an abstraction with variable consequences, depending upon its application. The theory and practice of collectivism, pursuing the ideal of freedom of the people from privilege and privation, insists as a necessary consequence upon the extinction of personal freedom, the levels of society being reduced to a just gradation by an equality of servitude. In a collectivist state, the only man its masters fear is the man who himself is free. So it comes about that if the respondent and his followers had staged this civil insurrection in some of the black republics whose cause they had adopted, they would certainly have been imprisoned, and may thereafter have been led away to face an even graver ordeal. But the paradox, although curious, is irrelevant. Anglo-Saxon societies have clung with similar tenacity to the principles of individual liberty, and have crystallized those principles into personal rights qualified only by a corresponding duty not to infringe those same rights vested in everyone else. The respondent therefore, as a corollary to his right to personal freedom, was legally immune from arbitrary arrest. He could be lawfully detained by the police if his conduct in being present in this public place, on this occasion, created a reasonable apprehension of a breach of the peace. The right of arrest in those circumstances is not controlled by uncertain standards, or disfigured by fluctuating jurisprudence. It is closely limited and clearly defined, so much so that in all cases similar to this, the ultimate answer is the legal response to a question of fact. The point of the present appeal is whether that question of fact was correctly answered in favour of the respondent.

It is not extraordinary here that Peter would connect protest with communism. At the time of the tour I remember well the urban myth that the students along with the middle-aged members of our free society and academics who stood firm on the Hamilton football ground were communist stooges being paid twenty dollars a piece to be there. There had to be an evil influence involved somewhere and that influence could only have been the old booger man from the East. These days it would have been Osama and the protesters would, of course, have been labelled terrorists. It was not for my father to remind those who were protesting against apartheid that freedom to protest was restricted in some black countries. It would have been as silly as to remind Karl Popper that he would not be able to teach his philosophies in Nazi Germany, an Anglo-Saxon society by all accounts. There was something here that Peter just could not resolve, and in this case he seemed to have made a conscious decision to remain uninformed. There was only ever one other time I observed this level of obstinacy in him; it was when he knew he was ill, but didn't want to confront what was happening to him. I sat at the edge of the room a little appalled while his friends supported him in his condemnation of the medical advice he was receiving. It was absurd, but then it was ill health, his ill health, his one fear. It was the one thing a well-turned phrase could not cure.

It is interesting that while he brashly declared his view that mental illness was a weakness for which he had no time, he would make an exception for his friend Clint Roper:

(Letter to John Burn)

...I note what you say about Roper declining to hear any further submissions after 4pm, and I hope he is not becoming unduly weighed down with trying to handle the Christchurch work under the present conditions. Despite his attitude of indomitable physical vigour, he is of brittle constitution, and should not be subjected to these pressures...

Clearly, he also admired Dr Kay Bradford, the eminent Nelson psychiatrist, (godmother to my sister) whom he regarded as an exemplary court witness and a woman of extraordinary common sense. Again and again in his judgments he makes allowances for weakness of the human spirit. I remember his description of a farmer who had come before the court on a charge of wilful damage to property. His father and he had fought bitterly over something at breakfast and then both had gone off to their separate duties, the son to discing a twenty-acre fallow paddock. 'It's an unhealthy thing,' said my father, 'to be too much on one's own. There he was, going round and round in diminishing circles with that breakfast argument going round and round in his head with no apparent resolution until suddenly something snapped, at which point he turned the machine and drove it and the discs clean through his old man's living room.'

Peter loved the bleak Greene realism of le Carré's stories, and his masterful prose. But what he missed was le Carré's own sense of social justice. Above all, Peter admired *Tinker Tailor Soldier Spy*. He regarded it as le Carré's masterpiece, and yet, somehow, he missed Haydon's (Philby's) soliloquy in the last chapter.

'Do you know what's killing western democracy, George? Greed, and constipation – moral, political, aesthetic.

'We live in an age where only fundamental issues matter... The United States is no longer capable of undertaking its own revolution... The political posture of the United Kingdom is without relevance or moral visibility in world affairs... In capitalist America economic repression of the masses is institutionalised to a point which not even Lenin could have foreseen... The Cold War began in 1917 but the bitterest struggles lie ahead of us as America's deathbed paranoia drives her to greater excesses abroad... Until the mid-fifties I still had hopes. Self-delusion of course. We were already America's street walkers.'

He hated America very deeply, he said, and Smiley supposed he did.

Le Carré is using part of his own voice here. He has never held the fundamentalist's view of good and evil, and while he could not excuse Philby's actions in the way Graham Greene could, he believes America's foreign policy to be dangerously flawed. Haydon's speech had to be convincing; why otherwise would any intelligent man seek to undermine the structures of his own country? But to a large extent, evidenced by recent interviews, they are also le Carré's feelings.

It is evident also that Peter thought the media had been captured by the Left, just as they were traditionally supposed to have captured the education system.

(Letter to Lloyd Brown, 1977)

Muldoon arrived back from his world tour the day before yesterday and needless to say the TV reporters were waiting for him. He made some brief statement but declined to appear on last night's television programme run by Gordon Dryden. This programme ran along accustomed lines. First of all there was a long speech by Rowling [Labour Party leader] to an enthusiastic Labour Party audience, in which he catalogued the inflation rate, unemployment, adverse balance of trade, etc. Then there was a short monologue from Dryden pointing out all the defects of the Muldoon administration. This was then followed by a dialogue between Dryden and Chapman, the chairman of the National Party.

Dryden put a series of about 15 loaded questions, which prevented Chapman giving any coherent explanation, and upon that note the proceeding closed. I think there should be a statutory requirement in the Broadcasting Act that there be at least one television interviewer who is not a socialist.

He had a distaste for Ian Fraser in particular. Perhaps it was because Ian, arguably the most astute interviewer of that time, scored so well against Muldoon that the Prime Minister refused to be interviewed by him. I was listening to Fraser one evening when my father came downstairs for yet another coffee. He paused while the water boiled, bent and rested his hands against his knees and frowned as he cocked his ear for the dialogue. Then he straightened and turned a pair of sad eyes on me. 'Samuel,' he said, 'what on earth are you listening to this pinko for?'

And then, a few years later, when Muldoon turned on my father and the structures of civilisation started to fall apart for him, I heard him utter these remarkable words, 'Ian Fraser. That's the man. I must get an interview with Ian, he'll sort it all out.' He had been confronted by the facts at last and his view had been turned around. Muldoon was not at all the fair man my father had judged him to be, and neither, when it came down to it, was Ian. When Peter at last found himself in a studio with Ian Fraser, he was surprised to find that the seasoned journalist did exactly what he does best: he offered him no favours at all but played devil's advocate to the very limit, leading my father into a series of cul de sacs that offered him no room to gather momentum. If my father had walked into the room while I was watching that interview he might have remarked, 'What on earth are you listening to this Muldoonist for?'

If he felt let down you could not see it in his face. He held his ground and courageously played a defensive game for which he was entirely unprepared. 'That must have been hard for him,' I said to my partner after it was over. I felt sick.

'I didn't notice,' she said. 'He looks so good. He's an aristocrat. I love him.'

A few years ago in an interview over a book I'd written, I was asked a question about human nature. I said that I believed people to be basically bad, but with a thin sugar coating of goodness. 'Really,' said my interviewer, 'well, I'm glad the rest of the world doesn't think that way.' She paused and added, 'But you'd probably be an interesting person to visit.' It was kind of her.

In *The Log from the Sea of Cortez*, Steinbeck writes: 'Man is a two-legged paradox. We admire people such as Ghandi, Christ and the Greeks, people who exhibit what we consider to be elements of goodness. But in our own lives we embrace the elements that are bad; such as graspingness, selfishness etc. This is because at base man needs to survive, and the elements of goodness are not those concomitant with survival.'

Here is Peter's letter to the reverend Bob Lowe, 1978:

…but all this is digressionary, as I am writing about your TV interview last night with David Lange [then Labour Prime Minister] whom I used to see now and then in the courts in Auckland. I followed with close attention his responses to your close interrogatories. He seemed to me to found his social and political philosophy upon a false major premise. He thinks that all people are inherently good, with an undeveloped devotion to the welfare of their neighbours. The law has failed to control the transgressions of society, so another system must be found. The remedy which David sees is the patient inculcation of public virtue by methods he did not clearly define, leading to the salutary abolition of magistrates, probation officers, police, and all the distasteful apparatus of legal restraints.

But all this is idealistic futility. The sombre experience of mankind, correctly identified by the church and by the law, points in the opposite direction. The generality of men abstain from breaking heads, and from breaking contracts, through fear of legal retribution, and that retribution is exacted by the law as an organ of society and with the approval of society. You correctly enquired whether the only alternative was totalitarian control, but like Pilate, another astute debater, David did not stay for an answer.

Your guest of last night is fluent, and friendly and sincere. But I think he needs a course in applied pragmatics. His own electorate enjoys the highest crime rate in New Zealand, and it is distinctly hazardous to walk anywhere within its confines at night. I can understand David's frustration at the systematic conviction and sentence of so many of his constituents and his wistful search for the Golden Grail, but unfortunately his search will be in vain. If there had ever been a Golden Grail in Mangere it would have been stolen by now and melted down, like copper wire belonging to the post office.

I am always interested in your TV interviews, and look forward to seeing more of them. Kind regards …

And this is so. He enjoyed Greene, le Carré and Somerset Maugham who all took a jaundiced view of their fellow man, whose every hero was flawed and where betrayal was all you could ever count on. Thus armed against any illusions of altruism in the world, he went about his job as an agent of the law, looking humanity in the eye and expecting the very worst.

Peter and his father fenced interminably, always trying each other. Neither would give in, both were forever seeking the advantage. In my experience, my father could never be pushed. If you applied a gentle pressure he would apply it back in equal measure. If you flung windmills at him he would offer a single dart in return that would go straight to the heart; he was a master of anatomy. At twenty-two he wrote this letter to his father from Japan:

(Yamaguchi 1946)
…the rainy season is almost finished and the weather is getting very hot. I am stationed over on the west coast so get a lot of swimming. As a matter of fact I have been away from there for two and a half weeks, engaged on courts martial, but am going back again today. There has been a bit of a crime wave here, and there is a lot of business for anyone with any legal qualifications. I was very unpopular with the president of a court martial the other day. It was a serious case and a full colonel was in charge of the court. I was prosecuting and he refused to let me call a certain witness, saying that he did not think that it was necessary. After an argument with him I gave up even though

I knew I was in the right. About ten minutes later when I had closed my case he asked me why I had not called a witness to prove a certain matter. I said that in my opinion it was not necessary. He then ordered me to call the witness. I refused, saying that as he would not let me call my witness, I was not going to call another one just to help him. He then asked me who was in charge of the court, he or I. I said that although he was in charge of the court, I was conducting the case for the prosecution and if he wanted a particular witness he could call that witness himself. He blew up then and told me I was insubordinate etc. But I would not shift, so we carried on the case without his witness, and I am pleased to say he had no option but to convict the prisoner on all counts. He wrote to my colonel saying that I was ill-mannered etc., but the colonel tore the letter up...

Many years later, when he was being pushed by the Muldoon government, he wrote in reply to a supporting letter from Sian Elias (now Chief Justice): 'Once, while on patrol in Italy, I was ambushed by a number of Germans who opened fire. Instead of diving for cover, I stood where I was and fired back.'

I have said somewhere that I don't remember that he asked questions. In his letters to us he was usually being instructive or amusing. I remember writing something to my sister once in which I was being perhaps a little overbearing. The next letter I received from my father contained an allusion to Laertes instructing his sister Ophelia before he left to join the war, and then of Polonius instructing Laertes: 'Give every man thine ear, but few thy voice.' Peter was being both humourous and instructive.

The Dante letter he wrote to my sister, (see page 27) is the best example I can find of how he tried to entice Janet, at least, into a close examination of things: of the world, of human nature. If it were at all possible, she would have been the one out of the three of us best placed to understand him. She was a daughter after all, and the eldest of his children.

His letter practises what Laurie Lee wrote about in his essay 'The first born', in which he promises the following for his baby daughter:

> I won't send her away to a [private] school to have her come home at weekends stiff as a hockey post and all sicklied o'er with the pale sense of cast. No, I will send her to the local school where she can acquire her conformity, and in the evenings we can unravel it together.

Well, Laurie, for all that he is loveable, was also a bit of a liar. I was very disappointed to read in his biography that he sent her to a private school after all. But I suppose, as parents, most of us set the bar far too high for ourselves. I'm not sure what Peter wanted for my sister, but presumably she felt his hand moving the carriages along the track of her life and shifting the rails ever so slightly. As I have said we tend to know what our parents want for us whether they put their thoughts into words or not.

I was playing guitar one day when he and my mother were entertaining a client in the next room. There was a pause in the conversation during which my careful picking must have filtered through. 'Is that your son?' asked the guest.

'Yes,' replied my mother.

'It's very nice,' he said.

My father, according to my mother, quickly rose from his seat, picked a trophy from the mantlepiece that I had won on the West Melton rifle range and handed it to him.

'He also shoots,' he said.

Janet travelled a good way down his road with him; she had lived in Italy for a while, she spoke Italian, and she studied law. And she was admitted to the bar just when he died. It wasn't fair, to either of them. The Dante letter was unusual. It was not written simply to entertain or written out of duty; it was a letter written with purpose and love and in it there is a wholeness of the man, not entire, but close to the thing I have been trying to discover. The man a little uncovered, and for once, a little off-guard.

Art, religion and philosophy

The immortality of the soul! What a boring conception! Can't think of anything worse than living for infinity in a great transcendental hotel, with nothing to do in the evenings …

(From *A Voyage Around My Father*, John Mortimer)

He was brought up a Catholic, apart from his sisters. He was brought up in that duality of contradiction that Thor Heyerdahl described when he spoke of leaving university with God in one hand and Darwin in the other. Peter was a thinking man who honoured his father and who could honour the church and be appalled by it at the same time. The wealth of the church in Italy bothered him, evidently, especially given that in 1945 a great number of people were starving. And the fundamental ethos of the Catholic Church provoked him to write, albeit with a slanted pen;

> …the concept of original sin is equivalent to an allegation of inherent vice unsupported by evidence.

And yet he was one of two New Zealanders to receive an audience with the pope in 1946. Writing to his parents he remarks; '…there is a small silver cross in the parcel. Hang onto it for me, it has received the papal blessing.'

When he returned home he attended mass only twice as far as my aunt can remember. Once with his father and once in the company of his beloved grandmother and her cat, the latter concealed inside his battle jacket.

Leaving Catholicism cost him dearly in some respects. Reg Bradley and John Mullins, whom he had described to his father as 'my best friends in the world' in a letter from the Mediterranean, never forgave him. When he married my mother in the Church of England, they could not bring themselves to attend. But he was a man continually evolving, as I have said.

Constantly changing trains. Perhaps he really believed that, in the end, 'nothing matters'.

'One night a priest came to the flat,' said my mother. 'It was shortly after we were married. He wanted to have a talk with Peter. When I told him a priest was at the door his face turned to stone. But he was polite and they had an hour together nevertheless.'

I remember him studying my paintings when I returned from Fontainebleau. He was a little amused by them, and a little puzzled. For him they were entertainments, like all art. But also there was perhaps in them a little of what had arrested his attention in the Uffizi. Something indescribable but of substance. Something that for me is a kind of intuition, but, for people like my father, needs to be given form. And form is a good word for it. It is one of the terms Plato uses in Popper's *The Open Society and Its Enemies*, along with pattern and idea.

(Peter's letter to Janet, 1980)

We were very pleased to get your letter from Rome and your description of the city was so good that the scenes almost came to life in the pages, especially the roast chestnut seller. We are looking forward to your first letter from Florence and hope that you have found congenial lodgings. I should not worry about the new law prohibiting long term tenancies to non-EEC persons. The Italians are not interested in laws or regulations. Sign up for three months and then sign up for another three months later. The landlady will curl a contemptuous lip at any official visitor. *'A basso gli ufficiali. …'*

During the hot days in Canterbury, with the nor'west winds blowing across the parched fairways at Shirley, I often thought of you in Florence with the Arno muddy and turbulent from the winter rains in the hills and the chill wind whipping across the city. But the winter cannot affect the beauty of Florence, and you can spend endless days looking at the galleries in your spare time, wandering through the Uffizi and the Pitti Palace over and over again, always seeking something new. And when you stand and look at Michelangelo's David, you will be astounded by the impression you are looking at something alive, a silent figure poised to strike, and yet it is carved out of cold marble…

This letter stands out amongst all his others for, I suppose, its sense of longing. Usually his letters are descriptive or instructive, but this one is different. He is the blind man and she his eyes. My sister is standing on his ground and he would like almost to place her feet for her, to direct her gaze. 'Wandering through the Uffizi and the Pitti Palace...' Is that how he spent his time when on leave during the war, or did he discover that timeless beauty later when he travelled to Europe for the Europa Oil case and stayed in Florence courtesy of big business? He talks about the David as if from a first-hand emotion, and yet not quite. He is impressed that it looks almost alive, but if it touches his heart he doesn't say so. And yet he says, '...endless days looking at the galleries over and over again, always seeking something new'. Seeking what? Why go back and back again? A simple tourist doesn't go back. What did he see? What did he feel?

I have just finished the plaster bust of a Japanese girl, Muyumi Kamegawa. I cannot explain how much I have enjoyed the process of sculpting her exquisite head; the best I can say is that when your hand finds the line and holds it, it is very much like love. I have seen it in Rodin's work, seen where his hands pressed the clay, the imprint of his thumb in that hollow between the bridge of the nose and the eye. I have seen, also, the secret white marble smile of his sleeping mistress, Camille Claudel. You have to stand behind and above the head and a little to the right to see it. And it is love, I would say; the sculptor's secret. Is that what my father discovered in the Uffizi? Something a little out of reach?

The creator of the 'Perseus', Benvenuto Cellini, was given a safe conduct by Pope Paul III, after he had murdered his rival Pompeo in reasonably cold blood. When criticised, the Pope answered: 'I must inform you that men who are masters in their profession, like Benvenuto, should not be subject to the laws...'

'The Italians are not interested in laws or regulations...' wrote my father. This must have interested him. The law was his one truth, and yet in his letters to colleagues it is clear that within the pure structure of law he had discovered considerable madness. Art, you could say, is a kind of madness within which can be found certain purities. I imagine he would have found this both confusing and interesting. 'You will be astounded by the impression you are looking at something alive...'

(Peter's letter to my brother, 1980)

Dear Tim,

The other day I read a new book published by professor Sir Karl Popper, and it reminded me of the time when he was a lecturer at Canterbury University in 1941 when I was a student.

In the early part of 1941, when I was in the army, leave was given to soldiers to attend two lectures a week in the evenings and, along with three or four other uniformed students, I used to appear at the lectures given under the heading of 'Philosophy 1', which was thought to be a soft touch for one of the BA subjects required as part of a Law degree. 'Philosophy 1' consisted of two parts – Psychology and Logic. Dr Popper was the senior lecturer in Logic. He was an Austrian who had left Austria when that country was threatened by Nazi domination, and he lectured at Canterbury University from 1937 to '45. The doctor was very well disposed towards the military students. I might almost say that he treated us with extreme indulgence.

My constant companion at these lectures was a powerfully built young soldier from the country, who had surprisingly been granted university entrance by some rustic high school. He had even more trouble than I in grasping the principles which the doctor endeavoured to convey. I can still remember a proposition which the doctor put to my military colleague. He asked him to comment on the significance of the following statement:

'No number of sightings of white swans can ever prove that all swans are white; the sight of only one black swan will refute the original theory.'

Upon being asked what he thought about this, my military colleague sat with folded arms and stared dumbly into the distance. After a minute of profound silence (it seemed longer), the doctor tactfully suspended the enquiry by intervening to say that he thought he knew the reply my military colleague was about to give – namely, that this was an illustrative analysis of the correlation between uncertain premises and false conclusions. Having then congratulated my colleague on his percipience, the doctor ceremoniously inscribed in his notebook a commendatory mark for the answer which my military colleague had, in theory, been about to give. At the end of the year, he and I, along with the other two or three uniformed students, all received marks of over 60 per cent. How my military colleague got over 60 per cent I do not know. He said he did not understand one question.

This story interests me on several levels; First, it acknowledges his admiration of James Thurber in paralleling Thurber's autobiographical incident of professor Bassum and the star tackle for the university football team:

(From *My Life and Hard Times*, Harper & Brothers, 1933)
…at that time Ohio State University had one of the best football teams in the country and B, was one of its outstanding stars. In order for him to be eligible to play it was necessary for him to keep up in his studies, a very difficult matter, for while he was not dumber than an ox he was not any smarter. Most of his professors were lenient and helped him along. No one gave him more hints than Professor Bassum. One day, when we were on the subject of transportation and distribution, it came B's turn to answer a question. 'Name one means of transportation,' the professor said to him. No light came into the big tackle's eyes. 'Just any means of transportation,' said the professor. B sat staring at him. 'That is,' pursued the professor, 'any means, agency or method of going from one place to another.' B had the look of a man who is being led into a trap. 'You may choose between steam, horse-drawn or electrically propelled vehicles,' said the instructor. 'I might suggest the one in which we make long journeys across land.' There was a profound silence in which everyone stirred uneasily, including B and Mr Bassum. Mr Bassum abruptly broke this silence in an amazing manner. 'Choo-choo-choo,' he said in a low voice, and turned instantly scarlet…

Secondly, the story about Popper indicates my father's unease around subjects that touch on the metaphysical. He was likely more than not to make fun of psychology. Those afflicted by mental illness were often dismissed as mad, with the exception of his old friend Clint whose stability of mind the war had temporarily broken. Popper was not a psychologist, he was a logician and logic attracted my father. Still, he must have his fun with him anyway: '…illustrative analysis of the correlation between uncertain premises and false conclusions…' These are my father's words, certainly not the words the clear-minded professor would have used to describe his famous theorem that, 'All observation is selective'. Popper particularly disliked 'philosophical obscuration and pretension'.

I think my father would have been doing my brother more of a service by being true to the professor rather than making fun of him, or rather, making fun of the abstract arts. And herein lies the nub of my strained relationship with my father: the abstract arts became my life.

During my first year at university I spent a great deal of time with an old college friend, a mathematician called Gary Newsam. We made a good pair. Always in my life I have sought out empiricists for company rather than artists. I need the balance.

One evening, at my parents' home in Remuera, Gary and my father and I were sitting in the living room with the fire crackling comfortingly in the background and something in a glass near at hand. I was proud to have my distinguished friend staying with us. Gary was about to embark on a scholarship at Harvard to complete a PhD in maths and had called in on his way up from Christchurch. I remember sitting watching Gary discussing the makeup of the Privy Council with my father and my father paying him close attention, enjoying a level of discussion he and I never could. I felt envious and a little sad.

Gary departed the next day and left me with a sheaf of drawings we had worked on some time earlier in which we had been trying vainly to comprehend why da Vinci's brilliant perpetual motion machines couldn't work. On paper they looked entirely possible. But the Renaissance genius hadn't reckoned on Newton who pointed out in due course that just as energy cannot be lost neither can it be created out of nothing, thus confining perpetual motion to fancy. It was a shame. Even Gary could not see why our intricate sketches would not come to life.

I could hear my father hammering tacks into the edge of a lifted piece of carpet on the stairs. I gathered up the sheets of paper and descended from my room to where he was poised between floors. I showed him the papers. He glanced at them. I began to explain the puzzle, but before I could get very far into the theory he raised an eyebrow and tossed off some small, humorous yet bitter remark that shattered the moment irrecoverably. And he was excellent at this. I imagine it was one of the things that made him so devastating in court. I stared at the papers in front of me unable to say anything for a moment and then just walked away.

Again, there was the time I discovered de Bono's definition of the adversary system.* It was extraordinary to me. I took it to my father, I wanted to know what he thought. And in a word he dismissed it leaving me standing with the book in my hand and a question unanswered.

I suppose I was hoping that he might take into account the syllogism from which Popper's counter-theorem evolved. 'All swans are white. That is a swan, therefore it is white.' I wanted my father to allow for the one that goes, 'Friends share each others' ideas. Gary is Sam's friend. Therefore Sam shares Gary's ideas.' Major premise, minor premise, conclusion. But no, I sat in my room, heartbroken, bewildered, listening to the distant tapping of a tack hammer.

He avoided where he could, discussing anything about which he had no intimate knowledge, especially music and the fine arts. Poetry was easier for him; poetry had to do with words and words were his medium. Where he felt uncertain he would often refer to a higher authority or perversely introduce some ironic element in order to trivialise it, to put it out of the way. I recall the advent of *The Bone People* on the literary scene. At the time I found Hulme's book very hard to read. It took me three beginnings to catch the rhythm of it but in the end I think I quite liked it. And it was

---

* 'The German philosopher Hegel proposed that all development was a matter of thesis which was opposed by antithesis and from the clash emerged a synthesis. But long before Hegel, Western thought had been dominated by the adversary system ... which has penetrated so deeply into our culture that we could be said to be dependent on it. Intellectually the adversary system is childish in the extreme. Both parties spend their time attempting to pick holes in the argument of the other party instead of exploring the matter itself. The overriding limitation of this system is that it is negative. It has no constructive element at all.' (Edward de Bono, *Word Power*, Penguin [1979])

controversial, of course. I mentioned it to my father once when I was in Auckland visiting. He tilted his head back, expelled a veil of smoke and pronounced it unreadable.

'You've read it?' I asked.

'I'm told it's unreadable,' he replied.

'By whom?'

Evidently some professor of English at the university. Oh, so an expert witness had proved the case and that was the end of the discussion. I was angry. I waited. A week later we met at a friend's house to celebrate my birthday. My parents came. Then when the time was right I slipped the Hulme book into the conversation. I asked around if anyone had read it. Of course I knew the answer. They were all very pleased with *The Bone People*. 'Well,' I said, 'Dad says it's unreadable.' There was a long and awkward moment in which everyone turned to him for an argued case. He had none of course, how could he have? Shortly after this he and my mother left. I was very content that on my birthday I had got the better of him at last. I had placed him before a jury and he had lost.

But I had done too well. I had hurt him very much. He was ill and it had been hard for him to come to the dinner. He had come for me, for my birthday. It had been his gift.

Part Five

End

I was living in a farm cottage near Lake Ellesmere. My uncle had found it for me when I left Gore at last to come home. He knew everyone on the peninsula. All the old names, the incumbent, the retired, the eager young waiting their turn. He picked up the phone in his big hand, lifted the cigarette to his other ear and bawled down the line in a voice that could be heard an acre away and who could deny his gruff charm, that inimitable laugh blooming like a fat bouquet of roses round a thorn of common sense. So he found his errant nephew a cottage, a refuge in the hills. And I was grateful. For six months I was very happy.

It was August when Gillian came. Caroline and our daughter Tess would be home soon from America and we would embark on a brand new, dangerous life. I was working at the easel, I had paintings leaning against the wall, I had a show imminent. I heard her car come briskly up the drive and saw her through the window turning in at the door, heard the creak, her firm step and felt the sudden shift of air as it opened to her sure hand. Her bright eye met mine and her smile creased a face fashioned over sixty years by absolute goodness. I was filling the kettle. She placed a freshly baked loaf of bread on the bench and hugged me like one of her own. She stood back a little, and in that very clear schoolroom voice of hers, a voice she used to instruct a faltering child or impart the arcane sense of a Bach flower remedy, she told me that my father had died.

She told me that I would never be able to ask him the questions I am asking now, that I would never be able to fight him again or be quite old enough to meet him as a man: she told me that I would never be able to ask his forgiveness, to apologise for crimes I never committed but to apologise anyway because that's all it ever comes down to, this never-ending paean of regret, the unaccomplished duty to the unremitting demands of those people who brought us unasked into the world.

She told me this, every bit of it, but in the simple words: 'Your father died.' And then she made me a cup of tea.

I remember the hills beyond my window, the scratched, fly-stained sky, the gum trees hanging against a windless day and every grass blade in place as if the world was, for a moment, too embarrassed to move. My mother, five hundred miles away, had woken in the night and realised, suddenly, that she was alone.

These moments are stolen from us by well-meaning souls, the same people who steal birth, who make dishonourable ceremony out of the simple honest ends of our lives. It's like Christmas in a way: tinsel and lies to mark the birth of a simple man, a man who went hungry and half-clothed through a bitter world.

I was determined they wouldn't take my father's death and do the same, make it into some Christmas pageant.

'I want to read this,' I said. The dean, his gold and white robe hanging stiffly against his thick body, the crucifix looking far too heavy against his chest, took the book from me and turned a little aside while he scanned the bracketed text. 'Yes,' he said. 'I think that will be all right,' handing it back to me unsmiling, a little suspicious. And I'm thinking, I don't care what you suppose. I will ruin your special day if I wish. This cathedral is not your house, this is not your father. I will read what I like. I will dance on his flag-draped coffin if I feel the need.

I have already recounted that I stood at the lectern and read Robert Bolt's interpretation of Thomas More's rationale. What I did not say was that as I walked back to our pew I glanced across the aisle where stood the leader of the opposition. Tears were tracking down his face. As I say, I have a memory for paradox. Was the shadow minister of law, the Honourable Jim McLay, brokenhearted for my father's sake, because he had run with the pack who had harried him for telling the inconvenient truth? Or was he upset for himself, realising too late that his unequivocal loyalty to the prime minister threatened to cast him irretrievably into the trashcan of political history? I don't know. I still think he was at heart a good man coerced.

Politics never suited him. I particularly remember that unnerving habit of his, when being interviewed on television, of nodding his head when he was denying something and shaking it when he was being affirmative. I don't think he ever knew quite who he was.

It wasn't many weeks later that the sale of the Mill went through and I moved my meagre possessions to the other windswept end of Canterbury. I stood in the dry crisp grass amid the broken discarded milling machinery and stared up at the abandoned concrete edifice that was to be my home for the next twenty years. Its empty windows stared back and I felt tired before I'd even begun.

There followed months of pulling down and building up, of de-nailing endless rimu boards, scraping the residue of neglect from the high beams. Standing over bonfires of debris just as I had watched my father, rake in hand. There was the oily smell of putty, slivers of glass, buckets of white-wash sloshed against walls and hours on my knees scraping back the encrusted flour and dust from the raw wood floors. And once when I looked up from my work, aching, every sinew stretched, I saw the hills across the valley lit from the late afternoon sun and it shocked me. Yellow light was catching the folds of the hills and they were framed by the white sill of my huge empty window. It was mostly sky, that late pale pastel sky with the day washed out of it. I stared at it transfixed. I couldn't have imagined a better painting. I was on my knees with a steel wedge in my hands, tired and sore with tears in my eyes because my father would never see this, and for the first time I raged against it. It wasn't anger or regret. It was a forgivable kind of despair.

Later, as the sky began to darken, I went out to the roadside, to the long acre, where my horse had been tethered for the day. As I was leading him in through the gates I noticed two birds in erratic flight high above me. A falcon was hunting down a pigeon. The pigeon was darting all over the sky trying to shake off his pursuer. He was desperate. I stood still with the lead rope in one hand, enthralled. Suddenly the pigeon dropped and shot in behind the only tree available, an elder, growing flat against the Mill. The falcon braked in midair, hung there briefly on the slight westerly breeze, and then settled gracefully on a fence post about twenty yards away. He didn't seem worried about me at all, or the horse. He perched there turning his head this way and that, sometimes right over his shoulder, his yellow eye alert as we all waited. Maybe five minutes passed, it was a long time. I didn't want it to end. I had kept a harrier once for four months, jessed and leashed on the front lawn. Sometimes I would perch it on my fist and try to feed it meat, but it never quite trusted me. It would bend its head down toward the food at its feet, its beak open, panting, but never quite able in the end to take its eye from mine.

It was growing late and I guessed this wonderful creature would fly away soon. But still, he seemed to be waiting, knowing that his dinner was still sheltering behind the tree. I let the rope go loose and walked slowly across to the elder. The falcon hunched forward and followed my progress. I pulled back some lower branches and there was the pigeon, sitting on the earth, bobbing his pale grey head at me. 'Out,' I said, and flicked my fingers. In a flurry of wing beats he was back into the air and in a second he had disappeared over the roof. The falcon spread his dark wings and pulled away in pursuit. It was over, they'd gone. It had been marvellous.

I was grinning to myself. I made a cup of tea and settled in the frame of the big window, my legs lying out flat against the broad bottom sill, fourteen feet of emptiness below me. I wanted to watch the last light fade out of the day. But I had barely relaxed when the falcon came back to perch on the same post. I was amazed. He stood there, puffed out his feathers and preened, seemingly unbothered by my presence. I doubted if he had caught his prey. I remembered then the fresh corpse of a starling I had shot that morning. Every day started like that, a brief gunfight to re-establish ownership over the massive cement and iron aviary, ownership that hadn't been contested for ten years.

The body lay near. I reached down and picked it up by one stiff wing and flicked it out the window. The falcon turned his head quizzically on one side and then fell from his perch. He snatched the bird just as it touched the ground and flew with it down the fence line to a new post where he began, methodically, to tear it into pieces. And this is the story I would have told my father, more or less. Maybe I would have used a little more invention, a little more colour. But the essential story would be there and this is the highest currency that ever passed between us. He would have loved it. He would have read it out to his friends, especially to his golfing partner who couldn't tell a shag from an egret. For he was a naturalist, as I have said, and it was our common ground. It would be foolish, I think, not to acknowledge that this incident occurred at the one moment I missed him most. And ever since, when something momentous happens in my life, the falcon comes. No, you're right, it can't be explained. And I don't care to. I just accept it without prejudice.

Lago Como

Sympathy with the fluttering alder and poplar leaves almost takes away my breath; yet, like the lake, my serenity is rippled, but not ruffled. These small waves raised by the evening wind are as remote from storm as the smooth reflecting surface.

(From *Walden*, Henry Thoreau.)

The wind lifts off the lake like a feather. It's warm, it's evening and again I'm sitting alone watching the lights across the water with an empty coffee cup in front of me. It's my last *cappuccino* in Italy, tomorrow I take the morning train to Switzerland, to Fanny. An hour ago I went to bed, but the night was too urgent and I couldn't sleep. On my way here I crossed the *piazza* where some of the tables were still out, their white cloths milky under the light of candles, wine in every glass, tourists draped and glittering, seeming like me, reluctant to leave the day. Flick-eyed waiters stand guard.

The evening's too hot for sleep. By the lake there's not so much light and the trees make a sombre promenade. There are yellow globes along the rails by the lake edge where I sit and the boats rock gently on Como's languid belly. To my right there's a couple bickering like paradise ducks. She's bubbling in a high key, he's demuring. Something shifts in the corner of my eye; a large rat, even by Mill standards, sneaks from shadow to shadow checking the flower boxes for scraps of the day. The woman keeps up her plaintive chirruping filled with all the accusations of old acquaintance. A young couple saunter over and pause by the rail to examine the black water. He's eating an ice-cream, she's stroking back her hair with both hands, methodically, staring out at the distant lights. He has one foot on the rail. She leans close and puts her cheek against his neck. His free arm goes around her waist.

A man comes briskly past carrying a large bunch of roses. Before I can warn him he's at the couple's table. The chirruping ceases like a cicada about to fly. She stares at him, at the proffered rose, she's poised, back arched, a little bewildered. Her husband does nothing. She's caught. She half wants it; after all it's Como, they're together, there have been better times. The pause is long enough to be embarrassing. She shakes her head. The young couple are gone. I take my cup inside. It's too good to leave, the night is too rich.

I buy a beer and return. 'Try this wine,' he would have said. 'I don't like wine,' I would have replied. He wouldn't have argued. He would have just raised his eyebrows and looked off to one side, maybe drummed his fingers lightly on the table top. That's all. I only just like beer. There have been three I have really liked: the one after Mt Rolleston, the one at Springfield, and the one on Brunate. This one's okay, this one's fine. I can feel the fizz against my tongue. The lake is perfection. The rat darts away and when I look across, the table is empty.

Epilogue

When I have fears that I may cease to be
Before my pen has gleaned my teaming brain…
Before high-piled books, in charactery,
Hold like rich garners the full ripen'd grain…

(John Keats)

We stood filling in time gazing out across the runway. The sky over Zürich was muddy and a light shower of rain had stained the tarmac grey and black. It was a dismal outlook that even the livery of the aeroplanes could not relieve. Fanny leaned against the glass beside me. 'Did you get everything you wanted?' she asked.

'Yes, I think so,' I said. 'I stole a flake of brick from the cathedral at Faenza, and I have the two daisies Gianna picked for me, and a cobble from the street in Como. The name for daisy is Margarita, did you know? It's my mother's name. And, of course, the stone…'

'Pietro,' she said.

I nodded. 'But really all I wanted was background, some way to glue together all the cameos, especially the war,' I said, 'You see, I have no narrative this time. It's not my story, it's not in my head. If it were it would be easy, it would just fall out onto the paper. But I've had to read about him, ask about him, try to make sense of it, and I was never a scholar, Fanny, you know that.'

She smiled and then walked away to get something from the café. A hundred yards off I could see a bird fluttering, seemingly suspended fifty feet above the verge of the concourse. I wondered if it were a tethered kite, one of those bird-scarers they use around vineyards. But there was no wind. And then I watched it dive to the grass and back into the air again to take up a new position, its wings trembling like a tern.

There was a tension between my father and me by the time he went back to Auckland, to take up his new work at the law school. It was never really resolved. And then when it was obvious he was ill, a friend told me that I should make it up with him while there was still time. I didn't want to. I thought he would prefer an honest dislike to a dishonest reconciliation. He used to say that when Voltaire was lying on his deathbed a priest came to see him, to offer him the last rights. 'And do you renounce the devil, my son?' asked the priest.

'Father,' said Voltaire, 'this is no time to make enemies.' Houdon's portrait of Voltaire shows a hollow-eyed, gaunt face above a mischievous smile.

I didn't want to mention to him the subject of Caroline. The relationship was fraught with difficulties and his illness was enough for him to worry about. She and I were in Auckland for ostensible reasons, and I found myself filling in time at my parents' home. I was sitting in the sun with a cup of coffee. My mother came to get me.

'Your father wants you,' she said. I went through to him. He was sitting up in bed. It reminded me of the time of the professor's birds' eggs. He spoke to me with his eyes a little away, as if what he had to say was too brittle to be taken on a straight bat.

'Caroline's an attractive, intelligent girl,' he said. 'You get on very well.' He shook his head, 'You mustn't worry about hurting people's feelings. You only have this one life, and you have to make the best of it.'

He had seen very easily what I had tried very hard to keep hidden from him, and he had sensed my anxiety and wanted to take the burden of it away. It was a kind of blessing and a forgiveness. There was nothing I could say. I leaned forward and hugged him for what seemed like the first and only time. It was the nearest I ever got to him.

Judge Speight, an old friend and colleague, sat with him one afternoon. He asked how it was for him. My father was silent for a while and then answered, as always, obliquely: 'I nightly pitch my moving tent a day's march nearer home.'

They tell me that the night before he died he stood outside, alone, and stared for a long time at the sky.

... When I behold, upon the night's starr'd face,
Huge cloudy symbols of a high romance,
And think that I may never live to trace
Their shadow with the magic hand of chance;
And when I feel, fair creature of an hour,
That I shall never look upon thee more,
Never have relish in the fairy power
Of unreflecting love; then on the shore
Of the wide world I stand alone, and think
Till love and fame to nothingness do sink.

But when I close my eyes I remember him most clearly that day we sailed our copper-mesh fire guard across an infinite sea. When, suddenly, he appeared on the horizon running toward us, and leaped over the entire ship. I can see him still. It takes my breath away.

Fanny returned with croissants and coffee.

'What's that?' I said, pointing. 'That bird?'

It took her a moment to see. 'Oh,' she said, 'I can't remember its name. But you'd call it a falcon.'

APPENDIX I
Letters

The defence has been cross-examining for half an hour and he's still going on. I haven't the faintest idea what he's talking about and nor has the jury, but it won't make any difference to what I say, so I thought I'd just drop you a line...

Unlike his domestic collection of carefully edited letters in *Dear Sam*, it is in his letters to lawyers and other judges that Peter most clearly reveals himself. They are humorous, of course; but sometimes, like the pictures he lightly sketched for us of the war, you only have to shift the frame a little to find the bleak landscape against which they were set.

Peter's criticisms are many and they edge on bitterness a little sometimes, perhaps born of the frustration of having, occasionally, to 'rub up against second-rate minds' while trying to get on with the job of conducting the law with considerable acumen. But even his critiques are designed above all to entertain, while at the same time leaving us a clear and unique view of a pompous hierarchy bedevilled by a degree of political machination never imagined by the average citizen.

(Letter to Garth Gould: 1973)

My dear Ham, your amusing and instructive letter has been received and I congratulate you on the domestic freedom, comparatively speaking, which now prevails. Your sense of controlled elation at the departure of your in-laws would be similar to that of one of the early Popes as the Visigoths reluctantly withdrew from Rome. By the time this letter arrives, the household may have been increased by one more little hostage to fortune, and with any luck you may spend a few rapturous evenings in the company and perhaps in the arms of a complaisant Karitane with sun-bronzed limbs, pale golden hair, and the sensuous charms of a Circassian slave-girl, but knowing your wife's protective interest, I doubt it. You are more likely to encounter the reincarnation of Irma Grese, head wardress of Ravensbruck.

I wrote to Burn not long ago, suggesting that he cultivate his already close acquaintanceship with Snow Hall, with the purpose of unveiling at last the dim mysterious temple of Weston, Ward and Lascelles. He replies with some preliminary disclosures but I should imagine that the full enormity of Tub's [Leggat's] professional manoeuvres will not become apparent until next year, by which time a number of angry clients would have wrested away their files by main force and delivered them to the fascinated and horrified inspection of other eyes. If I may change slightly my original metaphor, I always saw WWL as an opaque turbid pool, with occasionally a sudden swirling on the surface to indicate the Herculean hidden struggle of preventing a scandal from reaching the surface, with now and then the bland, courteous figure of Tub, in a frog-man's suit, coming briefly up for air. But from now on one may confidently anticipate a series of vain threshings on the surface, the participants coming plainly into view, and I hope and expect that there will be no lack of observers as this interesting phenomenon unfolds. As a matter of fact I saw something only yesterday which brought back a fleeting vision of Tub's past. I was driving along Grafton Road, and as I stopped at some traffic lights I saw in front of me a Holden station wagon with a legend printed across the back – 'Smith Ltd'. I recognised the driver. This was 'Smith' who suffered bad injuries in a car accident twenty years ago, and who endured in consequence many hours under the arc lights of the Burwood Hospital operating table as the surgeons valiantly stitched flaps of skin over his lacerated features which looked as if they had been worked over by Jomo Kenyatta's henchmen at a midnight séance in a Kenyan forest during the Mau Mau rebellion. Tub duly appeared for 'Smith' in a jury action for about £10,000. There was an offer of £4,000 which Tub not only declined, but did not disclose to his client, and there was a verdict for the defendant. By some mischance, 'Smith' senior discovered the deception but there was only a swirl on the surface, my dear fellow, only a swirl on the surface.

To advert to my own hum drum way of life, I have been in Hamilton for three weeks, cooped up in a hot humid courtroom with my shirt sticking to my back as I patiently transcribed into logical sequence numerous groups of complex submissions. It was a great relief to return to the air-conditioned courtrooms of Auckland where cases are propounded with brisk economy of presentation in order that counsel may hurry back to their offices so as to sign up a personal syndicate option for an old warehouse site on Karangahape Road. Just the same, the Hamilton assizes are not without their interesting moments. A motorist was charged in the Taupo Magistrates Court with passing on an intersection. The facts were clear and undisputed. But his counsel, a young fellow with bushy red hair, pointed out to Tom Birks that the regulation dealing with this matter also prohibited, in the next paragraph, the act of overtaking another vehicle with less that 300 feet of visibility, and he submitted that reading the regulation as a whole, it only disclosed one offence, to wit, overtaking on an intersection with less than 300 feet of vision ahead. 'Quite right,' said Tom, and dismissed the information. The Transport Department indignantly appealed. After I had allowed the appeal the red-haired young counsel objected to the department's application for costs. When I suggested that he himself was the true culprit, having advanced to the magistrate an untenable submission, he smiled genially like a trapped wolf and said that a defendant should not have to pay for the process of clarifying the law. I replied to the effect that the regulation was clear enough until he laid hands on it, directed the payment of $40 costs, and the proceedings terminated.

Nigel Wilson was in Hamilton last week, trying criminal cases. I saw him on the weekend and he advised that on reading the depositions relating to ten cases he had summarily dismissed four of the indictments before trial, leaving only six to proceed. I deferentially suggested that 40 per cent seemed a high proportion of unwarranted committals and he said, Oh yes, the police wanted a good ticking off. I think the chief should send him around the country to do all the criminal cases with the rank of General Commissioner of Gaol Delivery which, after all, would not be a wholly inaccurate description. Nigel also told me that after one verdict was returned he ticked off the jury for taking too long in their deliberations. By holding a cupped hand to my ear, and listening intently, I was just able to hear the rustling of the reeds at Runnymede.

Some time ago I found it necessary to make a request to the head office of the Justice Department for a copy of my IR12 tax certificate for the year ended 31 March 1972, the copy sent to me having been unaccountably mislaid. Now somewhere in Head Office there is an accounts clerk to which this inquiry was referred. I will never know his identity or appearance but I see him as a quiet middle-aged man thoughtfully smoking a metal-stemmed pipe and travelling to work each morning from Kelburn on a Honda motor-scooter. In the office he will wear a sports-coat bought at Kirkcaldie and Stains twenty years ago for £3.5, the leather inserts at the elbows shiny and worn. It was this loyal and devoted public servant, working selflessly in the interests of the state, who discovered by a departmental error Mr Justice Mahon had been underpaid a gross total of $2,420.

If ever a man deserves, along with the present writer, the cost of living increase back-dated to October 1972, then this man is that man. Naturally by the time the tax collector has imposed his levy I will only receive about $1200 but this will surely justify the careless purchase of new curtains for the lounge and a few crystal mice from Arpèges.

O'Regan J recently presided over a criminal trial in Dunedin in which the prosecution was conducted by Denis Wood, who elicited the whole of the Crown evidence by a series of highly improper leading questions. 'I've thought of a good name for you,' said Barry to Wood later – ' "Kindly Light." '

Reverting to the matter of Leggat's demise, I reflected the other day on the unfortunate situation of Snow Hall as he stands in the Supreme Court attempting to present a case founded on one of Tub's files, with the testimony of each witness in deep conflict with Tub's written report to the insurance company. It seemed however that there were some lines of Alfred Lord Tennyson which supported the possibility of Tub lending a helping hand from his listening post in Death's dark dominion:

> *So word by word and line by line*
> *The dead man touched me from the past,*
> *And all at once it seemed at last*
> *The living soul was flashed on mine.*

I know, my dear fellow, that you will not think these touches of macabre humour entirely misplaced. After all, Tub worked assiduously year by year for the elevation of his own prestige and for the simultaneous denigration of all his professional friends. Far better to have followed Churchill's precept and concentrated his attention only on doing his work as best he could all the time. Ambition is a faithless companion. And in the end, when the race is run, what is left?

These our actors,
As I foretold you were all spirits
And are melted into air, into thin air:
And, like the baseless fabric of this vision,
The cloud capp'd towers, the gorgeous palaces,
The solemn temples, the great globe itself,
Yes, all which it inherit, shall dissolve
And, like this insubstantial pageant faded,
Leave not a wrack behind...

This is not to say, of course, that the ultimate dissolution should not be survived by suitably constructed trusts created in a form not in conflict with s.5 of the Estate and Gift Duties Act, but that is another matter. Subject to that exception, my own credo is contained in the lines last quoted.

Thank you again for your letter, my regards to Liz, and I hope her mission is soon and safely accomplished.

APPENDIX II

A long time ago, during my art school years, a particularly lovely flat mate of mine, dressed it seemed perpetually in gossamer and smelling of Samarkand, used to wander about our cheap digs absorbed in Hermann Hesse. It annoyed me.

'Why do you read him?' I asked.

'Because he tells me what I know,' she replied.

'Ha,' I said. 'If you already know what he's trying to tell you, why bother to read him?'

She sighed and marked her place. 'Because,' she replied, 'although I know what he is saying, before I read him I never had the words to express it.'

It took me a long time to read *Das Glasperlenspiel* and *Narcissus and Goldmund* and I'm glad I finally did. I have read other works by Hesse but it is these that have impressed me most. In *The Glass Bead Game*, Joseph Knecht aspires to become a member of an elite, a master of intellect, a discoverer and defender of truth. Their game is played in an institution separate from the common world where the players assume a kind of aristocratic governance.

However, Knecht's friend Plinio Designori interrupts his meditations to remind him of the struggling world beyond his cloistered existence and in the end prevails and draws him out.

Joseph to Plinio: It might be asserted that every human being on earth can fundamentally hold a dialogue with every other human being, and it might also be asserted that there are no two persons in the world between whom genuine, whole, intimate understanding is possible – the one statement is as true as the other. But though you and I may speak different languages, if we are men of good will we shall have a great deal to say to each other, and beyond what is precisely communicable we can guess and sense a great deal about each other. At any rate let us try.

Plinio: I don't know whether my life has been useless and merely a misunderstanding, or whether it has a meaning. Body and soul, ideal and reality have moved apart in our country; they know little about each other or want to know. If I had one task or ideal in life, it was to make myself a synthesis of the two principles, to be a mediator, interpreter, and arbitrator between the two.

Hesse is concerned with a dialogue between these two parts of human nature; the pursuit of truth through abstinence, meditation, theism, and the pursuit of truth by honing one's soul against the rough edge of life; two paths with the same destination in mind. Almost equally, Narcissus devotes his life to the priesthood, while his friend Goldmund throws himself into the earthly world to experience 'a sea of blood and lust' to cut 'a picaresque swathe through plague, storm and murder, always chasing a fugitive vision of artistic perfection.'

When Hesse writes of these two men, in both stories, I like to think he is writing of one man struggling with the two halves of his nature.

My father was a man of two natures: a scholar of law who defended legal principle in the same way that Sir Thomas More defended it, as a lattice on which we hang civilised society, and yet he was also a scholar of romantic verse wherein the only principles that matter seem to be the occasional rhyming couplet and a sense of meter.

Peter had passed through storm and murder, the plague of his time, and possibly like the rest of his generation he adhered himself afterwards to order against the possibility of disorder ever happening to him again.

APPENDIX III

It is interesting to reflect on the variety of rulings concerning perceived bias and the debate surrounding the principle that a man must not be a judge in his own cause. Academic opinion on this subject does not seem at all fixed: while the spectrum of debate is narrow, it would fill more than the pages of this book. However, it is still, at times, as rigorously applied as it was by Sir Arthur Donnelly in 1955: recently, a judgment in the House of Lords involving the extradition of General Pinochet was thrown out after it was discovered that one of the judges, Lord Hoffman, was on the board of directors of a charity connected to Amnesty International. It is also of some interest to find that Sian Elias recused herself from a case involving drug charges against a jockey who had ridden a horse of which the judge was part owner. The judge's connection to the case was tenuous: there was no suggestion of pecuniary interest, simply the possibility that in the mind of the reasonable man there might exist a perception of 'own cause'.

The rule also extends to provide that a judge should not decide a case affecting the interests of friends, family or business associates. Bearing this in mind, it is reasonable to assume that my father would have been a little annoyed that McMullin, one of the appeal judges who found against Peter's costs judgment, was hosting a junior counsel for the airline at his house while the Erebus hearing was taking place, and although challenged by counsel for ALPA, refused to recuse himself. It was not revealed until some time after the event that Owen Woodhouse's daughter was, at the time of the commission hearings, employed as a public relations officer for Air New Zealand.